Placing Latin America

Placing Latin America

Contemporary Themes in Human Geography

Edited by
Edward L. Jackiewicz and
Fernando J. Bosco

ROWMAN & LITTLEFIELD PUBLISHERS, INC.
Lanham • Boulder • New York • Toronto • Plymouth, UK

ROWMAN & LITTLEFIELD PUBLISHERS, INC.

Published in the United States of America
by Rowman & Littlefield Publishers, Inc.
A wholly owned subsidiary of The Rowman & Littlefield Publishing Group, Inc.
4501 Forbes Boulevard, Suite 200, Lanham, Maryland 20706
www.rowmanlittlefield.com

Estover Road, Plymouth PL6 7PY, United Kingdom

British Library Cataloguing in Publication Information Available

Library of Congress Cataloging-in-Publication Data

Placing Latin America : contemporary themes in human geography / edited by
Edward L. Jackiewicz and Fernando J. Bosco.
    p. cm.
  Includes bibliographical references and index.
  ISBN-13: 978-0-7425-5642-3 (cloth : alk. paper)
  ISBN-10: 0-7425-5642-5 (cloth : alk. paper)
  ISBN-13: 978-0-7425-5643-0 (pbk. : alk. paper)
  ISBN-10: 0-7425-5643-3 (pbk. : alk. paper)
  1. Human geography—Latin America. 2. Globalization—Economic aspects—
Latin America. 3. Latin America—Economic conditions. I. Jackiewicz, Edward L.
II. Bosco, Fernando J., 1971–
  GF514.P53 2008
  304.2098—dc22

                                                      2007038794

Printed in the United States of America

⊗™ The paper used in this publication meets the minimum requirements of
American National Standard for Information Sciences—Permanence of Paper for
Printed Library Materials, ANSI/NISO Z39.48-1992.

Contents

Figures and Tables

FIGURES

TABLES

Acknowledgments

We would like to thank several people who helped us see this project to fruition. Most important were the great folks at Rowman & Littlefield. Susan McEachern and Jessica Gribble provided us with helpful suggestions, much needed guidance, and perhaps best of all, friendly voices to speak with to get through the more troubling aspects of compiling this book. David Deis, staff cartographer at California State University, Northridge, assisted us with many of the maps and images that appear in this book, and Lisa Baughn handled indexing responsibilities.

Ed dedicates this book to his lovely wife, Diana, and daughter, Olivia. They bring love, support, friendship, and laughter into his life every day and provide much needed balance to his life.

Fernando thanks Tyler Hower for his excellent editorial assistance and for his encouragement and support when things turned more complicated than expected. He dedicates this book to his family and friends in Argentina.

Introduction

A Roadmap to *Placing Latin America*

Fernando J. Bosco and Edward L. Jackiewicz

As the twenty-first century begins, Latin America finds itself increasingly integrated in economic, social, political, and cultural networks that transcend regional and national boundaries and span the world. Transnational networks of migrants link small villages in Central America with cities all across North America, international tourism links the local economies of places throughout the region to the consumption patterns and needs of visitors from places in the "global north," and the transnational strategies of firms and corporations reach more places in the region than ever before. Such increased global interconnections of places and people are taking place together with profound changes in the political and economic organization of countries in the region. At the beginning of the twenty-first century, many Latin American countries are experiencing changes in leadership and political orientation while continuing with a difficult process of democratization and strengthening of civil society. Politically, some states are challenging the basic tenets of globalization, while others are embracing them more directly. Grassroots social and political movements are also active participants in promoting change from the ground up locally, nationally, and globally. Add to this the ebb and flow of relations of Latin American countries with the United States: the push on the one hand for greater economic integration and free trade and on the other hand the attempts to tighten security along the U.S. border and reduce immigrant rights. These issues, among several others, provide the driving force behind *Placing Latin America*, a collection of essays that discuss many current themes from an explicit human geographic perspective in an effort to summarize and contextualize the global and local dimensions of economic, political, cultural, and social change in the region.

The geographic perspective that informs this volume pays close attention to the richness and diversity of Latin American places, from cities to border regions to nations. *Placing Latin America* examines the nexus of economy, politics, society, and culture and documents how these interactions manifest themselves geographically in different places in the region. The collection brings a number of essays that were written specifically with such goals in mind, and in that sense it is different from other existing textbooks on Latin America, which tend to follow regional and historical approaches. The approach of *Placing Latin America* is geographic and thematic, but it is not regional in the traditional sense. Much has changed in the discipline of geography in the past two decades; human geography in particular has become more dynamic, and geographers writing about Latin America have been thinking geographically about a host of new issues, from environmental politics to cinema and media, from tourism to the illicit drug trade in the region. These issues have joined more common research topics that have been central to geographers working on Latin America for quite some time, such as economic development and urbanization. But given the dynamic character of the region, even writing about development and urbanization in Latin America today involves revisiting some conventional ideas and reexamining them in light of changing local, regional, and global conditions. Thus, the contributors to this volume were asked to think about Latin America's most pressing and interesting issues and themes and to write about them in summary chapters that are rich in detail, conceptually current, and that provide room for further thought, reading, and exploration. Finally, despite its thematic approach, *Placing Latin America* is also different from volumes that bring together previously published academic papers, though each new chapter in the collection is firmly positioned in the current literature on the region.

Overall, the chapters in this volume seek to provide an account of the human geographies of the region that balances the negative impacts of globalization (which characterizes much academic writing on Latin America in the last decade) and the more inspiring ways in which people and communities are responding to these changes. This volume speaks of human geograph*ies* (in the plural form) because of the many juxtapositions of landscapes and social relations that characterize the region: poor people collecting cans and cardboard from Dumpsters roam elite residential and commercial enclaves in global cities like Buenos Aires and Mexico City in the evenings; peasants who engage in subsistence agriculture compete for land with large-scale landholdings that are part of the commercial agricultural complex that has catapulted Latin America as a global exporter of food and resources.

Two important themes of this volume are issues of continuity and change in Latin America. The contributors to this volume were asked to highlight the changing and dynamic human geographies of Latin America and at the same time to recognize the historical legacy and the continuity of many place-based phenomena across the region. Despite the changes and challenges confronting Latin America, some things have remained constant over the years, some would say to a fault. A few decades ago, scholars writing on the development trajectories of Latin America drew heavily from theories of economic dependency that emphasized that most of the region was mostly an exporter of primary products under the watchful eye of the United States, mired in extreme poverty and inequality, and a source of cheap labor for transnational corporations. Many of such conditions still remain, but there have also been alternative accounts of the trajectories of economic and social development in the region that have attempted to explain the myriad ways in which governments, NGOs (nongovernmental organizations), and people in the region have been working to change long-standing structural inequalities, rethinking strategies for social change, and imagining alternative futures. As geographers, we are keenly aware of, and most interested in, the way all of these issues of continuity and change play out on the landscape of the region at different scales. We are interested in how people experience globalization in place and we are also particularly interested in how people attempt to change their conditions and create new geographies. We are also interested in understanding and positioning these issues of continuity and change from global, hemispheric, and regional perspectives.

LATIN AMERICA: BOUNDED REGION OR OPEN PLACE?

A volume on the dynamic human geographies of Latin America begs the question of where Latin America begins and ends. What exactly is the extent of Latin America? There are some common (but also contested) answers to this question. Many geographic textbooks on Latin America define the region as a coherent unit that extends from the southernmost tips of Argentina and Chile in Tierra del Fuego to Mexico in the north, thus including both South America and Middle (or Central) America. This definition emphasizes the shared experience of Iberian colonialism (Spain and Portugal) and its legacy in the region as a unifying force that holds the region together despite the different trajectories that countries have followed since independence.

While some scholars include the Caribbean as part of Latin America, many others treat it as a distinct region. The argument is that the economic and cultural histories of the islands of the Caribbean are fundamentally different from those of mainland Latin America. Many point to the larger African legacy and the impact of other European colonial powers in the

Caribbean landscape as two fundamental variables that render the Caribbean a separate geographic realm, distinct from the rest of Latin America. Yet, it could be easily argued that emphasizing the African heritage in the Caribbean as a differentiating factor is misleading because this position fails to recognize the many ways in which Africans and African customs and traditions have played a significant role in shaping the character of places in Latin America, from Brazil to the Pacific coast of Colombia to the Atlantic region of Costa Rica, to name just a few. There are many other places where there might be no visible traces of an African past because of the brutality of slavery and independence and "frontier" wars, yet an African influence is undeniably a part of many unique Latin American cultural traits. This can be observed in food and musical traditions all the way to the Southern Cone; even Argentine tangos and milongas owe much of their style to African rhythms.

The colonial histories of the Caribbean and of Middle and South America might have been different, but there was no real unity of colonial experience in Middle and South America either. Spain and Portugal followed different colonial strategies in different places, from slave plantation economies in Brazil and in their Caribbean possessions to ranch economies in the interior of the continent, where European aristocracies lived alongside indigenous populations and pushed territorial frontiers further and further as time went by. There is a time dimension that also is often forgotten. For example, the colonial objectives and emphasis of Spain in Latin America changed over time. In the sixteenth century, Spain was driven both by economic and evangelical motives. This is the period that coincides with the "Black Legend" of Spanish colonialism in Latin America (i.e., the "conquistadores" annihilating native populations and leading to their demographic and cultural collapse, the attempts to spread a more pure and strict form of Catholicism among the natives, and so on). But these economic and evangelical motives were often in tension. While the devastating effects on the native population are undeniable, conflicting and complementary intentions created divergent colonial experiences in different places. Colonial power was contested among dominant elites and also by the popular classes (Adelman, 1999).

By the eighteenth century, the Spanish evangelical idea was almost abandoned and replaced with an imperial (and much more secular) objective. At this point in time, Spain was competing fiercely with other European powers for colonial domination and expansion, and the imperial objectives of Spain in Latin America were clashing with those of Portugal, England, and other European powers (Difrieri, 1980). Also at this time, the colonial experience in Latin America and the Caribbean became much more similar and convergent than in the past, and the argument that colonialism in the Caribbean was fundamentally different than in Middle or South America loses some explanatory power. Hence, it may not be so clear-cut that Latin America is different from the Caribbean as a result of the African legacy or of the colonial experience.

It is not the intention of this volume to enter into an in-depth debate about the boundaries of the region, but it should be noted that the idea of Latin America that inspires this collection is one of an expanded region. We are not really interested in delineating boundaries; rather we are more interested in the flows and connections between places that are made by shared social, cultural, economic, political, and environmental dimensions and that create Latin American spaces in Middle and South America, in the Caribbean, and even beyond. As geographers, we are inspired by ideas of place as open and porous, and notions of place as an expression of the global in the local. Latin America seems to us a perfect example of a porous region that is difficult to pin down in terms of tangible boundaries, in particular in the context of contemporary globalization. For example, this volume includes discussion of the Caribbean in the context of Latin America and with respect to tourism and economic development; the trends the authors recognize in the Caribbean (in terms of tourist flows, economic strategies for development, and so on) are shared also by other places in continental Latin America.

This volume also goes beyond the imagined but also very real line that separates Latin America from lands further north: the boundary between Mexico and the United States of America. On the one hand, this border is tangible, material. One can visit the border region from either side—though it is far easier to cross the border coming from the United States than the other way around. In this sense, the border acts as the real boundary between Latin America and North America. On the other hand, the border also is an artificial line, the product of the territorial geopolitics of modern nation-states. The border also is a porous contour that over the years has allowed those Latin Americans who have crossed it to begin creating Latin American spaces in North America (those places that in the United States we recognize as "Latino" and "Hispanic"). This is why in this volume we do not talk about a border, but rather about a border region that extends along the official boundary between the United States and Mexico. That transnational border region is also a part of different Latin American human geographies. Latin American cultural critic Nestor Garcia Canclini describes Latin American cultures as "hybrid cultures" (1990), an intertwining of premodernity, modernity, and postmodernity; of races and ethnicities; of religions; of symbolisms; of colonial pasts and postcolonial presents. Following Garcia Canclini, we see the border region from a geographic perspective and as a hybrid place that also encapsulates such intricate mixtures. But then again, because we recognize the openness of place in the context of globalization, the border region between the United States and Mexico is no more of a hybrid place than São Paulo in Brazil or Puerto Vallarta in Mexico. Thus, we see all of Latin America as a hybrid region, constantly changing and being transformed in the context of globalization.

LATIN AMERICA: CONTINUITY AND CHANGE

While the majority of this book focuses on the present, it is important to recognize important historical underpinnings to place the human geographies that this volume explores in context. As the above discussion regarding the commonly perceived boundaries of the region indicates, it has long been recognized that the legacies of colonialism in Latin America have an enduring effect on the present. Indeed, much scholarly historical research on Latin America identifies the legacy of colonialism and the *persistence* of history as one of the main problems the region has yet to overcome. For example, in the beginning of a discussion about the problem of persistence in Latin American history, historian Jeremy Adelman argues that:

> Latin America seems condemned to repetition. Troubled politics, boom-and-bust economics, a healthy passion for personal loyalties over impersonal identities all appear as common features of the region. . . . If the United States constantly adapted to future horizons, Latin America remained anchored to social relations, modes of behavior, and cultures of an earlier era. Where the United States made perpetual ruptures the hallmark of its history, Latin America forged its historic time lines out of deep continuities. Latin America still bears the shackles of its birth. The past is destiny. (Adelman, 1999:1)

Many other scholars disagree with such pessimistic and deterministic accounts of Latin American history and provide alternative, sometimes more hopeful, explanations. For example, anthropologist Arturo Escobar (1995) has also attacked traditional, top-down economic development efforts that have been tried in the region for decades and has dissected the inefficiencies of a development industry that often is more concerned with creating and maintaining bureaucratic and institutional structures rather than with effecting real economic and social change. But Escobar also has offered more hopeful accounts of the future of the region based on evidence from people in the region who are increasingly working together locally (in the form of social and grassroots movements, for example) to create real and effective change.

The evidence regarding deterministic or optimistic accounts of the trajectories of development in Latin America is mixed. For instance, the current contributions that Latin American countries make to the global economy are a good example of the persistence of history discussed above. Table I.1 shows the two leading exports of selected Latin American countries in 1913 and 2005. In 1913, all countries were exporting primary products. Whether it was coffee, bananas, or minerals, they were all shipped out in their raw form and then often transformed into a more valuable product overseas, a process known as "value added." To illustrate, one of Brazil's leading exports was rubber. That rubber was shipped to countries of the global north, which then converted that rubber into a tire, thus adding value to the rubber. In this process, the Brazilian economy and more precisely the rubber tappers make a small amount of money from the rubber while the tire manufacturers make a handsome profit from tire sales. A similar process occurs with many other Latin American exports. When a consumer in the United States pays $4.00 for a café latte at a fancy coffee shop, very little of that (in fact, pennies) actually goes back to the farmer who does the backbreaking work of picking the beans.

The other problem associated with reliance on the export of primary products is that these countries are vulnerable to world market prices for the commodities, which can fluctuate quite a bit. For example, as a legacy from the colonial period, sugar was an important export of many Caribbean countries, but when artificial sweeteners and high fructose corn syrup became cheaper and/or more desirable substitutes, this industry crashed, forcing short- to medium-term economic recession and the need to restructure economies and agricultural bases. At the same time, fluctuation in world market prices for commodities many times has benefited countries in the region. For example, in the past years the world has experienced increased prices for oil and copper, and two countries in the region, Venezuela and Chile, have been able to reap the benefits of such higher prices and experienced sustained economic growth.

It is also important to recognize that there have been attempts to alleviate the disadvantages related to Latin America's "peripheral" position in the global economy, most notably during the import substitution period and through a focus on exports of assembled manufactures in some countries (discussed in greater detail in chapter 1). The outcomes of industrialization in the region are also a mixture of success and failures. Many Latin American countries are still exporting primary products; indeed, six of the region's countries still have coffee as one of their top two exports. There are however, a few exceptions. Brazil has found a global market niche in the export of transport equipment. Mexico has expanded its export of manufactured goods largely through the assistance of NAFTA (North American Free Trade Agreement), although, as discussed later in the book, this should not be confused with substantive gains in the material well-being of its citizenry, as even a cursory overview of the border region will illustrate.

Similarly, a few other countries list "offshore assembly exports" (El Salvador) or "manufactures" (Haiti) as one of their leading exports. These industries have developed because of the low wages found in these countries, which allow transnational corporations, which typically contract with employers in these places, to have their goods produced at very low cost. This process has been roundly criticized; some have referred to it as "a race to the bottom," as investment capital can seek out the cheapest labor around the globe, thereby forcing and keeping the wages down. Thus, while this "fast" capital can speed around the globe and set up operations wherever they can be most lucrative, labor can only move at a fraction of that speed. Moreover, efforts are increasingly being made to restrict labor flows while at the same time capital continues to move with little resistance or regulation.

The diversity of experiences of continuity and change in Latin America's economic development mirrors the structure and ideas that inspire many of the chapters in this volume. The contributors to *Placing Latin America* recognize that studying the past can help shed light on contemporary conditions. They also recognize that change is possible, and that human agency can go a long way in affecting and modifying deep-seated structural conditions. The contributions to this volume are indeed much more about the present, in particular about changes in the present that challenge the problems of historical persistence that so many scholars have described as characterizing Latin America. As geographers or scholars who follow a geographic perspective, the contributors to this volume also explain situa-

Table I.1.   Latin America's Leading Exports, 1913 and 2005

Country	1913	2005
Argentina	Maize, Wheat	Edible Oils, Fuels/Energy
Bolivia	Tin, Silver	Natural Gas, Soy products
Brazil	Coffee, Rubber	Transport Equipment, Iron Ore
Chile	Nitrates, Copper	Copper, Fruit
Colombia	Coffee, Gold	Petroleum, Coffee
Costa Rica	Bananas, Coffee	Coffee, Bananas
Cuba	Sugar, Tobacco	Sugar, Nickel
Dominican Rep.	Cacao, Sugar	Nickel, Sugar
Ecuador	Cacao, Coffee	Petroleum, Bananas
El Salvador	Coffee, Precious Metals	Offshore Assembly Exports, Coffee
Guatemala	Coffee, Bananas	Coffee, Sugar
Haiti	Coffee, Cacao	Manufactures, Coffee
Honduras	Bananas, Precious Metals	Coffee, Shrimp
Mexico	Silver, Copper	Manufactured Goods, Oil
Nicaragua	Coffee, Precious Metals	Coffee, Beef
Panama	Bananas, Coconuts	Bananas, Shrimp
Paraguay	Yerba Mate, Tobacco	Soybeans, Feed
Peru	Copper, Sugar	Copper, Gold
Puerto Rico	Sugar, Coffee	Chemicals, Electronics
Uruguay	Wool, Meat	Meat, Rice
Venezuela	Coffee, Cacao	Petroleum, Bauxite/Aluminum

Sources: Bulmer-Thomas and Knight (2003:58); https://www.cia.gov/cia/publications/factbook.

tions of continuity and change in Latin America by paying close attention to the relations between people and place and society and space. Our point of departure in creating this collection is that geographic thinking can help us better understand continuity and change. For example, it is difficult to understand environmental politics and the mobilization of social movements in contemporary Latin America without recognizing people's claims to land and territory, or in other words, the need for people to have their own spaces for (re)production and representation.

PLACING LATIN AMERICA: A ROADMAP

The chapters in *Placing Latin America* provide a geographic perspective on the region's political and economic development as well as on its changing urban landscape, on the mobilization of civil society and on the cultural dimensions of one of the most diverse regions of the world. Several contributions to this volume focus on the dynamic relation between economy and society at different geographic scales, and on the resulting changes in the landscape and human geographies of Latin America. Other chapters speak to the idea of an "expanded" Latin America, focusing on the way in which Latin American spaces are fluid, crossing artificial and imagined boundaries as Latin American people (in many cases migrants) carry their traditions with them to different places that often challenge the sustainability of their livelihoods, whether in the U.S.-Mexico border region, in the streets of a Latino neighborhood in the midwestern United States, or in the cinematic spaces of Latin American movies. Finally, another group of chapters focus specifically on the struggles of people to shape their own geographies through their associations with others. In this set of chapters, the authors examine the dynamism of Latin American civil society in the context of globalization and of continuity and change that we described above. Together, all the chapters in this collection provide a window into life in Latin America at different scales, from the local to the global.

Chapter 1 by Ed Jackiewicz and Linda Quiquivix provides an overview of the economic changes that occurred during the twentieth century and the pattern of development trajectories followed by different countries in the region. The authors present a typology of developmental trajectories for the region, and suggest that Latin America today may be witnessing the transition to a new, uncertain phase of political and economic development characterized by a "turn to the left" and an antiglobalization stand. But, as the authors are also quick to point out, the presence of foreign capital and sentiments against it are nothing new in Latin America; the current neoliberal transformation and challenges to it are only the latest chapters in the saga of continuity and change in the region.

In chapter 2, Thomas Klak further develops the theme of continuity and change in Latin America through an analysis of the risks and vulnerabilities of trade dependency, in particular in the context of the region's embrace of neoliberalism as a developmental strategy. Klak focuses on Mexico, Central America, and the Caribbean because these are places that exhibit higher trade dependency in the larger region. He illustrates his arguments with examples from agricultural production (such as banana plantations), labor intensive but low-value-added assembly manufacturing (such as maquiladoras), and even advanced consumer services (such as online gambling and tourism). Klak argues that despite the apparent diversity of economic activity in the region, there is still a marked lack of sustained social and economic development. Much like the authors in chapter 1, Klak remains suspicious of neoliberalism as capable of producing sustained development for everyone because of the model's connections with powerful economic interests both locally and abroad.

In chapter 3, Adrian Guillermo Aguilar and Antonio Vieyra are interested in studying how relations between economy and society have material, tangible effects on the region's landscapes. Aguilar and Vieyra are specifically interested in impacts occurring at the urban scale. Analyzing a wealth of data from the region, Aguilar and Vieyra explain how the transformation of Latin American urban centers and an increase in rural to urban migration are tied to the changing dynamics of industrialization and economic restructuring, further supporting the general trends established in chapter 1. Aguilar and Vieyra demonstrate that despite the sustained growth of urban areas in Latin America, "megacities" (often publicized as the context for major social ills) are not growing as rapidly and still account for a small percentage of Latin America's population. Instead, they argue that the growth is being experienced in smaller urban areas, where unemployment unfortunately also remains high. Aguilar and Vieyra then examine how economic restructuring has resulted in changes in employment in urban labor markets in Latin America, leading to an increase in informal employment. Finally, they introduce the concept of employment *precariousness* and describe how women are disproportionately affected by labor conditions that unfortunately do not lead to positive social change.

The changes in development strategies in the context of economic adjustment programs have also resulted in urban areas characterized by a diverse, if somehow static, built environment. Geographer Larry Ford is interested in analyzing this changing Latin American urban landscape in historical and comparative perspective in chapter 4. As an urban geographer with an interest in architecture and urban design, Ford examines the changing phases and faces of urban planning and planning strategies in Latin American cities. Ford argues that Latin America's most important cities have lost some of the exciting and cutting-edge urban imagery that they exhibited a few decades ago. For example, he shows that Latin American cities no longer play an important role in world-city skylines and have lagged behind other world regions. Ford sees the lack of skyscraper construction in Latin America in recent decades as a possible sign of diminished urban dynamism. He also documents how Latin American urban planning and construction of "architectural icons" is lagging relative to other regions of the world. But he is also interested in explaining how these changes relate to the argument regarding continuity and change that *Placing Latin America* develops. Specifically, he argues that Latin American cities are still full of powerful architectural icons and symbolic spaces for which there is great appreciation today, in particular as heritage sites and urban tourism are growing in many urban centers of the region in the context of globalization.

In chapter 5 Altha Cravey provides an in-depth account of the U.S.-Mexico borderlands region, a region that in recent years has become more treacherous as migration to the north increases and the tangible effects of neoliberalism are intensified with the industrialization of the border. Adding to the discussion of assembly manufacturing already introduced in chapter 2, Cravey provides a detailed and socially oriented account of the maquiladoras that have settled in the border region in the context of NAFTA. She is particularly interested in explaining how globalization affects daily life for people in the border region, and she focuses explicitly on issues of gender, class, and household dynamics. Cravey is also interested in the informal economy of the region, and her accounts of drug- and people-smuggling further illustrate the discussion of the effects of neoliberalism and economic reform that other authors tackle in this collection. Toward the end of her chapter, Cravey successfully shows how the border region is a place that operates at multiple scales simultaneously: it is place that penetrates deep into ordinary spaces of both the United States and Mexico, but it is also a place to live, where many people work and raise families.

Chapter 6, by John Davenport and Ed Jackiewicz, analyzes Latin America through the eyes of the tourism industry. The authors provide a general account of the newly found importance of tourism as a strategy for economic development in the region. The chapter details many of the different ways in which the tourism industry is reshaping landscapes in the region, from ecotourism in Costa Rica to the "surf, sand, and sun" offers of Mexico, Brazil, and Venezuela. This chapter (as well as chapter 4 by Larry Ford, discussed above) also points out the importance of urban tourism as an economic development strategy that is tied to the resurgence of architectural historical preservation in cities. Davenport and Jackiewicz end on a cautionary note: despite the optimism of tourism boosters in Latin America, the authors indicate that the industry remains highly competitive, is often poorly managed, and more importantly, is still heavily dependent on foreign investment and visitors from abroad.

Thomas Klak and Ross Flynn tackle the topic of tourism as an alternative development strategy in more detail in chapter 7. They discuss ecotourism as an emerging alternative to conventional development policies in Latin America and the Caribbean, arguing that the shift to sustainable tourism in the region has tended to be inadequately inclusive in terms of the social groups affected and notably limited in terms of ecological protection. Through a case study of ecotourism in Dominica (the self-proclaimed "Nature Island of the Caribbean"), they point to some hopeful signs and suggest that decisions made in the near future will determine whether the strategies adopted in Dominica are sustainable over the long term.

If tourism provides a rich imaginary and analytical material to analyze globalization in Latin America, the same could be said about the illegal drug industry. In chapter 8, Kent Mathewson tackles this topic by analyzing how psychoactive drugs have been and continue to be both a force and a factor in the production of Latin America's economic, political, and cultural conditions. Mathewson's goal is to show what a comprehensive geography of drug making, taking, and trading for Latin America might entail. His comprehensive analysis is unique in its historical and geographic approach, and shows how entire Latin American landscapes and livelihoods have been made and remade in relation to the cultivation of drugs, and how local, regional, and national economies have been affected by the imperative of drug commerce. Mathewson's chapter demonstrates one particular way in which the relations between society, culture, and economy are an active part in the construction of unique human geographies in the region.

Large-scale changes on the politics and economies of Latin America during the last century also have changed the face of Latin America's civil society. This is the theme developed by several chapters in *Placing Latin America*. The authors of these chapters explicitly shift from examination of issues of *continuity* to examination of issues of *change*, with an eye toward developing a geographic perspective on contemporary Latin American civil society. Christopher Brown begins this project in chapter 9 by examining the growing role that NGOs play in Latin American civil society. Moreover, he ties what he calls an ongoing "associational revolution" in the region to the development of the "politics of scale"—one of the main concerns of theory in human geography in the past decade. Brown documents the efforts of NGOs to effect change in people's livelihoods in the region, and he explains how these often formal modern institutions that have roots in pre-Columbian civilizations operate at local, national, and global levels. He argues that NGOs respond to the challenges presented by the actions of the state and capitalism and that their actions reveal much about how ordinary citizens confront globalization.

Whereas Brown's focus is on formal organizations, in chapter 10 Fernando Bosco focuses exclusively on informal ones, specifically on social movements—which are the responses of civil society to perceived injustices. Like Brown, Bosco takes an explicitly geographic perspective to describe those acts of resistance that take place outside the sphere of formal institutions. He focuses on the ways in which Latin American social movements are better understood in relation to the symbolic places they create and that help sustain them and to the spatial strategies that they enact in order to change society. Bosco provides several examples, from indigenous movements in Guatemala to human rights movements in Argentina. He finds a common thread in the explanation of their mobilization through an analysis of the social movements' strategies in places such as plazas and historic sites (important sites also highlighted by Ford in chapter 4) and of networking with other actors of civil society across space and scales.

Adding to the analysis of the dynamism of civil society in the region, Sarah A. Moore provides a narrative regarding urban environmental politics in Latin America in chapter 11. Moore ties the ecological and environmental changes that are occurring in urban areas of Latin America in the context of neoliberal adjustment and restructuring to the environmental activities of residents and citizens of the region's urban areas. Focusing on conflicts over the management of trash in Oaxaca, Mexico; access to water in Bolivia; and successful environmental management in Curitiba, Brazil, she illustrates the complexity of the relationship between urban ecologies and urban politics and, again, reaffirms how geography is woven into the mobilization of civil society. Together, Brown, Bosco, and Moore provide a framework and detailed examples of how contemporary Latin American civil society, in order to improve livelihoods, is resisting some of the detrimental dimensions of global capitalism and neoliberalism and attempting to find alternatives believed to be more just and equitable.

The remaining chapters of *Placing Latin America* speak of the geography of the region in an expanded way, from the material spaces of the border region to the cinematic spaces of Latin American movies. In chapter 12, Susan Mains develops an account of Latin American transnationalism in the context of both migration and mobility of Latin American people. By drawing on different examples from different types of transnational relations that both Latin American governments and people build over time, Mains explains how Latin America can be understood as a transnational imagined community that has ties both to places and cultural norms within the traditional boundaries of the region and beyond. Mains expands the discussion of mobility and migration that was developed in chapter 5 in relation to the U.S.-Mexico border with further examples from transnational life in Colombia and even in the streets of cities in the United States, whether in the border or beyond.

The following chapter, by Joel Jennings, continues the discussion of the transnational lives of Latin American people with a discussion of Latinos in the United States, and more specifically, in the city of St. Louis. The chapter is presented in the context of an ongoing debate regarding immigration in the United States in which Latin American immigrants are center stage. Jennings first examines the demographic and political contexts of Latino/a immigration in the United States and moves down to the local scale to examine Latino demography and landscapes in the city of St. Louis. Like several other authors in this collection, Jennings uses the framework of the social construction of geography to argue that the struggles for Latino/a citizenship currently being advanced at *subnational* scales (at a scale other than that of the nation-state) in the United States have significant implications for the future of Latino/a citizenship. The chapter clarifies that Latino immigrants in the United States now live not just in the larger cities on the East and West Coast, but also in inland cities and rural communities. Jennings explains how it is in these places that the notion of citizenship is being redefined, through immigrants' struggles to obtain driver's licenses and the right to education and work.

Finally, in chapter 14, James Craine and Mirek Lipinski examine Latin American cinema with the goal of explaining how movies can shape perceptions of place and play a central role in the constitution and sustainability of Latin American landscapes and identities. As they argue, geographers are often concerned with the ways in which landscape is shaped by multiple articulations of cultural memory and identity. Craine and Lipinski view Latin American cinema as a cultural production that itself reproduces the spatial interpretations of the filmmakers as well as dominant relations of power and representations of space. As such, they argue that Latin American cinema provides insights into how both Latin American society and space are ordered. The arguments are put in context by examining two different important figures of Brazilian and Mexican cinema: the *Za do Caixao* (a dark, horrific movie character that has become ingrained in Brazilian national consciousness) and the *Santo* (a masked character in Mexican wrestling). Through their analysis of several movies, Craine and Lipinski show how the *Za do Caixao* has been used as a tool for self-analysis and expression and the *Santo* as a representation of the possibility of broader geographical change (the possibility of political and economic transformation in Mexico). In the end, much like Cravey's chapter on the border, this demonstrates how Latin American cinema can be seen as a visual representation that both contains and transgresses the geographies of the region.

NOTE TO THE READER

All together, the chapters in *Placing Latin America* describe the continuity and change of general and specific patterns on human geography in the region, the conditions that give rise to such patterns, and the actions of people (in the region and abroad) that either challenge or reaffirm such patterns. The readers of *Placing Latin America* should not consider the road-map to the book given above as the only way to read this collection. While this introduction has made explicit some of the many points of connections among all the chapters in an attempt to provide a cohesive narrative, the book can be read in other ways. Readers are encouraged to approach this collection either by reading it in its entirety and in the order presented, or to choose chapters according to a thematic preference. We have asked each of the contributors to write chapters that would be satisfying to the reader if read individually but that also would make an independent contribution in the context of the human geographies of the larger region. The contributors have different writing styles, but all the chapters are clear and approachable and follow a similar structure. Some authors provide substantial references in the text, while others have chosen to keep the narrative simple by minimizing text citations. Nevertheless, at the end of most chapters the authors provide a list of suggested readings that expand the topics of each chapter. We believe those references are an important resource that, together with the chapters in this collection, will lead readers to their own conclusions regarding how to *place* the human geographies of Latin America.

BIBLIOGRAPHY

Adelman, J., ed. *Colonial Legacies: The Problem of Persistence in Latin American History.* New York: Routledge, 1999.

Bulmer-Thomas, Victor, and Alan Knight. *The Economic History of Latin America since Independence.* 2nd edition. Cambridge: Cambridge University Press, 2003.

Difrieri, Horacio. *El virreinato del Rio de la Plata: Ensayo de geografía histórica.* Buenos Aires: Ediciones Universidad del Salvador, 1980.

Escobar, Arturo. *Encountering Development: The Making and Unmaking of the Third World.* Princeton, N.J.: Princeton University Press, 1995.

García Canclini, Nestor. *Culturas híbridas.* Mexico City: Editorial Grijalbo, 1990.

1

Eras and Errors

A Historical and Geographical Overview of Latin America's Economic and Political Development

Edward L. Jackiewicz and Linda Quiquivix

In this chapter we trace the evolution of Latin America's economic and political development over the past century, highlighting key character-istics of three dominant phases: modern/liberal, import substitution, and neoliberal. We also introduce the idea that Latin America may be transitioning out of the neoliberal era into a new phase spearheaded by the antiglobalization stance of some Latin American leaders. We focus on the respective policies of each era, the crises that provided the impetus for change, and how policies impacted the region's landscape in highly uneven ways. The greatest emphasis, as a prelude to the rest of the book, is placed on the last years of the twentieth century and the early part of the twenty-first century, as significant events such as the economic crisis in Argentina, elections of several antineoliberal presidents, and various left-ist uprisings throughout the region may be indications that Latin America is indeed transitioning.

The chapter builds a conceptual framework for understanding Latin America's developmental trajectory and illustrates the dynamic nature of such policies over time. For example, this chapter argues that, especially as Latin America and the Caribbean are concerned, today's dominating pres-ence of foreign capital and ideas is nothing new. Paul Streeten (2001) points out that the world economy was actually more integrated at the end of the nineteenth century than it is today. Further, the region's own history shows that economic policies are not permanent. Placing the current neoliberal period in context, we illustrate that this political and economic transforma-tion over the last twenty years is just the latest episode in Latin America's developmental history. Indeed, over the past century, the region's economic policy has gone through (at least) three phases, all leaving a similar pattern of first growth and then collapse—and always the miserable footprint of inequality. Each phase has been characterized by significant policy changes driven by the current dominant paradigm; the transition to each new phase signaled by some type of economic crisis. It is important to remember the role of *agency* in this process—that is, how individuals are responding to macro-level changes and how the interaction between the global and the local alters the landscape of the region. This is also discussed in many other chapters throughout this volume.

Before we discuss the various eras, it is necessary to outline the parameters and limitations of this chapter. The dates used here to delineate the various eras are intended to provide a general time reference and not precise points in time when one period ends and another begins. Also worth mentioning is that all countries throughout the region did not embrace policies at the same time or in the same way. Some were much more aggressive in their adherence to certain policies, while others approached them more cautiously. It is beyond the scope of this chapter to illustrate the range of experiences. Rather, we draw on specific examples from around the region to illustrate the major points.

THE MODERN/LIBERAL PERIOD IN LATIN AMERICA
(1880s–1930s)

The modern/liberal period in Latin America emerged after independence and, in some ways, marked a significant break with the region's colonial history. This period quickly saw an expansion of world trade dominated by primary product exports such as coffee, bananas, sugar, and beef. These products, among many others, were the entry point into the global economy and in some cases provided handsome returns. Indeed, Argentina entered the twentieth century one of the richest countries in the world, ranking ahead of the United States and Great Britain and only slightly behind France in terms of per capita gold reserves in 1910.

In other cases, however, export gains were less than adequate, in many ways determined by geographic factors. Countries blessed with the right climate, soils, natural resources, ports, and/or proximity to chief trading partners fared well in their abilities to produce primary products. Brazil and Colombia saw success in coffee, Cuba in sugar, Argentina in wheat and livestock, Mexico in minerals, and Venezuela in oil. The majority of the small, "geographically challenged" countries, however, struggled to find a niche in the increasingly globalized economy. One notable exception was Panama—although too small to export substantial quantities of primary goods, its tiny size became its greatest asset during the construction of its canal—a precious trading route between the Atlantic and Pacific oceans.

The export-led model was supposed to expand domestic economies by creating jobs not directly related to exports—the "commodity lottery" deciding which countries fared well. Products like Argentinean beef, for example, required many separate processes (e.g., pasture, fencing, fattening, slaughtering, and packing), making this type of growth possible, illustrating that the export-led model could work well as a stimulus for development. Conversely, those countries exporting bananas in Central America and the Caribbean did so in enclaves, separating industry from the rest of the internal economy; thus, the model would give these countries little chance of growth (Bulmer-Thomas and Knight, 2003:83).

While securing its interests in these primary products, countries from the global North, most notably the United States and Great Britain, would invest in infrastructure in these countries. Direct foreign investment (DFI) was substantial not only in those regions that held vested economic interests, but also in those that had diplomatic ties and were deemed politically stable (Thorp, 1998:51). It was Argentina, Brazil, Uruguay, Cuba, and Chile that ranked the highest in DFI (Bulmer-Thomas and Knight, 2003). One important result of this investment was the construction of railroads, designed primarily to transport export products to the port city and out into the global economy.

Latin America's break from colonialism allowed the region to enter the global marketplace. However, fundamental aspects of the colonial economy remained in place. While foreigners came to invest, they did not do so as simple gestures of goodwill. Many of the foreign corporations dependent on Latin America's exports would come to buy the large amounts of land and infrastructure they relied on so heavily, oftentimes via government occupation or through backroom deals that cut or even abolished taxes and duties. Land was sold to them at "bargain prices" and workers' rights were almost nonexistent. These conditions were ideal for foreign domination, allowing the previous attitudes of colonialism to permeate, spurring an era of "neocolonialism." In 1899 the United Fruit Company, banana exporter and U.S. multinational (the predecessor of Chiquita Brands International), came to own 112 miles of Central America's railroad and well over 212,000 acres of land throughout the Caribbean and Central America (Schlesinger and Kinzer, 1998:67). By 1913 British investors owned approximately two-thirds of the total foreign investment in Latin America (Skidmore and Smith, 2001:44). In Cuba, where sugar dominated the country's exports, U.S. sugar mills owned 22 percent of Cuban national territory (Thorp, 1998:78); and in Puerto Rico, the country's three main exports—coffee, sugar, and tobacco—became dominated by U.S. corporations (Thorp, 1998:80).

Another legacy from the colonial period that was perpetuated was the highly uneven pattern of development which is evident today throughout the region. Most of the economic growth was occurring in coastal areas, or major cities near coastal areas, except for situations where it was necessary to develop other parts of the country (for example, the extraction of minerals). These economic enclaves were designed to export products as quickly and cheaply as possible and did little to develop the vast hinterlands of the region. Even though all Latin American countries were politically independent, they were still tied economically to countries of the North Atlantic, and most important was the increasing influence of the United States within the region. Perhaps this is best illustrated by the presence of the aforementioned American-based United Fruit Company, which proved to have not only a strong economic impact, but also a vigorous political might. This U.S. multinational would come to successfully request that the CIA overthrow Guatemala's democratically elected government due to policy differences, in turn sparking a bloody civil war that lasted over thirty years (see Schlesinger and Kinzer, 2001).

This vulnerability of economic and political dependency became increasingly evident in World War I and then more fatally during the Great Depression and World War II, pushing Latin America toward a new internally driven paradigm.

THE PERIOD OF IMPORT SUBSTITUTION INDUSTRIALIZATION (1940s–1970s)

The crash of the New York Stock Exchange in 1929 underscored Latin America's dependency on, and vulnerability to, the global North's economic policies. The crash, and later World War II, proved to be a *global* economic disturbance reducing the North's demand of nonessential primary products such as cacao, bananas, and coffee (Thorp, 1998:97–98). With this drop in foreign exchange, Latin America's capacity to buy imports decreased by approximately half (Kay, 1989:36). As Cardoso and Helwege (1995:84) state, this crisis backed Latin America by default into its second significant economic era.

Import substitution industrialization (ISI) held the guiding principle that a developing country should stop relying on imports and should produce substitutes at home. The ISI movement, seeking to grow national industry and offer protection from foreign competition as a means to reduce external dependencies and improve local economies, involved considerable state intervention—government subsidies and high tariffs and quotas on imported goods. The motivations behind ISI were the perceived flaws of the previous period. Chief among these was the economic asymmetry between the global North and Latin America, whereby primary goods were exported to developed countries that would transform them into finished goods (i.e., value added), and then sell them back to Latin America.

At the United Nation's Economic Commission for Latin America and the Caribbean (ECLAC, originally ECLA), Argentine economist Raúl Prebisch became ISI's primary champion by concluding that it was to Latin America's advantage to isolate itself from the global economy until it could build a strong domestic economy. While serving as ECLAC's executive secretary from 1949 to 1963, Prebisch argued that domestic industrialization would foster the spread of technology, increase employment, enhance the productivity of the labor force, and reduce the region's vulnerability to the international economic system (Birdsall and Lozada, 1998).

ISI proved to be most successful in the largest countries with the highest populations (notably Brazil, but also Argentina and Mexico), primarily because they had the greatest growth potential, the most resources, and relatively diversified economies and were thus able to borrow startup funds to expand their industrial capacity. Moreover, these countries with a large consumer base and bigger markets were able to sell their manufactured goods more successfully. Yet while these countries experienced greater economic growth than their smaller regional counterparts, they also took greater risks—the money borrowed to start these industries could not be repaid from the revenues received, and thus began their debt crises.

Despite the success in certain countries, the inherent flaws in these policies were soon exposed. The demise of ISI was attributable to ill-conceived policies with regard to both the production and consumption of domestic goods. First, because Latin America did not possess the necessary financial resources or the technological capabilities to implement a vast industrial program, the region was still reliant on foreign assistance. Thus, it was not possible for them to entirely break away from the burdens of dependency that characterized the previous period. The success of ISI was also hindered by the poor quality of products produced in the region, arguably because of the lack of competition in the state-run sectors. This generated little demand, as elites preferred and could afford imported products even if they had to leave the region to buy them. A substantial middle class never materialized and the poor could not afford to buy much, thereby limiting consumption and stunting the success of local industry. ISI's problems were further exacerbated by the lack of cooperation within the region, a legacy from the colonial period and something that has only been remedied slightly since then. Limited transportation linkages, historical rivalries between countries, and vast natural barriers all contributed to the limited interaction between the region's countries. This meant, to a large extent, that all countries were experimenting with ISI independently. This was especially detrimental to the smaller Latin American countries.

Industrialization programs focused on the largest cities, making these places magnets for employment as great emphasis was put on the industrial sector at the expense of the agricultural region. Not surprisingly, a mass rural-to-urban migration ensued as ISI's new factories promised the opportunity for many to move away from the exploitative rural working conditions to higher wages and a more modern lifestyle in the city. Soon the cities were overrun with would-be workers, and even when the factories could no longer absorb the workers, the rural refugees continued to come. This was the onset of "overurbanization" putting a strain on the urban infrastructure (housing, schools, as well as jobs), leading to the informal city, where many found work and housing outside of the formal sector. This fundamental shift in the region's social and economic geography led to a highly urbanized Latin America (see chapter 3) without the concomitant industrialization to achieve stable economic growth (as had previously occurred in the United States).

These flaws would become evident in the 1960s and manifest in greater social unrest, which opened the door for the period's first military dictatorship, Brazil, in 1964. By the mid-1970s, military rule was commonplace throughout the region and economies were stagnating. ISI did little to eliminate regional and class disparities in the region, and the now increasingly urban population began to voice its dissatisfaction.

Although the ISI period was a protectionist one, it was still heavily dependent on foreign investment. This was highlighted when as the region's economic instability led foreign investors and many international banks to reduce their presence in Latin America. Between 1980 and 1986, net capital inflows into the region dropped by 40 percent, and private net flows from international banks declined a whopping 80 percent (Gwynne, Klak, and Shaw, 2003), forcing governments to borrow monies from international lenders, most notably the World Bank and the International Monetary Fund (IMF). The World Bank, whose original undertaking was to aid in the recovery of World War II–ravaged countries in Europe, later modified its mission into working for "a world free of poverty" by injecting money into less developed countries to help expand their economies. Because the World Bank was under the marked political influence of free-market countries like the United States, these loans often imposed strict conditionalities, broadly known as structural adjustment programs (SAPs), that reinstilled the liberal economic policies and reduced role of the state reminiscent of the modern/liberal period.

Perhaps the death knell for ISI was in 1982, when Mexico declared that it was no longer able to service its debt and the peso was devalued. The country's debt crisis had a contagion effect throughout Latin America, triggering a crisis. The last years of ISI were plagued by military regimes and highly unstable economies characterized by large debts and hyperinflation. Subsequently, an alternative model was sought to alleviate the region's economic woes, although this time the policies came from abroad. However, in retrospect this period should be remembered as a relative bright spot in the region's development, with Brazil leading the way with an average growth rate during the period of 8.5 percent.

THE NEOLIBERAL PERIOD (1980s–?)

ISI's failure allowed advocates of free trade to reintroduce their agenda into Latin America. The model was first implemented in the region under the military rule of Augusto Pinochet in Chile. Pinochet took office after the bloody CIA-sponsored coup and bombing of the presidential palace of Salvador Allende on September 11, 1973. Two years later, Pinochet hired the "Chicago Boys" to restructure the economy. Dubbed so because of their postgraduate education at the University of Chicago, this group of economists called for the privatization of the country's state-owned enterprises as well as the tearing down of any trade barriers put up during ISI. As journalist Greg Palast (1998) outlines, Pinochet came to "abolish the minimum wage, outlaw trade union bargaining rights, privatize the pension system, abolish all taxes on wealth and on business profits, slash public employment, and privatize 212 state industries and 66 banks." Silva (2004) points out that it is important to remember that this economic project was first introduced to the region under the context of an American-backed military coup (p. 158), casting further doubt (and perhaps limited support) among the region's residents as well as outside observers to its legitimacy.

Neoliberalism was in many ways a return to the pre-ISI, modern/liberal period. Neoliberalism nearly eliminates state intervention in the economy and forces markets to be left unregulated and freely open to global capital (see chapter 2). During this period, the state was determined to be at the center of ISI's failure and therefore needed to be relegated to a less important role in economic development. Any impediments to trade (i.e., tariffs, quotas) were anathema to the development strategy and were quickly scrapped. The hyperinflation scared off many investors and greatly reduced the purchasing power of many residents. By the mid- to late-1980s, nearly all countries were on board, mostly because high debt had greatly reduced their economic sovereignty, and the region had entered into a new development paradigm despite the obvious parallels to an earlier failed era. Controversial policies such as privatization (selling off of state-owned industries) and trade liberalization (the elimination of tariffs and other trade barriers) were paramount throughout the region. Latin America was advised (some would say coerced) to integrate into the global economy as quickly as possible. Neoliberalism's proponents in the global North were led by a supranational triumvirate: the World Bank, the IMF, and the World Trade Organization (WTO). This collection of powerful decision-makers insists that the fall of the Soviet Union in the late 1980s signaled that conservative ideals triumphing over the socialist endeavors of communism should be interpreted as "capitalism is here to stay."

By 1989, the ideas of these supranational organizations came to be known as the "Washington Consensus," a recipe for stimulating economic growth and development in Latin America that included reforms like cutting public spending, lowering tariffs, decreasing regulation, promoting privatization, and opening up to foreign investment and trade. This cadre of individuals, believing these methods of globalization to be original, was instead committing itself to a set of principles and guidelines that already had a history of failing in Latin America and elsewhere. Countries of the region were now subordinate to supranational organizations who forced them to swallow some "bitter pills" to reduce the ills that plagued the region. Of course, some countries were more aggressive than others in their implementation of these policies, but it was not really a question of whether to adopt these policies or not, but rather how deeply to embrace them.

The success of neoliberalism was to be based primarily on the notion of efficiency. States were seen as inefficient, while the profit-seeking private sector was not and thus could rectify the problems of ISI. Proponents of these policies viewed any short-term hardships as necessary growing pains, while critics saw them as fundamental flaws that would have adverse effects on an increasing number of people. Privatization was one of the most controversial aspects of these reforms. The selling off of state industries allowed the state to quickly receive a significant amount of capital while at the same time relieving it of the responsibility of operating a diverse array of industries. It was expected that the private sector would come in and manage these enterprises more efficiently and profitably. In order to sell off these industries, the state had to find buyers/investors which, not surprisingly, were mostly based in the global North. Inflation was curtailed, and the trade-oriented policy adjustments once again began to lure investors. Giant U.S. and European corporations soon had critical links into the region: between the years 1990 and 2001, Latin America received private investment in infrastructure amounting to $360.5 billion, mainly in telecommunications (44 percent), energy (33 percent), and transport (18 percent) (Campos and Jimenez, 2003).

But the pitfalls associated with privatization proved to be more than "growing pains." Local populations felt the sting as soon as they found themselves without employment, as one of the quickest and easiest ways to make these industries more efficient was to cut costs, often achieved by laying off workers. Privatization and the subsequent layoffs occurred at a time when many social subsidies were being cut (also to become more efficient), placing an added burden on the already marginalized populations.

Proponents of neoliberal policies frequently point to how these policies lowered the hyperinflation of the 1980s, yet there was little else to illustrate their success, particularly as the century came to a close.

Although adhering to the neoliberal prescription, Latin America had not reaped the benefits long overdue. In the 1980s, Latin America's income per person, the most basic measure of economic well-being, actually shrank (by 3.1 percent). Inflation skyrocketed throughout the region, peaking at over 7,000 percent annually in Bolivia (1985), Nicaragua (1990), and Peru (1990), and exceeding 2,000 percent in both Argentina and Brazil. In fact, Bolivia and Peru both *averaged* an inflation rate of more than 1,000 percent between 1984 and 1993 (see Franko, 1999; Gwynne, Klak, and Shaw, 2003). The hardships that befell the local citizens during this period resulted in the moniker the "lost decade." ECLAC (2000) goes further to point out that the term "lost decade" falls short. At the end of 1989, the real per capita product stood at the level not of ten but of thirteen years earlier, and even earlier in some economies. While the 1990s saw some growth, it "was accompanied by negative characteristics from unemployment to volatility" (Grynspan, 2004), leaving the latter part of the decade to witness an increase in poverty and growing inequality, enough so that it was christened as the "lost half-decade" of 1997–2002 (Grynspan, 2004). In line with each period's history of growth and then collapse, were these distress signals flagging that the time had come to transition from the neoliberal era to a new phase?

THE EMERGENCE OF A NEW ERA?

During the neoliberal period, much of the power within the global economy shifted from the nation-state to transnational corporations. The neoliberal prescription, with promises of improving the standard of living among the masses, echoed facets of the liberal period and even the colonial era. During this era, the influence of transnational corporations and global capitalists escalated throughout the region. Increases in poverty and inequality led to widespread dissatisfaction among residents, with political ramifications.

In 1998, Venezuela elected left-wing populist Hugo Chávez as president. Chávez first came into prominence in 1992 for being jailed after heading a failed coup attempt against then president Carlos Andrés Pérez. Perez had initially campaigned against the neoliberal agenda and, indeed, while keeping his promise to nationalize the country's oil, did an about-face during his second term and embraced the Washington Consensus. Pérez would be impeached a year later for mishandling $17 million, used to aid the anti-Sandinista movement in Nicaragua.

Soon after Chávez's election, leading U.S. newspapers such as the *New York Times* and the *Washington Post* referred to Chávez as "Venezuela's rambunctious president" and a "firebrand," and his movement as containing "anti-American elements" (Ellner, 2001:6). The strong backing by Venezuela's impoverished majority helped Chávez survive a failed coup attempt in 2002 and a U.S.-backed recall referendum in 2004. While Chávez accused the Bush administration of aiding in his removal, reminiscent of Chile's socialist president Salvador Allende in 1973, the United States claimed at the time to have had neither participation nor knowledge of the incident. This would later be proven false when CIA documents were uncovered in late 2004 showing that, in fact, the United States had knowledge of the coup days before the attempt.

Chávez is seen as a major obstacle to the free-market agenda, as Venezuela accounts for about 15 percent of U.S. crude oil supplies and also has the largest proven reserves in the Western Hemisphere (Webb-Vidal and Cameron, 2005). His attempts to renegotiate the 60-year agreement with U.S. and British oil companies, which charges them as little as one percent in royalties and hands out huge tax breaks (Tucker, 2002), render Chávez a major threat to foreign interests.

Chávez would soon be joined by others around the continent. One of Latin America's most powerful neoliberal antagonists, Brazil's antiglobalization Workers Party (Partido dos Trabalhadores) candidate Luiz Inácio "Lula" da Silva, was elected president in 2002. Lula presented himself as a genuine alternative to neoliberalism. The Brazilian president described the economic model of the 1990s as "perverse," which, instead of bringing about financial stability and creating jobs, "strangles us" (Scheman, 2004). If not a total neoliberal adversary (he successfully campaigned and has governed closer to the center than his ideological history would have predicted), Lula has at least proven himself a key challenger to globalization's unfair playing field. Perhaps more significant was the election in 2005 of Evo Morales as president of Bolivia. The former coca farmer first gained notoriety for being elected executive secretary of the coca growers' union and is the first indigenous president in the country's history. All three of these presidents share their resistance and disdain of many aspects of globalization, and their desire to have more national control over strategic natural resources such as oil and gas, thus, in many ways, revisiting aspects of ISI. They all also emphasize a progressive social agenda (increase public expenditures to help poor and marginalized populations), which has earned them widespread support.

It is difficult to dismiss Venezuela's Chávez and the others as simply the region's menaces when considering that neoliberalism's most obvious failure materialized in Argentina, which exploded into a massive uprising leaving 36 dead (North and Huber, 2004:1). In late 2001–early 2002, the country spiraled into an economic meltdown after declaring a record default of $140 billion in public debt, resulting in massive unemployment and a poverty rate of greater than 50 percent (Hershberg, 2002). It is important to note that not all of Argentina's (or any country in the region, for that matter) ills are attributable solely to external actors, as corruption and mismanagement have been endemic to Latin America and a significant contributor to most if not all crises that have plagued the region. While Argentina had long supported the United States in global politics, it hardly received the concern it warranted from its northerly neighbor during its suffocating downturn as the United States' attention became concentrated in the Middle East and on the global "war on terror." A stunned Argentinean body politic, experiencing the worst depression in its history, went through four presidents in just a few weeks during December 2001 and opted for policies that defied the Washington Consensus. By stimulating internal consumption and ignoring IMF recommendations to pay its creditors first, Argentina's economy grew in 2003 and 2004 by 8 percent, its exports zoomed, its currency stabilized, unemployment rates dropped, and investors gradually returned (Rother, 2004). Asian countries, with China and South Korea in the lead, have now begun to move in. During a state visit in November 2004, the Chinese president, Hu Jintao, announced that his country plans to invest $20 billion in Argentina over the next decade (Rother, 2004).

Perhaps most important is the new regional axis between Brazil, Argentina, and Venezuela, with the latter becoming a member of the MERCOSUR trade group in 2006, thus moving toward a regionally comprehensive development strategy and perhaps trying to overcome one of the major pitfalls of ISI. It should also be noted that the narrow defeat of Mexico's leftist candidate, Manuel Lopez Obrador, in 2006, brings into question whether or not there is a cohesive Latin American turn to the left.

The first decades of the twenty-first century in Latin America promise to be eventful. At the forefront of this drama is Chávez promoting his "Bolivarian Revolution" as a socialist and regionally based alternative to neoliberalism. As this decade continues to unfold we will be able to see more clearly whether or not he will lead the way into a new paradigm or be relegated to pariah status while the neoliberal trend carries on.

CONCLUSION

Today's dominating presence of foreign capital and ideas in Latin America is nothing new. The current neoliberal transformation over the last twenty years, already following the predetermined pattern of growth and then collapse, is only the latest era in Latin America's developmental history. Thus, numerous questions persist:

Have the crises in Mexico, Brazil, and Argentina proven dismal enough to warrant an urgent need for reform? Do the elections of left-leaning leaders Chávez, Morales, Lula, and others, and the increasing presence of antiglobalization uprisings throughout the region signal the end of the overpowering and omnipresent Washington Consensus? Are these gestures toward regional cohesion viable enough to change the development trajectory? The region's historical transition into a new phase after experiencing an economic crisis might have already spelled this out. Granted, the neoliberal paradigm is heavily espoused by the global financial community and entrenched in the region; it will be much more difficult for Latin America to "come out from under" this recent period than it was in past episodes. But will these recent political movements be substantial enough to overturn the dominant paradigm of U.S.-led neoliberalization and globalization?

In the July/August 2003 issue of *Foreign Policy*, Jorge Domínguez points out that "the Yale University class of 1968 had no geography requirement for graduation, and Bush has looked east and west, not south." Indeed, while the United States concerns itself with the Middle East and the global "war on terror," it neglects to realize that conditions are ripe for Latin America to transcend the Washington Consensus and emerge into a new era—this time one led by individuals and grassroots organizations highly mobilized and influential in challenging the elite domination and transformation of the Latin American landscape.

SUGGESTED READINGS

Bulmer-Thomas, Victor, and Alan Knight. *The Economic History of Latin America since Independence.* 2nd edition. Cambridge: Cambridge University Press, 2003.

Cardoso, Eliana, and Ann Helwege. *Latin America's Economy: Diversity, Trends, and Conflicts.* Cambridge, Mass.: MIT Press, 1992.

Gwynne, Robert, and Cristóbal Kay. *Latin America Transformed: Globalization and Modernity.* 2nd edition. New York: Oxford University Press, 2004.

Schlesinger, Stephen, and Stephen Kinzer. *Bitter Fruit: The Story of the American Coup in Guatemala.* Cambridge, Mass.: Harvard University Press, 1999.

Skidmore, Thomas E., and Peter H. Smith. *Modern Latin America.* 5th edition. New York: Oxford University Press, 2001.

Thorp, Rosemary. *Progress, Poverty, and Exclusion: An Economic History of Latin America in the 20th Century.* Baltimore: Johns Hopkins University Press, 1998.

SUGGESTED FILMS

The Take (2004). Icarus Films. Directed by Avi Lewis and written by Naomi Klein.
Trinkets and Beads (1996). Icarus Films. Directed and written by Christopher Walker.

BIBLIOGRAPHY

Birdsall, Nancy, and Carlos Lozada. "Prebisch Reconsidered: Coping with External Shocks in Vulnerable Economies." *CEPAL Review*, October 1998.

Bulmer-Thomas, Victor, and Alan Knight. *The Economic History of Latin America since Independence*. 2nd edition. Cambridge: Cambridge University Press, 2003.

Campos, Javier, and Juan Luis Jimenéz. "Evaluating Rail Reform in Latin America: Competition and Investment Effects." *Conference on Railroad Industry Structure, Competition and Investment*. Toulouse, France, November 2003.

Cardoso, Eliana, and Ann Helwege. *Latin America's Economy: Diversity, Trends, and Conflicts*. Cambridge, Mass.: MIT Press, 1992.

Domínguez, Jorge I. "Grading the President: A View from Latin America." *Foreign Policy*, July/August 2003.

ECLAC. "Changing Production Patterns with Social Equity." November 2000.

Ellner, Steve. "Hugo Chavez: Radical Populist or Neopopulist?" *Prepared for Delivery at the 2001 Meeting of the Latin American Studies Association Washington, D.C.*, September 6–8, 2001.

Franko, Patrice. *The Puzzle of Latin American Economic Development*. Lanham, Md.: Rowman & Littlefield, 1999.

Grynspan, Rebecca. "Economic and Social Trends in Latin America: The Bases for Social Discontent." *International Review of Administrative Sciences* 70, no. 4 (2004): 693–709.

Gwynne, Robert N., Thomas Klak, and Dennis J. B. Shaw. *Alternative Capitalisms*. London: Edward Arnold Publishers, 2003.

Hershberg, Eric. "Why Argentina Crashed—And Is Still Crashing." *NACLA Report on the Americas* 36, no. 1 (2002): 30–33.

Kay, Cristóbal. *Latin American Theories of Development and Underdevelopment*. New York: Routledge, 1989.

North, Peter, and Ulli Huber. "Alternative Spaces of the 'Argentinazo'." *Antipode* 36, no. 5 (2004): 963–984.

Palast, Greg. "Tinker Bell Pinochet and the Fairy Tale Miracle of Chile." *The London Observer*, Sunday, November 22, 1998.

Rother, Larry. "Argentina's Economic Rally Defies Forecasts." *New York Times*, December 26, 2004.

Scheman, L. Ronald. "Reform US Neighborhood Bully Image." Commentary. *Christian Science Monitor*, December 29, 2004.

Schlesinger, Stephen, and Stephen Kinzer. *Bitter Fruit: The Story of the American Coup in Guatemala*. Cambridge, Mass.: Harvard University Press, 1999.

Silva, Patricio. "The New Political Order: Toward Technocratic Democracies?" In *Latin America Transformed: Globalization and Modernity*, 2nd edition, edited by R. N. Gwynne and C. Kay. New York: Oxford University Press, 2004.

Skidmore, Thomas E., and Peter H. Smith. *Modern Latin America*. 5th edition. New York: Oxford University Press, 2001.

Streeten, Paul. "Integration, Interdependence, and Globalization." *Finance and Development: The Quarterly Magazine of the IMF* 38, no. 2 (2001).

Thorp, Rosemary. *Progress, Poverty, and Exclusion: An Economic History of Latin America in the 20th Century*. Baltimore: Johns Hopkins University Press, 1998.

Tucker, Calvin. "US Fingerprints on Venezuelan Coup." *Trinicenter.com*, April 22, 2002.

Webb-Vidal, Andy, and Doug Cameron. "US Investigates Risk of Losing Oil Supplies from Venezuela." *Financial Times*, January 13, 2005.

2

Neoliberal Exports and Regional Vulnerability

Overview and Critical Assessment

Thomas Klak

Central America and the Caribbean can be characterized as a region of small, economically vulnerable, and trade dependent countries. The region is sandwiched between larger and more industrialized and economically diversified countries to the north and south. Together with Mexico, Central America and the Caribbean are economically dependent on the United States. This is an important regional commonality, as distinct from the situation in South America. Central America and the Caribbean's high levels of trade dependency distinguish the impacts of neoliberalism there compared to most of South America. Namely, neoliberalism puts pressure on these already highly trade-dependent countries to open their economies further and to export more.

This chapter provides an overview of the economic and geopolitical vulnerabilities that have constrained development in Central America and the Caribbean in recent decades. Since the 1980s international agencies and national governments in the region have pursued neoliberal policies that have introduced a range of new development schemes for the purpose of generating new sources of foreign exchange and employment. These include maquiladoras and free zones, export market niche agriculture, and offshore services. The chapter reviews the experience with these targeted sectors to understand why they have not delivered their promised development.

ENDURING DEPENDENCY

Whatever the theoretical paradigm adopted to examine the development conditions in Central American and Caribbean countries, their position as colonial, neocolonial, dependent, peripheral, or "price takers" within the international political and economic communities is a necessary point of departure. This chapter employs a theoretical perspective that extends from the dependency theory tradition and that is informed by contemporary world-systems theory (Gwynne, Klak, and Shaw, 2003). This perspective takes seriously the range of constraints on development policy options and the vulnerability to exogenous factors in Central America and the Caribbean due to the region's position in the global economic periphery (Klak, 1998; Potter et al., 2004).

While trade dependence is a key economic characteristic for all Central American and Caribbean countries, the smaller islands of the Eastern Caribbean are significantly more trade dependent than the larger islands and mainland countries. The United States is both the largest importer and exporter for virtually every Central American and Caribbean country, with the obvious exception of Cuba, against which the United States has had a trade embargo since the 1960s. At the same time, the United States is among the world's least trade dependent countries (Klak, 2004). This extreme contrast in the account ledgers and therefore at the negotiating table has enormous implications in the neoliberal "free trade" era. Trade is not really free unless all participants can choose *not* to trade (Ikerd, 2002). When one side holds the vast majority of the economic and geopolitical power, "coerced trade" might be a more apt descriptor than "free trade."

A major contributor to the region's contemporary weakness in policy negotiations was its foreign debt crisis, which began in the early 1980s but which endures to the present (Robotham, 2005). The neoliberal development policy paradigm was proposed as a solution to the debt crisis (Klak, 2004). It originated in the governments of Ronald Reagan in the United States and Margaret Thatcher in the United Kingdom, and has since been spread globally through the World Bank and the IMF (International Monetary Fund; Harvey, 2005). Dick Peet aptly summarizes the neoliberal paradigm in the process of critically reviewing the work of Jeffrey Sachs, the world's most influential development economist:

> Under all existing aid and debt relief schemes, to get their money poor countries have to agree to open their markets to foreign competition, privatize public enterprises, withdraw the state from service provision, reduce state budget deficits, reorient their economies to export orientation, flexibilize their labor markets, and so on down a list written under the belief that markets and free competition can guide any economy into the magic realm of growth, up the ladder of development. (Peet, 2006:452)

For more than two decades now, representatives of the World Bank and the IMF have regularly visited the capital cities not only of Central America and the Caribbean but also of the larger countries of Latin America. During these visits, financial aid and debt restructuring are exchanged for commitments to the neoliberal transition, which is in the process moved slowly, incrementally, but irreversibly along (Hey and Klak, 1999). Since the 1980s Latin American policymakers have placed great emphasis on attracting foreign investors, especially ones proposing to earn foreign exchange. The Latin American state's role has therefore shifted away from direct ownership, production, and the provision of social services, and toward subsidizing export-oriented investors. The state's new role under neoliberalism is sometimes portrayed as one of downsizing, if not retrenchment (Ohmae, 1995). However, it is more accurately viewed as a qualitatively different relation between the state, investors, popular classes, and territories. For some neoliberal activities, such as promoting exports, creating and managing free zones, and competing to attract investment, the Latin American state's role has actually expanded considerably (Peck, 2004).

The main point of this section is to place contemporary Latin American development policy in its recent historical context. The Latin American debt crisis since 1980 opened the way for a new era of development policy called neoliberalism, which continues to the present. Neoliberalism, judged to be "the most successful ideology in world history" (Anderson, 2000:17), has profoundly shaped the role of states and the organization of societies throughout Latin America, and indeed the world. However, it has had its greatest impact on smaller and more trade-dependent and thus vulnerable states such as those of Central America and the Caribbean.

THE BANANA WAR

Banana exports were economically prominent during the twentieth century in many parts of the Western Hemisphere, and led to the banana war that began in 1996. Beginning in 1899, the United Fruit Company (called Chiquita since 1968) amassed more than 3.4 million acres of rainforest in Central America and the Colombian Caribbean. It cleared large sections of these exceptionally biodiverse regions, and created plantations and vertically integrated production systems that brought bananas to stores in the United States and throughout the world. After 1958, Standard Fruit (Dole) and Del Monte joined Chiquita to become the three major banana suppliers of global markets (Wiley, 2007).

The origin of banana exports from the Caribbean was different. Beginning in the 1950s, Britain instructed small farmers in its Caribbean colonies such as St. Lucia, Dominica, and St. Vincent (all part of the Windward Islands) to plant bananas and to export them to a guaranteed market in the United Kingdom through the British company Geest. This British policy was part of a series of international trade agreements, the name of which changed over time. Europe's Banana Protocols began in 1957 and were followed by four successive Lomé Conventions and one Cotonou Agreement. France, Greece, Italy, Portugal, and Spain have also provided protected markets to former or current colonies (Gonzalez-Perez and McDonough, 2006). Taken together, these policies have provided special market access to more than seventy former European colonies, which are now called the ACP (Africa-Caribbean-Pacific) countries. The special market access applies mainly to commodities such as coffee, sugar, and bananas. Only twelve ACP countries export bananas to Europe, and seven of these are members of CARICOM (the Caribbean Common Market).

The guaranteed British/European Union (EU) market for bananas from its former colonies created one of the few exceptions in the Western Hemisphere to the rule of U.S. trade dependency. For years, St. Lucia, Dominica, and St. Vincent each earned more than half of all their foreign exchange from bananas, which placed them among the countries of the world most dependent on the export of a single cash crop (Cater, 1996). Perhaps even more telling of banana dependence, in 1993 banana farmers in Dominica, for example, were 20 percent of the entire labor force (Wiley, 1998). In addition to bananas, agricultural products that generate foreign exchange for these Eastern Caribbean countries and that are also grown by small farmers include coffee, cocoa, vanilla beans, citrus fruit, soap, and bay oil. These same farmers also grow a host of traditional Caribbean subsistence crops that are crucial to local survival.

Europe's guaranteed import of Eastern Caribbean bananas made it an advantageous form of trade dependency, at least in the medium term. Although farmers have felt powerless against Geest (and, since 1995, against Fyffes, which acquired its Caribbean operations), bananas fueled significant growth in middle-class prosperity on the islands. Gains were especially solid for the three islands' 50,000 banana farmers, whose prominence and vitality are unusual in Central America and the Caribbean region dominated by large landholdings (Barrow, 1992). Banana exports helped Dominica, St. Vincent, and St. Lucia climb to the top half of countries of the world ranked by the Human Development Index. In addition, the public educational systems of these three Caribbean islands among others in the region have for long been national assets. This reservoir of human capital offers potential when looking toward an uncertain and vulnerable, but hopefully more sustainable, future.

The British banana trade arrangement, by creating opportunities for thousands of smallholders to earn steady livable incomes by farming in ways that did not severely degrade the land, contributed to social development. It could have contributed to longer-term national sustainable development but it came under scrutiny in light of the global neoliberal paradigm. The implementation of the Single European Market in 1993 and the creation in

1995 of the World Trade Organization (WTO) were institutional manifestations of a global trend toward neoliberalism. Managed trade arrangements like those offered by Lomé/Cotonou essentially violated WTO principles. Unfortunately for the Eastern Caribbean islands, their lack of trade dependency on the United States created a bigger problem. The United States successfully argued to the WTO on behalf of Central America and Ecuador that the guaranteed banana market in the EU is illegal and must be terminated (Klak, 2004).

European Union trade preferences for bananas expired on January 1, 2006, and were replaced by a tariff system that offers just a 176 euro per ton preference for Windward Island bananas. This is considered insufficient to preserve their banana industries. Preferences on their other agricultural exports to the EU are due to expire by the end of 2008. The immediacy of the situation leaves little time to adjust to the harsh economic realities imposed by neoliberalism. Thanks to the WTO ruling against the EU, the Eastern Caribbean banana sector has severely contracted. By 2003 Dominica's banana earnings had fallen to U.S.$5 million, down from $30 million in 1992 (*Economist*, 2004), and the decline has only continued since then. Unemployment already exceeded 20 percent in recent years and the banana sector collapse has significantly worsened the problem. Unemployment in St. Lucia and St. Vincent has similarly risen to over 15.5 percent (UN, 2000). These countries have also lost a key middle-class sector in the form of small banana farmers that worked the land in relatively benign ways compared to the large-scale Central American, Colombian, and Ecuadoran banana plantations that have now usurped most of their European market share (Barrow, 1992; Grossman, 1998; Wiley, 2007).

Central America, Colombia, and Ecuador are on the "winning" side in this banana war, and therefore can expect strong global demand for their bananas in the future. However, unlike the "losing" side that includes the former British colonies, Central American, Colombian, and Ecuadoran banana workers generally do not own their own small farms. Instead, they toil for low wages on huge plantations that sell their product to the world's largest and oligopolistic fruit companies (Chiquita, Dole, and Del Monte). Throughout the twentieth century, these workers' collective actions to improve their conditions have met serious resistance from owners supported by the state. Pesticide dangers and poisonings have also been well documented (Gallagher and McWhirter, 1998; Gonzalez-Perez and Mc-Donough, 2006). Thus, judged in terms of sustainable development, both sides of the dispute in Latin America are losers. U.S. banana corporations have won greater access to the EU, and EU consumers have won cheaper bananas. Neither of these victories advances sustainability in Latin America or in the core countries. For Latin America, the banana war illustrates the many vulnerabilities and obstacles in the way of sustainable development.

The Eastern Caribbean region in particular now needs to vigorously expand other sources of foreign exchange.

THE NEOLIBERAL TRANSITION AND NONTRADITIONAL AGRICULTURAL EXPORTS

Neoliberal policies have had many impacts on agriculture besides bananas, and also on a range of urban economic sectors. In the 1980s, most Central American and Caribbean countries shifted the axes of their economies away from traditional agriculture toward a new focus on promoting the export of higher-value manufactured and "market niche" agricultural products. In the 1990s, there was yet another economic shift. The focus became international services, including tourism (already central to many economies), but also offshore financial services and other telecommunications-based services. Through these shifts, the region continues to face the monumental challenge of replacing traditional sources of income with new ones suitable to the present neoliberal era of more open trade relationships, and shielding itself from the vulnerability associated with relying on a relatively few products and North Atlantic markets.

These multifaceted neoliberal development policy efforts can be seen as a "shatter-shot" approach to searching out export market niches in agricultural and beyond (Klak, 1998). The strategy has been to diversify crops and the economy as a whole in order to generate new sources of foreign exchange and to help protect themselves from any particular volatile markets. Even in the smallest countries, policymakers are actively promoting investment in a host of nontraditional activities. In tiny Dominica, for example, these range from tourism (see chapter 6), assembly operations, and data processing, to vegetables, fruits, seafood, and cut flowers (Wiley, 1998). Such experimentation raises the essential question of whether product niches with considerable foreign exchange earning power and stability can be secured, or whether they are replacing monocrop and single-market dependence with new forms of neoliberal vulnerability. In other words, are exporters and the state behind them trying to do too many very challenging things at once while doing little to build toward a sustainable future?

Under neoliberalism, Central American and Caribbean countries have also been under pressure to reduce the trade barriers that have protected labor-absorbing domestic producers. This includes farmers who have traditionally served domestic markets. Farmers now find themselves unable to compete in the U.S. market and against U.S. imports. U.S. crops are produced on a larger scale, with more chemical inputs, and are underwritten with federal subsidies (Ikerd, 2002). The results have not been encouraging in Central America and the Caribbean, but governments have continued to follow the neoliberal approach of aggressively promoting and subsidizing an array of nontraditional exports (Klak, 2004).

The exports of fruits, vegetables, and flowers, labeled NTAEs (nontraditional agricultural exports), by definition have high value by volume and area under cultivation. Central America has been more successful than the Caribbean in meeting the demand for NTAEs in the United States and other North Atlantic markets. However, the NTAE sector has had several problems that have restricted benefits, even in Central America. The sector is characterized by dominance by firms from the United States and other core countries, inadequate state support to develop the sector, shaky performance and low to no growth for small-scale local producers, and poor working conditions for the employees (Thrupp, 1995).

THE RISE AND FALL OF MAQUILADORAS

Over recent decades international development agencies and national governments in Central America and the Caribbean have promoted and pursued many nonagricultural exports for the purpose of earning foreign exchange and generating employment. These include maquiladoras (assembly plants for such things as clothing, electronics, plastic goods, shoes, and sporting goods) and the so-called free zones, many of which are state subsidized, that house the maquiladoras (see also chapter 5). New sources of foreign exchange also include data processing and other offshore services. Maquiladoras are discussed in this section followed by an overview of offshore services placed in the context of U.S. global financial policies in response to 9/11.

Haiti was one of the earliest entries into the maquiladora sector in the region. Employment expanded between 1970 and 1984 under the Duvalier dictatorship, after which jobs began to move elsewhere as Haiti became less stable and other countries opened free zones as a component of the neoliberal transition. Even during peak maquiladora employment, however, Haiti was a net exporter of capital. This is because foreign investors and Haitian managers moved most of their profits abroad, and more consumer and producer goods came in than were exported as manufactured products (Dupuy, 2005). Since the 1990s Haiti's political instability has repelled more maquiladora investment than its sub-fifty-cents-an-hour wages have attracted. Wages are already minimized; any lower and workers literally could not survive (McGowan, 1997).

Elsewhere in Central America and the Caribbean, maquiladora employment peaked in the early 1990s. Tens of thousands of mainly young females were employed in factories in Jamaica, Haiti, and each Central American country. Most of the Eastern Caribbean countries had more than a thousand

workers each. The Dominican Republic attracted the most assembly operations and had over 160,000 factory workers. But even there, the assembly
plants were low-paying economic enclaves with minimal positive impact
on the Dominican economy (Willmore, 1994; Kaplinsky, 1995). Since the
mid-1990s, maquiladora employment has declined throughout Central
America and the Caribbean. More and more noncore countries, particularly
in Asia, have sought assembly operations and lured investors away from the
region with promises of state support, lower wages, and more abundant
nonunion workers.

Observing the rise and fall of the maquiladora sector in St. Lucia, one official in the ministry overseeing the promotion of foreign industrial investment lamented, "many establishments that came here in the early days were
what are called 'footloose'" (Richardson, 1998). But the English-speaking
Caribbean has virtually no maneuvering room to attract and keep manufacturers. Prevailing wages of $1–2 per hour are the absolute minimum needed
to offset the high cost of living on the import-dependent islands. However,
these rates are uncompetitive in the global South, where there is so much
poverty. State subsidies to investors are ubiquitous in Central America, the
Caribbean, and beyond. They therefore simply cancel each other out and
undermine the effort to generate foreign exchange.

Economic globalization has increased capital mobility, and there are now
too many low-wage countries competing for the same limited maquiladora
investment. Even low-wage Central America began to lose jobs when NAFTA
(North American Free Trade Agreement) came on line in 1994 and shifted
much of the free zone employment to Mexico. The many garment producers that have abandoned Central America and the Caribbean left behind
tens of thousands of unemployed workers and many vacant factory shells,
a good share of which were built when governments took international
loans they have been unable to repay. Governments have had to admit
that "the move to diversify the economy to include export-oriented services
(and increasing tourism), as well as non-traditional exports such as apparel
manufacturing has not yielded the economic development gains expected"
(Government of Jamaica, 2002:18). Central American and Caribbean states
therefore have not been able to provide decent and long-term income opportunities through the maquiladora sector. The sector's rise and fall over
time, and its "race to the bottom" logic, demonstrates its fundamental flaws
(Klak and Das, 1999; Klak, 2004).

Anticipating the negative impact of NAFTA for export manufacturing,
Caribbean governments and international institutions such as the World
Bank's Caribbean Group for Cooperation in Economic Development
(CGCED) began exploring economic alternatives, as discussed in the next
section. But even in Mexico, maquiladora employment peaked at over 1.5
million in 2000. Since then, hundreds of thousands of jobs have moved to

Asia, particularly China, where there is a vastly greater supply of laborers earning around twenty-five cents an hour (Ross, 2002). Further, the kind of investment and other neoliberal economic changes that NAFTA has brought to Mexico has increased productivity and exports, but also lowered real wages, particularly in manufacturing, and sent millions more people to live in poverty (Anderson and Cavanagh, 2003).

ONLINE GAMBLING

In the mid-1990s, CGCED recommended that Caribbean governments promote international service industries such as tourism, offshore banking, data processing, and offshore services as alternative economic activities to the failed ones discussed above (World Bank, 1994). Offshore services have taken many forms, ranging from insurance and ship registration to psychic healers, phone sex, and Internet gambling. Central American and Caribbean countries established some of the world's first offshore regulatory environments for Internet gambling (Martin, 2001). As of May 2001, there were about 1,400 offshore gambling sites worldwide, operated by about 250 companies. All of these online gambling sites are located outside of the United States, and most are in Central America and the Caribbean.

Costa Rica hosts about 15 percent of all gambling sites. In Costa Rica, about 3,000 workers, mostly college students and foreigners staying on after teaching English, earn U.S.$4–5 per hour taking bets or answering customer queries over the phone. Worldwide, online wagers were about $300 million in 1997 and $1.6–2.2 billion in 2000, and were projected to reach $100 billion in 2006. Note that no U.S. law explicitly prohibits gambling over the Internet inside the United States. What is invoked is a 1961 U.S. law called the "Wire Wage Act" that prohibits gambling operations to use interstate telephone lines. The prohibition is generally understood to include the Internet.

Big U.S. casinos have for years lobbied the U.S. government to legalize online gambling inside the country. For its part, the U.S. Congress has in recent years considered legislation that would more directly criminalize online gambling in two ways. Legislation would explicitly prohibit and prosecute Internet gambling operations and customers, and it would force Internet providers to attempt what computer specialists say is not technologically feasible: to block access to offshore gambling sites. For now, so long as U.S. law restricts Internet gambling within its borders, Central American and Caribbean countries that host offshore gambling sites can earn some foreign exchange and create some jobs for foreign language–proficient residents. But this equates to a highly tenuous offshore services sector because its advantages would be eliminated if the United States were to legalize domestic Internet gambling or prosecute it internationally. The events of 9/11 and U.S. policy responses to it have revealed additional aspects of regional vulnerability, including the fragility of other offshore services, to which we now turn.

POST-9/11 VULNERABILITIES AND OFFSHORE SERVICES

The events of 9/11 occurred as the U.S. economy was beginning a downturn after nearly eight years of sustained growth. The convergence of recession and the fear of terrorism in the United States created a heightened sense of socioeconomic, as well as strategic, insecurity. President Bush's calls to American citizens to go on with their lives, travel, and spend, translated into more domestic travel and spending, rather than foreign travel and spending (CTO, 2004). The reduction of U.S. international travel after 9/11 followed a pattern seen after the first war with Iraq in 1991. Then U.S. citizens became more fearful of flying abroad and the Caribbean's vulnerable tourism sector, otherwise unrelated to the source of fear, suffered.

Similarly, an immediate effect of 9/11 was a generalized fear of flying internationally among citizens of the United States and also some parts of the EU (e.g., Britain, France, Germany). The stricter security measures adopted after 9/11 may also have discouraged leisure travel. Caribbean tourism contracted even in locations where Europeans outnumber Americans, such as Barbados, the Dominican Republic, and Cuba. During the first semester of 2002, European tourist arrivals to the Dominican Republic declined by 17.1 percent and to Barbados by 13.1 percent (CTO, 2004). The second war with Iraq worsened the contraction in Caribbean tourism. The Caribbean Tourism Organization (CTO) announced in a March 25, 2003, "War in Iraq" bulletin that there had been "fewer cancellations than expected." However, Air Jamaica, after surviving a U.S.$80 million financial loss in 2002, saw reservations fall by almost 40 percent during the first two weeks of hostilities. This decline forced Air Jamaica to reduce flights to some U.S. cities it regularly services, thereby worsening the decline in passengers. The Caribbean's regional airlines that serve the smaller islands went even further into arrears and required additional state subsidies to continue operating. Tourism reservations for Mexico similarly declined by 17.1 percent overall and by more than 30 percent from U.S. visitors (CTO, 2003). One needs to pause and consider the reverberating impacts of sudden exogenous-induced declines of this magnitude, even though they were temporary, throughout societies dependent on tourism revenue. Not until early in 2005 did international travel finally rebound to its pre-9/11 level. For the Caribbean region, so reliant on international tourism, this represents a three-and-one-half-year setback.

The global economic slowdown, the war on terrorism, and the war in Iraq have influenced the spending decisions of investors and citizens in the United states and in Europe. The flows of foreign direct investment (FDI) to Latin America and the Caribbean, which the region's neoliberal economic opening was supposed to increase, peaked in 1999 at $86.3 billion and then decreased consistently through 2003. FDI has rebounded since then, reaching $47.3 billion in 2005, but this is still below the $50.2 billion recorded in 2002 (ECLAC, various years). Part of the explanation for the tepid investor interest is that the most attractive targets for FDI are already gone. Many large state companies have been offered and purchased by foreign interests. Global investors are now focusing their attention on Asia (UNCTAD, 2004). This shift leaves most of Latin America, and particularly the smaller countries, in the periphery or the backwaters of the global economy. The region's main value to transnational corporations (TNCs) is its untapped consumer markets, which the neoliberal policy paradigm, most recently in the form of CAFTA (Central American Free Trade Agreement), has continued to nudge open.

The second Iraq war's predictable negative economic implications for the Caribbean region were enough to push CARICOM to issue a resolution in February 2003 opposing a U.S. invasion. The U.S. assistant secretary of state for hemispheric affairs, Otto Reich, responded to CARICOM's declaration with a thinly veiled threat:

> I would urge CARICOM to not only study very carefully what it says, but the consequences of what it says. . . . We are not going to take retaliatory action or punitive measures, but the American people do listen and our Congress listens. It is not just the executive branch. These kinds of resolutions and this kind of language doesn't help lead to a better understanding between our countries. (BBC, 2003)

Given CARICOM's preexisting vulnerability to exogenous forces and its trade and geopolitical dependence on the United States, Reich's warning is dire. It illustrates an enduring regional dilemma: Should the Caribbean support U.S. policies even when they are seen as contrary to regional interests (let alone policies seen as immoral or unlikely to promote global stability), or should it prepare to face additional "consequences"?

Since 9/11 the U.S. government, in concert with the OECD (Organization for Economic Cooperation and Development), has sought and achieved greater regulatory oversight of offshore financial centers (OFCs), a large portion of which are in Central America and the Caribbean (Klak, 2002). A major component of these efforts is directed at disclosing sources of money laundering. They include blacklisting suspected individuals and organizations, freezing of assets, and investigating the internal records of U.S. banks and their foreign affiliates. The Bush team is also pressuring OFCs with bank secrecy laws to cooperate with the FBI and other U.S. government agencies by providing information on depositors. Nearly all governments hosting OFCs are cooperating and some, such as Grenada, have gone as far as to shut down most of these banks. This results, according to a British international financial investigator quoted in *The Observer of London* (February 24, 2002), in treaties that "make your eyes water when you see them. It's classic U.S. extra-territorial lawmaking." One consequence is a reduction of capital flows through, and therefore revenues going to, the offshore centers, particularly the smaller, poorer, and less regulated ones (Klak, 2002).

To summarize, 9/11 occurred at the beginning of an economic recession in the United States and triggered a series of other events leading to a significant shift in U.S. domestic and foreign policies. What can be termed "the post-9/11 shift" refers to a combination of negative factors around the 9/11 critical event: fear of flying, tighter travel security measures, economic recession, the call to Americans to continue on with their lives and spend domestically, a crackdown on OFCs, and the war in Iraq. The post-9/11 shift has thus created a new international environment that negatively impacts Caribbean economies, particularly the international services sectors, that neoliberal policy had already weakened and made more vulnerable (Pantojas-García and Klak, 2004).

These post-9/11 vulnerabilities have not dissipated with time. Instead they have become institutionalized in U.S. policy and in its foreign policy. For example, tiny Dominica has recently needed to spend U.S.$3 million on upgrades to its port facilities in order to conform with U.S. requirements regarding ships entering U.S. ports. The impacts of 9/11 and the international campaign in response to it reveal how global priorities are set. The antiterrorism campaign demonstrates how a critical event in core countries can quickly and decisively shift global priorities, marginalize and effectively discredit other concerns, and dominate the global agenda. Further, the post-9/11 shift in U.S. policies laid bare the persistent vulnerability of Central America and the Caribbean to international economic and political events. Their governments and entrepreneurs cannot influence the international economic and political frameworks that condition their policy options. Even in their new role as international service centers, Central American and Caribbean economies remain highly vulnerable (arguably more so) to changes in the international prices of commodities and in the regulation of trade and banking.

REMITTANCE ECONOMIES AND PHANTOM LANDSCAPES

Taken together, the decline of most Central American and Caribbean economies successively as agricultural exporters, manufacturing export platforms, and now international service centers places them on the path to

Figure 2.1. Charred tree trunks are virtually all that remains of what was ten years ago vast tracts of the Petén rain forest in northern Guatemala.

what has been labeled "peripheral postindustrialization" (Pantojas-García, 2001). The obvious questions are, what can people do to make a living, and how can these countries generate foreign exchange?

Take the example of Guatemala, which has one of the strongest natural resource bases and economic profiles in the region (Klak, 2004). Official unemployment now exceeds 50 percent and unofficially may be 75 percent. The civil war that killed over 100,000 people finally ended in 1996. The peace opened previously remote and dangerous parts of the country for increased settlement. The huge Petén rain forest region of northern Guatemala has received thousands of peasant migrants who have come to clear and burn land for farming (figure 2.1). The supportive infrastructure needed to make these small farms viable, such as agricultural extension services, loans, and transportation to get products to market, is inadequate. Peasants therefore fail as farmers and sell their recently cleared parcels, which are now worth more on the market than when they grew trees, to cattle ranchers who consolidate them. The peasants then move on to clear more forest. This process has cleared hundreds of thousands of acres of rainforest during the last decade alone (figure 2.2).

With most agricultural and industrial sectors on the decline, Central America and the Caribbean countries now have essentially service and remittance economies. Services that are growing as a result of tourism promotion include the hotel and restaurant sectors, formal and informal

Figure 2.2. Peasants who clear Guatemalan rain forests have difficulty making a living off the land, so instead they sell off their parcels to cattle ranchers.

vendors, and taxi and tour drivers. Tourists from core countries also inadvertently bring with them the "demonstration effect," whereby locals are exposed and grow accustomed to an affluent consumer lifestyle (Pattullo, 1996). The dominance of U.S. television and films similarly carries with it this demonstration effect (Potter et al., 2004). Other services that have expanded in recent years include the standard array of other items associated with global consumer culture such as cable and satellite TV, shopping malls, fast-food chains, and U.S.-style subdivisions (figure 2.3).

Across Central America, the Caribbean, and Mexico as well, the principal export has become workers who migrate legally or illegally to the United States and other core countries (see also chapters 12 and 13). About 800,000 Haitians live in the United States and Canada and keep their homeland afloat through remittances. According to Mexico's president Vicente Fox, by 2003 remittances became Mexico's "biggest source of foreign income, bigger than oil, tourism or foreign investment." He added that "the 20 million Mexicans in the United States generate a gross product that is slightly higher than the $600 billion generated by [the 90 million] Mexicans in Mexico" (Alonso Lugo, 2003).

Figure 2.3. International fast-food chains arrived in Roseau, the capital of Dominica, in 2006.

Services are also driven by the remittance-receiving family members who have income-earning relatives in the United States and other core countries. These family members can consume at a middle-class level without the associated gainful employment. Their purchasing power is demonstrated by new homes and home additions, trendy clothes and electronic goods, high-tech appliances, fancy vehicles, and domestic service workers. These landscapes and their inhabitants convey the false impression that there is much local economic vibrancy, stability, and productivity, and hence earn the label "phantom landscapes."

Underneath the visual prosperity is economic malaise, or worse. In Jamaica, for example, neoliberalism has cut deep into public resources, so that the state is no longer financially capable of maintaining clientelistic relationships with constituents (Sives, 2002; Gray, 2004). In poorer parts of Kingston, the state has been upstaged by drug dons who now control neighborhoods and protect and provide for residents better than the state can (figure 2.4). The emergent wealth from drug trafficking also distorts the landscape, as Robotham (2005:211) observes: "we have witnessed prolonged contraction of the formal economy over the very same period that this frenzy of house construction and car buying has occurred."

CONCLUSION

Sustainable development requires a strong and secure set of economic activities in communities that do not degrade the environment. With this goal in mind, the chapter examined a variety of export sectors that have been pur-

Figure 2.4. Jamaican police, who traditionally carried only batons, are now equipped with AK-47s, military helmets, and bulletproof vests.

sued before and during the neoliberal policy transition. The small countries of Central America and the Caribbean have been particularly hard hit by the recent changes in the global trading regime that have led to sharp declines in their ability to generate foreign exchange through exports. It can be viewed as ironic that perhaps the most successful recent export from the region is their workforces, which have gone to core countries to earn and remit money back home. The neoliberal transition has been incompatible with sustainable development because it has undermined autonomy and empowerment at the national and local scales. Neoliberalism has created additional problems by pressuring already highly trade dependent countries to trade more and thereby decrease their self-sufficiency and self-determination.

From the perspective of world-systems theory, these results are unsurprising. Sustainable development policies are unlikely to be delivered by indebted, neoliberalizing, peripheral states with so little maneuvering room and so narrowly tied to powerful economic interests at home and abroad. Central American and Caribbean countries are therefore facing major challenges regarding how to cope with their new economic realities. Their ability to replace failed exports with new productive activities will determine the stability of those societies in the years ahead. With so few options, governments have felt compelled to embrace the "last resorts" (Pattullo, 1996), that is, various forms of tourism development. Chapter 11 examines mass tourism, whereas chapter 12 explores ecotourism-related sustainable development. These emerging policies are arguably the front-runners to replace the various fallen exports reviewed in this chapter.

BIBLIOGRAPHY

Alonso Lugo, Luis. "Remittances Are Mexico's Biggest Source of Income, Says Fox." *Associated Press*, 2003, at http://www.signonsandiego.com/news/mexico/20030924-2051-us-mexico.html (accessed May 14, 2007).

Anderson, Perry. "Renewals." *New Left Review* 1 (2000): 5–24.

Anderson, Sarah, and John Cavanagh. "Factsheet on the NAFTA Record: A 10th Anniversary Assessment." *ZNet*, 2003, at http://www.zmag.org/content/showarticle.cfm?ItemID=4865 (accessed May 13, 2007).

Barrow, Christine. *Family Land and Development in St. Lucia.* Cave Hill, Barbados: Institute of Social and Economic Research, University of the West Indies, 1992.

BBC (*BBC Monitoring International Reports*). "CARICOM Should Rethink Its Opposition to US-Led War on Iraq, USA's Reich Says," April 3, 2003.

Cater, E. "Ecotourism in the Caribbean: A Sustainable Option for Belize and Dominica?" In *Sustainable Tourism in Islands and Small States: Case Studies,* edited by L. Briguglio, R. Butler, D. Harrison, and W. L. Filho, pp. 122–146. London: Pinter, a Cassell imprint, 1996.

CTO (Caribbean Tourism Organization). "Mexico's Tourism Hit Hard by War," 2003, at http://www.onecaribbean.org/information/documentdownload.php?rowid=1226 (accessed May 13, 2007).

CTO. "Caribbean Tourism Performance 2003, Prospects for 2004," 2004, at http://www.onecaribbean.org/information/documentview.php?rowid=2391 (accessed May 14, 2007).

Dupuy, Alex. "Globalization, the World Bank, and the Haitian Economy." In *Contemporary Caribbean Cultures and Societies in a Global Context,* edited by Franklin W. Knight and Teresita Martínez-Vergne, pp. 43–70. Chapel Hill: University of North Carolina Press, 2005.

ECLAC. *Latin Business Chronicle,* various years, at http://www.latinbusinesschronicle.com/ (accessed May 14, 2007).

Economist. "Easy Money," April 7, 2004.

Gallagher, Mike, and Cameron McWhirter. "Chiquita: An Empire Built on Controversy." *The Cincinnati Enquirer,* May 3, 1998, at http://www.mindfully.org/Pesticide/chiquita/ (accessed May 13, 2007).

Gonzalez-Perez, Maria-Alejandra, and Terence McDonough. "Chiquita Brands and the Banana Business: Brands and Labour Relations Transformations." CISC (Centre for Innovation & Structural Change, National University of Ireland) Working Paper No. 23, January 2006, at http://www.cisc.ie/publications/detail.php?publication_code=7544 (accessed May 14, 2007).

Government of Jamaica. *A Five-Year Strategic Information Technology Plan for Jamaica.* Kingston: Government of Jamaica, 2002, at http://www.mct.gov.jm/GOJ%20IT%20Plan%20-%20Revised%20Version%20March%2020021.pdf (accessed May 13, 2007).

Gray, Obika. *Demeaned but Empowered: The Social Power of the Urban Poor in Jamaica.* Mona: University of West Indies Press, 2004.

Grossman, Lawrence. *The Political Ecology of Bananas: Contract Farming, Peasants, and Agrarian Change in the Eastern Caribbean.* Chapel Hill: University of North Carolina Press, 1998.

Gwynne, Robert, Thomas Klak, and Dennis J. B. Shaw. *Alternative Capitalisms: Geographies of Emerging Regions.* London: Edward Arnold Publishers, and New York: Oxford University Press, 2003.

Harvey, David. *A Brief History of Neoliberalism.* Oxford, U.K.: Oxford University Press, 2005.

Hey, Jeanne, and Thomas Klak. "From Protectionism toward Neoliberalism: Ecuador under Four Administrations (1981–1996)." *Studies in Comparative International Development* 34 (1999): 66–97.

Ikerd, John. "The Real Costs of Globalization to Farmers, Consumers and Our Food System," 2002, at http://www.ssu.missouri.edu/faculty/jikerd/papers/Globalization.html (accessed May 14, 2007).

Kaplinsky, Raphael. "A Reply to Willmore." *World Development* 23 (1995): 537–540.

Klak, Thomas, ed. *Globalization and Neoliberalism: The Caribbean Context.* Lanham, Md.: Rowman & Littlefield, 1998.

Klak, Thomas. "How Much Does the Caribbean Gain from Offshore Services?" In *The Association of Caribbean States (ACS) Yearbook,* 5th edition, edited by Mark Blacklock, pp. 88–103. Port of Spain and London: ACS and International Systems and Communications Limited, 2002.

Klak, Thomas. "Globalization, Neoliberalism and Economic Change in Central America and the Caribbean." In *Latin America Transformed: Globalization and Modernity,* 2nd edition, edited by Robert N. Gwynne and Cristóbal Kay, pp. 67–92. London: Edward Arnold Publishers and New York: Oxford University Press, 2004.

Klak, Thomas, and Raju Das. "The Underdevelopment of the Caribbean and Its Scholarship." *Latin American Research Review* 34, no. 3 (1999): 209–224.

Martin, A. "A Sure Thing." *Harper's Magazine,* April 2001, 96.

McGowan, Lisa. "Democracy Undermined, Economic Justice Denied: Structural Adjustment and the Aid Juggernaut in Haiti." The Development Group for Alternative Policies, Inc., 1997, at http://www.developmentgap.org/americas/Haiti/Democracy_Undermined_Economic_Justice_Denied_Structural_Adjustment_&_Aid_Juggernaut_in_Haiti.html (accessed May 14, 2007).

Ohmae, Kenichi. *The End of the Nation State: The Rise of Regional Economies.* New York: Free Press, 1995.

Pantojas-García, Emilio. "Trade Liberalization and Peripheral Post-Industrialization in the Caribbean." *Latin American Politics and Society* 43 (2001): 57–78.

Pantojas-García, Emilio, and Thomas Klak. "Globalization and Economic Vulnerability: The Caribbean and the Post-9/11 Shift." In *Caribbean Security in the Age of Terror: Challenge and Change,* edited by Ivelaw Griffith, pp. 176–198. Kingston, Jamaica: Ian Randle Publishers, 2004.

Pattullo, Polly. *Last Resorts: The Cost of Tourism in the Caribbean.* New York: Monthly Review Press, 1996.

Peck, Jamie. "Geography and Public Policy: Constructions of Neoliberalism." *Progress in Human Geography* 28 (2004): 392–405.

Peet, Richard. "Review of 'End of Poverty: Economic Possibilities for Our Time' by Jeffrey Sachs." *Annals of the Association of American Geographers* 96 (2006): 450–453.

Potter, Robert, David Barker, Dennis Conway, and Thomas Klak. *The Contemporary Caribbean*. Essex, U.K.: Addison Wesley Longman and Prentice Hall, 2004.

Richardson, Bonham. *The Caribbean in the Wider World, 1492–1992*. Cambridge: Cambridge University Press, 1998.

Robotham, Don. "Crime and Public Policy in Jamaica." In *Understanding Crime in Jamaica: New Challenges for Public Policy*, edited by Anthony Harriott, pp. 197–238. Mona: University of West Indies Press, 2005.

Ross, Jon. "Maquila Meltdown: Plants Flee Mexican Wages." *Now Toronto*, November 28, 2002, at http://www.nowtoronto.com/issues/2002-11-28/news_story4.php (accessed May 13, 2007).

Sives, Amanda. "Changing Patrons, from Politician to Drug Don: Clientelism in Downtown Kingston, Jamaica." *Latin American Perspectives* 29 (2002): 66–89.

Thrupp, Lori Ann. *Bittersweet Harvests for Global Supermarkets: Challenges in Latin America's Agricultural Export Boom*. Washington, D.C.: World Resources Institute, 1995.

UN. "Call for Action." Office of the UN Resident Coordinator, Barbados and the OECS, Bridgetown, 2000, at http://www.bb.undp.org/pdfs/call_for_action.pdf (accessed May 14, 2007).

UNCTAD. *World Investment Directory*. Volume 9: *Latin America and the Caribbean 2004*. Parts 1 and 2. New York: United Nations, 2004.

Wiley, James. "Dominica's Economic Diversification: Microstates in a Neoliberal Era?" In *Globalization and Neoliberalism*, edited by T. Klak, pp. 155–178. Lanham, Md.: Rowman & Littlefield, 1998.

Wiley, James. *From Banana Empire to Banana Split: Globalization and the Banana Industries of the Western Hemisphere*. Lincoln: University of Nebraska Press, 2007.

Willmore, Larry. "Export Processing in the Caribbean: Lessons from Four Case Studies." United Nations Economic Commission for Latin America and the Caribbean, Report Number LC/CAR/G.407, 1994.

World Bank, Caribbean Division. *Coping with Changes in the External Environment*. Washington, D.C.: World Bank Report no. 12821 LAC, 1994.

3

Urbanization, Migration, and Employment in Latin America

A Review of Trends

Adrian G. Aguilar and Antonio Vieyra

This chapter examines the rapid urbanization process that Latin America has experienced since the second half of the twentieth century to the present. The growth of the largest cities was related to industrialization in the past century (see chapter 1). This process was the outcome of high levels of rural-to-urban migration, in combination with similarly high rates of natural increase in the population. Decades later, with the arrival of neoliberal policies, some countries began to experience a process of urban deconcentration that led to a more balanced urban system. Nowadays, migration shows new trends in which urban-urban flows become more important.

Some of the main features of urbanization in Latin America include urban primacy, metropolitan expansion, and urban systems as functioning parts of the world economy. Urbanization in Latin America is also characterized by severe social problems often linked to globalization. Massive growth in urban areas, especially in intermediate cities, indicates the need for a policy agenda that addresses these urban conditions.

URBANIZATION IN A HISTORICAL PERSPECTIVE

Most major Latin American cities were established by the sixteenth century. In the colonial period, Latin America was divided into *core areas*, where European enterprises and the native population were concentrated, and *peripheries*, which remained largely unsettled (Newson, 1996:20). These urbanized core areas were symbols of territorial possession and centers from which the surrounding countryside could be administered and exploited. This was particularly the case in Spanish America. The most important towns in colonial Latin America were political and cultural centers. For example, Mexico City, Lima, and Buenos Aires were capitals of viceroyalties; they housed the seats of archbishops as well as universities, convents, and hospitals. Thus, they remained important cities in Latin America throughout the colonial period. Apart from main cities, a few towns such as the mining centers—for example, Potosí in Peru—and major ports performed important economic roles. Most important were the ports of call for the Spanish fleet, such as Veracruz, Portobello (Panama), Cartagena, Guayaquil, Lima-Callao, and Arica (the latter being the port through which the silver from Potosí was exported). Significantly, it is the political and administrative centers of the past that remain the major urban centers in Latin America today.

By the mid-twentieth century, there was considerable range in the level and nature of industrialization in Latin America. Countries such as Argentina, Brazil, and Mexico achieved rapid industrial growth. These nations had developed a fairly substantial and diverse industrial structure, with a variety of durable and nondurable consumer goods and some heavy industry (see Gwynne, 1996:218–219). Manufacturing activities were concentrated in the capital cities and chief ports. This pattern of concentration became significant in the post-1945 period and it had an impact on urban growth, migration patterns, and regional development strategies. Away from these manufacturing cores, export-processing industries created economic enclaves in peripheral areas.

Inward-oriented industrialization reinforced the spatially concentrated urbanization pattern in Latin America. Urban primacy became a distinctive geographic feature in most of Latin America as of the postcolonial era. For example, by 1980, after 80 years of industrialization, Lima and Buenos Aires were more than 11 times larger than their countries' second-largest city.[1]

In the early 1980s, the debt crisis reflected the economically unsustainable nature of ISI (the import substitution industrialization model) and its narrow range of exports. As discussed in chapter 1, free-market policies were strongly recommended by international organizations such as the International Monetary Fund (IMF), the World Bank, and the Inter-American Development Bank (IDB). The IMF particularly favored structural adjustment policies that involved macroeconomic stability, deregulation, privatization, and openness to trade. Such policies were assumed to be more in keeping with the increasing internationalization of the world economy (Gwynne, 1996:225).

Opening up national economies led to increasing deindustrialization, the growth of the informal sector, and an increase in urban poverty. This, in turn, shifted growth from large metropolitan areas toward urban centers that became more competitive in the global economy, such as capital cities, border towns, or tourist centers.

THE URBANIZATION PROCESS IN LATIN AMERICA

Latin America and the Caribbean have a high proportion of their population living in cities. Indeed, Latin America has been the most highly urbanized region of the less developed world since 1900. From 1950 to 2000, its urban population grew at a rate of 1.2 percent per year, more rapidly than those of Europe or North America. By 2000, Latin America was as urbanized as Europe or North America, with three out of every four inhabitants living in cities. According to United Nations population projections, by 2030 the urbanization rate in Latin America would reach 84 percent urban, making this the second most urbanized region after North America, with 600 million urban dwellers (Zlotnik, 2004:49).

The high rate of urbanization in Latin America does not imply that other social and economic changes have also been achieved. Although the concentration of population in large cities may be a prerequisite for development, it is not a sufficient condition. In fact, recent studies show that the level of urban poverty continues to grow (see CEPAL, 2004:ch. 1).

The evolution and dynamics of urban systems in Latin America can be characterized by three main processes:

1. *An accelerated urbanization process that has tended to slow down in recent years.*

    With an urban population of a little more than 350 million in the year 2000, Latin America's urbanization level rose from 54 percent in 1970 to 75 percent in 2000. Despite certain general trends, regional urban trends exhibit great heterogeneity. Table 3.1 illustrates four different categories of urbanization, reflecting two main points. First, the group of highly urbanized countries (high and medium-high) includes both the largest and most developed countries in the region. However, at present these countries (Argentina, Chile, Venezuela, Brazil, Mexico, and Colombia) are experiencing slower rates of urban growth. Other countries in this same group include small island-countries where most of the people live in the one or two important cities. Second, countries belonging to the medium and low categories are those that experienced the most rapid rates of growth in the 1990s. On average, these countries recorded rates of over 3 percent, almost double that of the highly urbanized countries. It is interesting to note that these countries also have higher growth rates for the rural population.

2. *A restructuring of urban systems with a slower but continued concentration in megacities, and a greater proportion of intermediate and large cities (with more than one million inhabitants).*

    The presence of cities with over one million inhabitants is one of the main features of Latin America's urban system. In thirty years, the

Table 3.1. Latin American and Caribbean Countries by Level of Urbanization, 1970–2025 (Percentage of Total Population)[a]

Level of Urbanization	Country	1970	1980	1990	2000	2015	2025
High							
	Anguilla	100.0	100.0	100.0	100.0	100.0	100.0
	Uruguay	82.0	86.1	90.5	92.6	93.9	94.2
	Argentina	78.4	83.0	86.9	89.6	92.0	92.9
	Bahamas	71.8	75.1	83.6	88.5	91.5	92.5
	Venezuela	71.8	78.9	83.9	87.4	90.8	92.1
	Chile	73.0	79.0	82.8	85.7	88.8	90.3
Medium-High							
	Brazil	55.6	67.3	74.7	79.9	84.2	85.6
	Cuba	60.1	68.0	74.8	79.9	84.7	86.5
	Mexico	58.9	65.5	71.4	75.4	80.2	82.3
	Puerto Rico	58.3	66.9	71.3	75.2	79.9	82.5
	Colombia	57.7	64.4	69.4	74.5	80.0	82.5
	Suriname	45.9	55.0	65.4	74.1	81.3	83.7
	Trinidad and Tobago	63.0	63.1	69.1	74.1	79.3	81.9
	Peru	58.1	64.2	68.7	72.3	75.5	77.1
	Dominica	46.9	63.4	67.7	71.0	76.0	79.1
Moderate							
	Netherlands Antilles	67.9	67.9	68.3	69.2	73.0	76.4
	Dominican Republic	40.3	50.5	58.3	65.0	72.6	76.2
	Bolivia	36.2	45.4	55.6	64.6	73.1	76.0
	Ecuador	39.5	47.1	55.4	62.7	70.7	74.0
	British Virgin Islands	28.7	38.8	50.2	61.1	71.4	75.1
	Panama	47.6	49.7	53.8	57.6	62.9	65.9
	Jamaica	41.5	46.8	51.5	56.1	63.5	68.2
	Paraguay	37.1	41.6	48.6	56.1	65.7	70.3
	Nicaragua	46.8	50.1	52.5	55.3	59.4	61.8
	El Salvador	39.0	44.1	49.8	55.2	62.6	66.6
	St. Vincent and the Grenadines	26.9	27.2	40.6	54.8	68.0	72.1
	Aruba	50.6	50.5	50.3	50.8	56.1	61.5
	Costa Rica	38.8	43.1	46.7	50.4	56.1	59.6
Low							
	Barbados	37.1	40.2	44.8	50.0	58.4	63.7
	Honduras	29.0	35.0	40.8	48.2	59.5	65.7
	Belize	51.0	49.4	48.1	48.0	51.7	57.0
	United States Virgin Islands	44.5	44.5	44.5	46.4	51.9	57.4
	Guatemala	36.2	37.2	38.0	39.4	41.2	42.4
	Haiti	19.7	24.5	30.5	38.1	48.4	53.8
	Grenada	32.2	32.9	34.2	37.9	47.2	53.4
	St. Lucia	40.0	37.3	37.2	37.8	43.6	50.1
	Antigua and Barbuda	33.8	34.6	35.4	36.8	43.3	49.7
	Guyana	29.4	30.5	33.2	36.3	44.0	50.4
	St. Kitts and Nevis	34.1	35.9	34.6	34.1	39.3	45.9
	Montserrat	11.1	12.4	12.5	13.0	16.9	22.0
	Total[b]	**57.4**	**65.3**	**71.0**	**74.9**	**79.1**	**80.9**

Source: ECLAC. *Statistical Yearbook for Latin America and the Caribbean 2003.*
[a]The term "urban" is defined as it is used in each country. For the classification of countries by level of urbanization, the year 2000 was taken as the main reference.
[b]Excluding Caribbean English-speaking countries.

number of such cities more than doubled: whereas in 1970 there were 21 cities of this size, by 2000 there were already 50 (table 3.2). This can be explained by their privileged position as recipients of national and foreign investment, as well as their achievements in linking local productive sectors with international markets. Some of the largest

Table 3.2.   Latin America and the Caribbean: Urban Population, Number of Cities, and Percentage of Urban Population

	1975	1980	1985	1990	1995	2000	2005	2010	2015
10 million or more									
Number of agglomerations	2	2	3	3	4	4	4	4	4
Population*	21,024	25,703	38,492	41,591	55,038	59,705	62,134	64,394	66,390
Percentage of urban population	10.6	10.9	14.1	13.3	15.6	15.0	14.4	13.7	13.1
Growth rates		4.10	8.41	1.56	5.76	1.64	0.80	0.72	0.61
5 to 10 million									
Number of agglomerations	2	2	2	2	3	3	3	4	5
Population*	17,106	18,732	14,330	15,514	17,413	19,681	21,648	28,503	35,515
Percentage of urban population	8.7	8.0	5.2	5.0	4.9	5.0	5.0	6.1	7.0
Growth rates		1.83	−5.22	1.60	2.34	2.48	1.92	5.66	4.50
1 to 5 million									
Number of agglomerations	17	22	27	32	36	43	54	61	69
Population*	32,388	43,834	51,285	63,407	68,329	85,822	108,596	124,065	139,425
Percentage of urban population	16.4	18.6	18.8	20.3	19.4	21.9	25.2	26.4	27.5
Growth rates		6.24	3.19	4.33	1.51	4.66	4.82	2.70	2.36
500,000 to 1 million									
Number of agglomerations	26	27	32	41	47	56	57	62	64
Population*	17,826	19,303	21,999	28,241	33,192	39,050	40,702	44,660	45,380
Percentage of urban population	9.0	8.2	8.1	9.0	9.4	10.0	9.4	9.5	8.9
Growth rates		1.60	2.65	5.12	3.28	3.30	0.83	1.87	0.32
Fewer than 500,000									
Population*	109,310	127,479	147,034	164,194	177,939	188,083	197,842	208,133	220,708
Percentage of urban population	55.3	54.2	53.8	52.5	50.6	48.1	45.9	44.3	43.5
Growth rates		3.12	15.34	11.67	8.37	5.70	5.19	5.20	6.04
Total*	179,828	215,748	251,141	284,706	318,719	353,291	390,220	425,095	462,038
Growth rates		3.71	3.08	2.54	2.28	2.08	2.01	1.73	1.68

Source: United Nations Population Division, Department of Economic and Social Affairs, *World Urbanization Prospects: The 1999 Revision* (2001:178).
*In thousands.

cities, like São Paulo or Mexico City, are considered "global cities" thanks to their importance beyond the region.

Patterns of growth in large cities vary. At least five primate cities (Buenos Aires, Montevideo, Caracas, Mexico City, and Asunción) have experienced a decrease in the percentage of their countries' respective total urban population since 1970. In other countries, the degree to which the urban population is still concentrated in the largest city seems to be growing, although at different paces. This is the case of cities like Santiago, Lima, Guayaquil, Panama City, and Guatemala City (see table 3.3). In any event, there appears to be a trend among the largest cities to lose part of their prominence, which is reflected in a reduction of their primacy index and in their percentage of urban population.

This decrease in the importance of urban concentration in the largest cities has been explained in several ways. First of all, there has been a more open and export-oriented strategy causing a more deconcentrated and dispersed urban pattern. Second, the economic crisis of the early 1980s affected large cities more severely, with more limited government action and higher living costs, pushing migrants to other urban destinations. Third, as a response to severe urban problems such as pollution, crime, and traffic, the attraction of larger cities diminished. Fourth, improvements in transportation infrastructure have helped connect main cities with smaller urban centers, thus facilitating a deconcentration of population and productive activities. Finally, the diminishing attraction of the largest cities is linked to the growing importance of intermediate cities and their growing attractiveness to potential migrants.

3. *Extended metropolitan areas with rapid growth in peripheral areas.*

Research in the last decade has suggested the emergence of new urban forms associated with the largest cities in Latin America. These forms have been the result of what can be described as region-based urbanization, as the influence of a city is expanded to a wider region facilitated by more advanced technology. Lower rates of metropolitan growth have coincided with a more intense circulation of commodities, people, and capital between the city center and its hinterland, with ever more diffuse frontiers between the urban and rural, and a manufacturing deconcentration toward the metropolitan periphery, and in particular beyond, into the peri-urban space that surrounds large cities (Aguilar and Ward, 2003:4).

In territorial terms, and particularly in the case of megacities, they present a more polycentric spatial expansion of urban centers and subcenters following a network pattern that tends to sprawl along major highways and/or railroad lines radiating out from the urban

Table 3.3.   Latin America and the Caribbean: Population in the Main Metropolitan Area (Percentage of Total Population)[a]

Level of Urbanization	Country	Main Metropolitan Area	1970	1980	1990	2000
High						
	Argentina	*Greater Buenos Aires*	35.6	35.7	34.5	32.3
	Bahamas	*Nassau*	60.1	64.6	67.6	71.4
	Chile	*Santiago*	32.3	34.8	35.4	36.0
	Uruguay	*Montevideo*	48.2	49.5	50.3	39.5
	Venezuela	*Caracas*	20.3	18.1	15.3	12.9
Medium-High						
	Brazil	São Paulo	8.4	10.2	10.2	10.1
	Colombia	*Bogotá*	14.0	14.8	15.8	16.3
	Cuba	*Havana*	20.8	19.8	20.0	20.2
	Dominica	*Roseau*	28.0	27.8	—	36.6
	Mexico	*Mexico City*	18.5	20.8	18.5	18.2
	Peru	*Lima*	24.4	25.9	27.9	29.1
	Suriname	*Paramaribo*	27.3	—	25.0	57.3
	Trinidad and Tobago	*Port of Spain*	30.4	32.2	—	4.2
Moderate						
	Bolivia	*La Paz*	13.0	13.8	17.4	17.6
	Costa Rica	*San José*	21.8	25.1	26.1	23.9
	Dominican Republic	*Santo Domingo*	16.7	23.3	21.9	30.9
	Ecuador	*Guayaquil*	13.0	14.9	15.6	17.9
	El Salvador	*San Salvador*	13.9	—	20.4	21.6
	Jamaica	*Kingston*	26.1	24.0	24.6	25.9
	Nicaragua	*Managua*	21.2	21.2	18.8	20.0
	Panama	*Panama City*	31.7	35.1	36.3	41.5
	Paraguay	*Asunción*	26.2	28.3	29.5	23.1
	St. Vincent and the Grenadines	*Kingstown*	27.0	25.7	24.3	24.6
Low						
	Antigua and Barbuda	*St. John's*	34.2	—	—	36.9
	Barbados	*Bridgetown*	47.0	46.6	44.8	50.7
	Belize	*Belize City*	32.6	27.9	26.5	21.2
	Grenada	*St. George's*	31.9	33.0	—	38.3
	Guatemala	*Guatemala City*	19.6	19.9	19.6	28.8
	Guyana	*Georgetown*	23.4	24.0	—	40.0
	Haiti	*Port-au-Prince*	11.5	14.3	16.1	22.2
	Honduras	*Tegucigalpa*	7.1	12.7	14.5	14.9
	St. Kitts and Nevis	*Basseterre*	30.9	33.0	—	31.6
	St. Lucia	*Castries*	40.5	37.9	45.9	38.3

Source: ECLAC. *Statistical Yearbook for Latin America and the Caribbean 2003.*
[a]Metropolitan area refers to the main city plus the high-density zones in its environs.
[b]The data refer to the years in which population and housing censuses were conducted in each country, that is, around the year at the top of the column.

core. In this pattern, mixed land uses are created in an expanded region where traditional agriculture is found side by side with new housing projects, industrial sites, recreational sites, and suburban developments. Thus, a new spatial configuration of metropolitan development has emerged, with two distinctive features: first, urban corridors, which are linear developments with a concentration of different activities (corporate developments, residential areas, etc.). Second, urban subcenters in the periphery of megacities that may be consolidating traditional towns once dominated by agricultural activities, or are the result of new developments in metropolitan municipalities (Aguilar, 2002b:130–131). In Latin America, this new territorial configuration has been described for the largest cities such as Mexico City, Buenos Aires, Santiago, São Paulo, and Rio de Janeiro. The terms used to describe these forms are "extended metropolitan areas," "mega-urbanization with a polycentric structure," or "expanded metropolitan peripheries" (see Aguilar, 2002a; Aguilar, 2002b; Aguilar and Ward, 2003; Campolina, 1994; Ciccolella, 1999; De Mattos, 1999; Lopes de Souza, 2001).

URBAN GROWTH AND MIGRATION

Labor considerations are clearly a vital component to understanding migration and the rural-urban transition in Latin America. In a context in which most Latin American governments have promoted policies encouraging urban-based industrialization and have neglected investment in rural areas, people have moved to towns as a result of declining opportunities for livelihood in rural areas.

All indications are that a possible increase in job opportunities, including better salaries, in a more informed world with better intercommunications will serve as a stimulus to migratory tendencies (see also chapter 12). Therefore, the erratic economic growth of countries that have traditionally exported their labor force, now assisted by foreign direct investment, helps generate an environment favorable to emigration (Villa and Martínez Pizarro, 2001:32).

People move toward areas where wage levels are high (cities) and where the quality of life—as expressed by housing availability and the degree of provision of health and education—is most satisfactory.[2] Urban settlements usually offer more employment and higher wages, and are better equipped with education and health facilities, thereby attracting people with young families (Chant, 1999:242). Figures on poverty in urban and rural areas regularly showed that city dwellers are better off than their rural counterparts. The United Nations estimated that in 1990, whereas 34 percent of city dwellers lived in poverty, 53 percent of rural Latin Americans were poor.

Insofar as it is possible to generalize, most migrants move for economic reasons. But, while most migrants are looking to improve their lives, migration is often highly selective. A majority of the surveys show that certain groups move more frequently: young adults, particularly women, the better educated, and those with skills (Gilbert, 1998:46). Another significant aspect of Latin America's migratory flows is that women are more likely to move than men. For every three rural-urban male migrants, there were four female migrants. The age pattern of female net urban in-migration resembles that of males, except that the peak age for female migration is approximately five years lower. The highest rates of net urban in-migration for females occur at the ages of 15–19 and 20–24 (Singelmann, 1993, cited in De Oliveira and Roberts, 1996:261).

For example, in the early 1990s in Mexico City there were only 88 men to every 100 women, and in Bogotá and Cali only 90. In general, women dominate the flows to most large cities, where there are plenty of jobs waiting for them in domestic service, office cleaning, shop work, street selling, and, unfortunately, prostitution. The large number of women working as domestic servants in middle-class homes is a significant feature of the job market, and young women are often recruited directly from the countryside for this purpose (Gilbert, 1998:47).

ECONOMIC RESTRUCTURING AND MIGRATION

Evidence suggests that economic restructuring in the 1980s and 1990s has reduced the pace of rural-urban migration, at least in the medium term. This is because structural adjustment programs led to a relative increase in poverty in urban versus rural areas because of their adverse effects on wages and employment through cutbacks in public expenditure and government bureaucracies (Chant, 1999:244).

From the 1970s onward, natural increase has tended to override migration as a contributor to urban growth in Latin America as a whole as well as in the largest cities. Rural-urban migration became a less important issue in urban development, while interurban, intraurban, and international movements became more significant themes. This tendency was clearest in those countries that had high levels of urbanization and in which the rural population had declined in absolute numbers, such as Argentina and Mexico.

In 2000, net rural-urban transference of population, including the effect of international migration and the reclassification of localities, has been diminishing over time in its contribution to urban growth. During the 1950s, it accounted for 46.4 percent of urban growth, whereas by the

1990s the proportion had fallen to 38.4 percent. At the same time, the role played by migration has varied greatly among countries: during the 1990s, for instance, it ranged from 8.8 percent in Guatemala to 51.7 percent in Honduras.

There is now much evidence indicating the growing weight of urban-to-urban migration as part of internal population movements in the region. This trend was already observed in the 1970s, and became much more apparent in the 1980s and 1990s (Lattes, Rodriguez, and Villa, 2004:96). For instance, from 1987 to 1992 almost half of the movements of residents among the states of Mexico had urban origins and destinations[3] (see CO-NAPO, 2001). A similar case was verified in Brazil, where it is estimated that more than 60 percent of the 26.9 million intermunicipal migrants from 1981 to 1991 moved among cities (see Baeninger, 1997). In more recent years, data confirm this trend, and once again the case of Mexico is highly representative. In terms of migratory flows in the period 1995–2000, nonurban migration represents only 18.1 percent of total migrants; on the contrary, urban and metropolitan migrants together represent more than 50 percent of all flows among municipalities. Clearly, in the case of Mexico, most migratory flows represented an exchange among the total of 364 urban centers existing at that time (see CONAPO, 2001:102).

Until the 1970s, most migrants from the countryside tended to settle in large, and particularly primate cities, usually capitals or major ports, which contained a disproportionate concentration of the national urban population. However, from the 1980s onward, there has been greater movement by migrants from both the countryside and large cities to "secondary" urban centers. Thus, although the proportion of the urban population living in cities of one million or more rose between 1980 and the mid-1990s, this had more to do with increased numbers of large cities than with the continued growth of primate centers. Nonetheless, it should be noted that urban dispersion is more common in larger, more urbanized countries than in smaller ones.

Secondary urbanization has been driven first and foremost by industrial relocation and/or the development and expansion of new economic activities associated with restructuring, such as international tourism and export manufacturing. This is certainly the case in Mexico, where there was net outmigration from Mexico City during the 1980s to smaller cities within a 200-kilometer radius, such as Querétaro, Toluca, Cuernavaca, and Puebla, and to core cities of the maquiladora industry on the northern border, such as Tijuana and Ciudad Juárez.

Nevertheless, tendencies toward metropolitan deconcentration in Latin America generally have been such that Gilbert (1995:323) argues that the recession has achieved in ten years what attempts at regional development had failed to do in thirty. Besides economic reasons for shifts away from primate cities, there is also evidence to suggest that middle-class groups are moving to secondary centers as a result of concerns about the environment and the quality of life.

PRODUCTIVE RESTRUCTURING AND URBAN LABOR MARKETS

Composition of Urban Employment

In recent history, the first major change in employment structures occurred between 1940 and 1960 with the shift from a national economy based on agriculture to one based on industry (see chapter 1). A second stage, according to De Oliveira and Roberts (1996), took place from the 1950s to the mid-1970s. At that time, Latin America witnessed the development of its economies through a consolidation of industrial activity, the shaping of a welfare state, and the arrival of multinational firms that diversified this sector and fostered growth in the production of intermediate consumer goods and capital goods. Under this economic model, urban growth privileged the development of national capitals, and a pattern with a great deal of primacy was established in terms of both demography and economics.

The last stage, spanning from the 1970s to present, has evidenced a continuous decline in the "inward-directed" growth model; the beginning of an internationalization of markets, especially in urban economies; the exit of capital beyond its national borders through multinational firms that began operating in the countries of this region; and, above all, the exit of financial capital, whose major repercussions have been in the service sector (see chapter 2). Similarly, major advances in technoproductive innovations and the launching of neoliberal national development policies were some of the highly significant changes marking a new economic-productive scenario characterized by the unprecedented rise of the tertiary (service) sector and a new composition of the sectoral structure of urban complexes in the countries of this region.

The tertiary sector has also been characterized by its growth rate in activities involving low levels of capitalization and productivity carried out by low-skilled and low-paid labor (Méndez, 1997). In other words, these are what are known as "precarious services." Under a new international division of labor, those services are identified with developing economies showing serious problems of unemployment and underemployment. In 1990, Latin America as a whole had 28.8 percent of its nonagricultural employment in the goods sector, whereas the remaining 71.2 percent was accounted for by the service sector. Thirteen years later, this marked disparity between the two sectors continued to increase, and so there was a drop of 3.8 percentage points for the former (25.0 percent in 2003) and, logically, a rise in the same proportion for the latter (75.0 percent in 2003).

The tertiarization process has affected both men and women. Although from 1990 to 2003 the increase in urban employment was higher in the case of men (4.5 percentage points) than in that of women (2.1 percentage points), it is interesting to note the marked difference between the proportions of workers employed in this sector. For the year 2003, men had a 67.8 percent share in the service sector, while the remaining 32.2 percent was employed in the goods sector. For their part, women had an 85.1 percent share in the former and a 14.9 percent share in the latter. Thus, women found greater access to the urban labor market performing work in the tertiary sector as compared to men, who are employed more frequently in the secondary sector.

It can be seen that the tertiarization process occurring in major Latin American urban areas is currently characterized by an expansion of unproductive services and, to a lesser extent, by the impact of productive services. For that reason, the growth recorded in this sector has mostly been in activities involving low levels of capitalization and productivity, carried out by low-skilled and low-paid labor, where women have been participating to an increasing degree.

BEHAVIOR OF URBAN LABOR MARKETS: UNEMPLOYMENT, INFORMALITY, AND PRECARIOUSNESS

In the 1990s, flexibilization of labor markets thanks to technological advances, the deregulation of labor relations stemming from new neoliberal policies, and the withdrawal of the state as a regulating agent for labor market conditions have all been translated into greater job insecurity and instability and a progressive degradation of labor conditions, a situation that has prevailed to date in Latin American countries (Berry, 1997; Serrano, 1998; Sheahan, 1997; and Ward and Pyle, 1995).

It is now recognized that unemployment is not a structural problem, but rather affects societies' structures because it has deep economic and social consequences. It generates losses in the production of goods and services, slows down economic growth, and produces major damage to affected individuals' morale and psychological well-being. This has repercussions on all of society through higher levels of crime, exclusion, insecurity, morbidity, and poverty, among other aspects (Freeman and Soete, 1994:39, cited later in Méndez, 1997:224; Gilbert, 1996).

The behavior of urban labor markets in Latin America, which began to show negative signs during the 1980s, also called the "lost decade" due to the lack of growth in the region's economies, is presently failing to exhibit substantial improvement: on the contrary, the situation of these markets has worsened.

Although Latin America has reported relatively "low" urban unemployment rates, these figures fail to reveal the true situation, since a large percentage of the population holds precarious jobs lacking certain guarantees such as social security or the rights that, by law, workers are entitled to. Thus, the dearth of "quality" employment represents one of the most serious problems confronted by this region, and is considered to be very difficult to solve.

During the 1985–2000 period, open urban unemployment tended to increase in the region as a whole: the rate went from 9.5 percent to 10.5 percent. For the year 2004, the regional urban unemployment rate accounted for approximately 19.5 million jobless urban workers (OIT, 2004). Urban unemployment also varies from one country to the next. Colombia had one of the highest rates for this region at 17.3 percent, followed by Argentina, Ecuador, Venezuela, and Uruguay, with rates of 15.1 percent, 14.1 percent, 13.9 percent, and 13.6 percent, respectively (OIT, 2004:91).

Urban unemployment, coupled with the erosion of household incomes, forces more family members to enter the labor market. This is a survival strategy to guarantee minimum earnings and to enable families to meet their needs, given the increasing difficulty of doing so on a single salary. Thus, the inclusion of women in labor markets has been fundamental. However, the circumstances under which women join the labor market are not the most favorable. The situation of women is highly vulnerable as they work precarious jobs, with long days with little or no fringe benefits and no access to social security. In the year 2000, the majority of urban areas in the region reported higher unemployment rates for women than for men. Only Peru evidenced a higher unemployment rate among men in comparison to women (8.2 percent and 7.4 percent, respectively). The higher level of unemployment rates among women is also attributable to lower possibilities for obtaining stable employment, since a large proportion of females have jobs in the informal sector.

Along with unemployment, an increase in the degree of informality[4] in urban labor markets is another of the major problems afflicting Latin American economies. Between 1990 and 2003, there was a rise in the size of the informal sector in the region as a whole (nearly 4 percentage points, from 42.8 percent to 46.7 percent). For every 100 new urban jobs created during this period, 61 were informal (OIT, 2004:37). Colombia and Venezuela recorded the highest increments, with 15.7 and 15.2 percentage points, respectively. And in the year 2003, those two countries, along with Ecuador and Peru, surpassed the threshold of 50 percent of their occupational structures in urban informal employment (61.4 percent, 53.8 percent, 56.5 percent, and 55.9 percent, respectively) (see table 3.4).

The share of the informal sector in urban labor markets is larger for women than it is for men. At the country level, the most pronounced case

Table 3.4. **Latin America, Selected Countries: Urban Employment by Formal and Informal Sectors and Gender, 1990–2003 (in Percentages)**

	1990			2003		
Country/Sector	Total	Men	Women	Total	Men	Women
Latin America	100.0	100.0	100.0	100.0	100.0	100.0
Formal Sector	57.2	60.6	52.6	53.3	55.9	49.9
Informal Sector	42.8	39.4	47.4	46.7	44.1	50.1
Argentina	100.0	100.0	100.0	100.0	100.0	100.0
Formal Sector	48.0	50.2	44.5	53.5	52.8	54.4
Informal Sector	52.0	49.8	55.5	46.5	47.2	45.6
Brazil	100.0	100.0	100.0	100.0	100.0	100.0
Formal Sector	59.4	63.9	52.4	55.4	59.5	50.2
Informal Sector	40.6	36.1	47.6	44.6	40.5	49.8
Chile	100.0	100.0	100.0	100.0	100.0	100.0
Formal Sector	62.1	66.5	54.1	61.2	65.8	54.1
Informal Sector	37.9	33.5	45.9	38.8	34.2	45.9
Colombia	100.0	100.0	100.0	100.0	100.0	100.0
Formal Sector	54.3	54.9	53.4	38.6	41.0	35.8
Informal Sector	45.7	45.1	46.6	61.4	59.0	64.2
Costa Rica	100.0	100.0	100.0	100.0	100.0	100.0
Formal Sector	58.8	62.3	52.5	56.6	60.8	50.2
Informal Sector	41.2	37.7	47.5	43.4	39.2	49.8
Ecuador	100.0	100.0	100.0	100.0	100.0	100.0
Formal Sector	44.4	48.3	37.9	43.5	47.6	37.9
Informal Sector	55.6	51.7	62.1	56.5	52.4	62.1
Mexico	100.0	100.0	100.0	100.0	100.0	100.0
Formal Sector	61.6	62.4	60.1	58.2	58.6	57.5
Informal Sector	38.4	37.6	39.9	41.8	41.4	42.5
Peru	100.0	100.0	100.0	100.0	100.0	100.0
Formal Sector	7.3	53.7	37.1	44.1	49.0	37.8
Informal Sector	52.7	46.3	62.9	55.9	51.0	62.2
Uruguay	100.0	100.0	100.0	100.0	100.0	100.0
Formal Sector	60.9	66.3	53.4	60.9	62.9	58.4
Informal Sector	39.1	33.7	46.6	39.1	37.1	41.6
Venezuela	100.0	100.0	100.0	100.0	100.0	100.0
Formal Sector	61.0	61.7	60.7	46.2	48.3	43.4
Informal Sector	38.6	38.3	39.3	53.8	51.7	56.6

Source: Based on data from OIT (2004), using country household interviews. Argentina (31 urban agglomerations); Brazil, Colombia, and Ecuador (national urban totals); Chile, Costa Rica, and Venezuela (national totals); Mexico (urban national—32 localities); Peru (Metropolitan Lima); Uruguay (1991 and 1995—Montevideo; 1999 onward—national urban total).

is Colombia, which concentrates 64.2 percent of female urban employment in the informal sector, followed very closely by Peru (62.2 percent) and Ecuador (62.1 percent), as well as Venezuela, whose rate is somewhat lower (56.6 percent). The other countries report figures of no lower than 41.6 percent.

This increase in informality gives rise to the precarious nature of employment, which can be observed in the decrease in government jobs, as well as a drop in social security coverage among workers. The public (government) sector was a victim of international financing organizations that pressured governments to cut back unsustainable bureaucracies and to privatize semistate enterprises (Chant, 1999). Such structural changes resulted in an increase of private vis-à-vis public employment under new working conditions. The deregulation or "thinning" of work contracts was one of the main causes of the privatization of employment and, therefore, of an increase in the precarious nature of those jobs. In the 1990–2003 period, 88 of every 100 new jobs created in the region's urban areas were in the private sector.

The evolution of the social security system is another factor that has been affected by the growth of informal employment and that has led to greater precariousness in employment. From 1990 to 2003, only 53 of every 100 new salaried workers were enrolled in the social security system. It stands to reason that the informal sector has been reporting a lower percentage of salaried workers in the social security system than the formal sector. However, the proportions exhibited by both these sectors vary widely. In the year 2003, nearly 80 percent of those working in the formal sector had social security, whereas only 26.2 percent did so in the informal one. The decrease in social security coverage that has occurred among salaried workers of both sexes affected urban residents and resulted in greater precariousness in employment.

CONCLUSION

This chapter has presented an overview of recent trends in urban and metropolitan growth. Urbanization levels in Latin America increased markedly during the late twentieth century, and will continue to rise. The region's urban population, estimated to have been 179.8 million in 1975, went to 353.2 million in 2000, and is expected to be 462.0 million in 2015. This constitutes a major transformation of society. Yet despite this tendency, it is evident that the rate of increase has declined from 3.7 percent in 1980 to 2.1 percent in 2000 (see table 3.3).

Most of the region's urban population growth has been absorbed by urban centers with more than 500,000 inhabitants, a pattern that is bound to continue. Megacities, while attracting much attention owing to their individual size and well-publicized problems, accounted for less than 20 percent of the region's urban population in 2000, and their share of the urban population seems likely to remain low in the foreseeable future.

Latin America's urban employment structure is currently characterized by a tertiarization process, with an expansion of labor in unproductive services. Therefore, the growth shown by this sector is in activities involving low levels of capitalization and productivity, carried out by low-skilled and low-paid labor, in a context of economies with high unemployment rates and increasing conditions of informality and precariousness.

Higher unemployment rates among women are also a consequence of their lesser possibilities of obtaining more stable work. To a very marked degree, the activities they engage in are related to jobs with limited guarantees of social security and where the turnover is very high, namely trade and unproductive services, with a high proportion of women in the informal sector. This increase in informality leads to the precarious nature of employment in the region's urban areas. That can be observed in the decrease in government employment as well as a drop in social security coverage among workers; this situation is even worse in the case of women.

NOTES

1. In most of the countries, with the exception of Ecuador and Brazil, for example, the primate city and the political capital have been one and the same.

2. Population censuses are the main resources available for quantifying migration and obtaining a profile of migrants. This information, although useful, has many limitations, since the data refer only to the accumulated stocks of migrants and not to the flows.

3. These data refer only to people moving to localities of 20,000 or more inhabitants, and exclude intrametropolitan movements.

4. For a wider discussion of the informal sector see: Bromley, 1978; De Soto, 1989; International Labour Office, 1972; Portes, Castells, and Benton, 1991; Santos, 1979; Thomas, 1995; Tokman, 1989.

BIBLIOGRAPHY

Aguilar, Adrian G. "Megaurbanization and Industrial Relocation in Mexico's Central Region." *Urban Geography* 23, no. 7 (2002a): 649–673.

Aguilar, Adrian G. "Las mega-ciudades y las periferias expandidas: Ampliando el concepto en la Ciudad de México." *EURE: Revista Latinoamericana de Estudios Urbanos y Regionales* 28, no. 85 (2002b): 121–149.

Aguilar, Adrian G., and P. Ward. "Globalization, Regional Development, and Mega-City Expansion in Latin America: Analyzing Mexico City's Peri-Urban

Hinterland." *Cities (The International Journal of Urban Policy and Planning)* 20, no. 1 (2003): 3–21.

Baeninger, R. "Redistribución espacial de la población: Características y tendencias del caso brasileño." *Notas de Población* 25, no. 65 (1997): 145–202.

Berry, A. "The Income Distribution Threat in Latin America." *Latin American Research Review* 32, no. 2 (1997): 3–40.

Bromley, R. "The Urban Informal Sector: Critical Perspectives." *World Development* 6 (1978): 1031–1198.

Campolina, C. "Polygonized Development in Brazil: Neither Decentralization nor Continued Polarization." *International Journal of Urban and Regional Research* 2, no. 18 (1994): 293–314.

CEPAL. *Panorama social de América Latina, 2002–2003.* Santiago de Chile: Comisión Económica para América Latina y el Caribe, 2004.

Chant, S. "Population, Migration, Employment, and Gender." In *Latin America Transformed: Globalization and Modernity*, edited by R. N. Gwynne and C. Kay, pp. 226–269. New York: Oxford University Press, 1999.

Ciccolella, P. "Globalización y dualización en la Región Metropolitana de Buenos Aires: Grandes inversiones y reestructuración socioterritorial en los años noventa." *EURE: Revista Latinoamericana de Estudios Urbanos y Regionales* 25, no. 76 (1999): 5–27.

CONAPO. *La población de México en el nuevo siglo.* Mexico City: Consejo Nacional de Población, 2001.

De Mattos, C. "Santiago de Chile, globalización y expansión metropolitana: Lo que existía sigue existiendo." *EURE: Revista Latinoamericana de Estudios Urbanos y Regionales* 25, no. 76 (1999): 29–56.

De Oliveira, O., and B. Roberts. "Urban Development and Social Inequality in Latin America." In *The Urban Transformation of the Developing World*, edited by J. Gugler, pp. 253–314. New York: Oxford University Press, 1996.

De Soto, H. *The Other Path: The Invisible Revolution in the Third World.* London: I. B. Tauris, 1989.

ECLAC. *Statistical Yearbook for Latin America and the Caribbean 2003*, United Nations, 2004.

Freeman, C., and L. Soete. *Work for All or Mass Unemployment?: Computerised Technical Change into the 21st Century.* London: Pinter Publishers, 1994.

Gilbert, A. "Debt, Poverty, and the Latin American City." *Geography* 80, no. 4 (1995): 323–333.

Gilbert, A. "Urban Growth, Employment, and Housing." In *Latin American Development: Geographical Perspectives*, 2nd edition, edited by D. Preston, pp. 246–271. London: Longman, 1996.

Gilbert, A. *The Latin American City.* 2nd edition. London: Latin America Bureau, 1998.

Green, D. *Faces of Latin America.* London: Latin America Bureau, 1991.

Gwynne, R. N. "Industrialization and Urbanization." In *Latin American Development: Geographical Perspectives*, 2nd edition, edited by D. Preston, pp. 216–245. London: Longman, 1996.

International Labour Office. *Employment, Incomes and Equality: A Strategy for Increasing Productive Employment in Kenya.* Geneva: International Labour Office Publications, 1972.

Lattes, A. E., J. Rodriguez, and M. Villa. "Population Dynamics and Urbanization in Latin America: Concepts and Data Limitations." In *New Forms of Urbanization: Beyond the Urban-Rural Dichotomy*, edited by T. Champion and H. Graeme, pp. 89–111. London: Ashgate, 2004.

Lopes de Souza, M. "Metropolitan Deconcentration, Socio-political Fragmentation, and Extended Urbanization: Brazilian Urbanization in the 1980s and 1990s." *Geoforum* 32, no. 4 (2001): 437–447.

Méndez, R. *Geografía económica: La lógica espacial del capitalismo global.* Barcelona: Ariel, 1997.

Newson, L. A. "The Latin American Colonial Experience." In *Latin American Development: Geographical Perspectives*, 2nd edition, edited by D. Preston, pp. 11–40. London: Longman, 1996.

OIT. *Panorama laboral, 2004: América Latina y el Caribe.* Lima: Organización Internacional del Trabajo, 2004.

Portes, A., M. Castells, and L. Benton, eds. *The Informal Economy: Studies in Advanced and Less Developed Countries.* Baltimore: Johns Hopkins University Press, 1991.

Santos, M. *The Shared Space: The Two Circuits of the Urban Economy in Underdeveloped Countries.* London: Methuen, 1979.

Serrano, A. "Representación del trabajo y socialización laboral." *Sociología del Trabajo* 33 (1998): 27–49.

Sheahan, J. "Effects of Liberalization Programs on Poverty and Inequality: Chile, Mexico, and Peru." *Latin American Research Review* 32, no. 3 (1997): 7–37.

Singelmann, J. "Levels and Trends of Female Internal Migration in Developing Countries 1960–1980." In *Internal Migration of Women in Developing Countries: Proceedings of the United Nations Expert Group Meeting on the Feminization of Internal Migration*, pp. 77–93. New York: United Nations, 1993.

Thomas, J. J. *Surviving in the City? The Urban Informal Sector in Latin America.* London: Pluto, 1995.

Tokman, V. "Policies for a Heterogeneous Informal Sector in Latin America." *World Development* 17, no. 7 (1989): 1067–1076.

United Nations Population Division. *World Urbanization Prospects: The 1999 Revision.* New York: Department of Economic and Social Affairs, United Nations, 2001. See pp. 120, 178.

Villa, M., and J. Martínez Pizarro. "International Migration Trends and Patterns in Latin America and the Caribbean." In *ECLAC: International Migration and Development in the Americas*, pp. 21–57. Seminarios y conferencias Series No. 15. Santiago de Chile: ECLAC, CELADE, IOM, IDB, UNFPA, 2001.

Ward, P., and J. Pyle. "Gender, Industrialization, Transnational Corporations, and Development: An Overview of Trends and Patterns." In *Women in the Latin American Development Process: From Structural Subordination to Empowerment*, edited by C. Bose and E. Acosta-Belén, pp. 37–64. Philadelphia: Temple University Press, 1995.

Zlotnik, H. "World Urbanization: Trends and Prospects." In *New Forms of Urbanization: Beyond the Urban-Rural Dichotomy*, edited by A. G. Champion and Graeme Hugo, pp. 43–64. Aldershot: Ashgate, 2004.

4

Architectural Icons and Urban Form

The Power of Place in Latin America

Larry R. Ford

When I first began to travel and study in Latin America back in the 1960s, I was impressed with what I saw as the very latest in sophisticated architecture and urban form. Mexico City, for example, not only had one of the tallest buildings outside of the United States but also many exciting new types of structures at its major university campus. When the Olympics were held there in 1968, avant-garde structures in the form of stadiums and arenas added to the progressive atmosphere of the metropolis. The new Museum of Anthropology near Chapultepec Park and the string of glass-walled skyscrapers along the impressive, traffic-circled Paseo de la Reforma gave me the impression that Mexico was leading the way toward a new type of city. A variety of very unusual, even utopian, residential structures in several of its upscale neighborhoods confirmed this view.

A few years later, I traveled through a number of South American cities and my favorable impressions of Latin American urbanism were largely reinforced. The sinuous skyscrapers of São Paulo, the high-rise beachfronts of Rio de Janeiro, and the broad avenues and interesting Art Nouveau buildings of Buenos Aires convinced me that urban design was a field worth pursuing in Latin America. Brasilia, although not everyone's cup of tea, epitomized the idea that Latin America was at the forefront in urban planning and design and that the modernist icons of the future were most evident there.

Many of the cities I had visited in North America seemed to lack the aesthetic coherence and mixture of architectural styles I found in the capitals of the south. I felt certain that the dynamic cities of Latin America would remain the focus of attention for those interested in urban morphology and iconic architectural statements for some time to come. I do not think that this came to pass. To a very real degree, I was overoptimistic. As I explored a wider range of Latin American cities and regions well beyond the major capitals, I became aware that the majestic icons I encountered in Mexico City and Buenos Aires were not as common as I once imagined. There were far more unpaved streets than Paseo de la Reforma's. Stunning architecture did exist, but examples were fewer and further between than I had thought. Over the years, I have tried to explore both the reality of architecture and urban design in Latin America and my own impressions of them. What follows is a somewhat subjective but I hope thoughtful and critical examination of some of the trends in the region.

I am concerned that much of the exciting urban imagery associated with Latin America has been surpassed by a number of other world regions and that recent developments have been more derivative than cutting edge. This is not to say that the cities of the region no longer contain great beauty and exciting architectural juxtapositions but only that they are not really "where it's at" in the race to create new types of urban places. Indeed, other authors have suggested that there is currently a crisis in Latin American architecture that did not seem to exist before. There are a number of reasons for this view, some dealing with the reality of what is being constructed and others dealing with the way Latin American cities are treated in academic and popular accounts. In fact, not long after my initial experiences in the region, much of the academic literature I encountered on Latin American cities increasingly focused on rampant population growth, squatter housing, and other topics that emphasized the unplanned peripheries of all but the most moribund urban places. The periphery came to dominate the center as a primary research topic in the region. The image of the Latin American city became darker and less optimistic.

Given the realities on the ground, it is hard to argue against this change in emphasis. After all, policies that facilitate the construction of self-built housing in poverty-stricken areas are more important than the aesthetic breakthroughs associated with a new anthropology museum or even a soccer stadium. Still, this does not mean that the latter should never be addressed and that the images of cities should be made up of more than just attempts to solve serious social and economic problems. In fact, this may be truer in Latin America than anyplace else, given the historic importance of symbolic landscapes there. But there is more involved than just changing academic interests. It would seem, at least for some of us who try to follow such things, that Latin American cities have ceased to be the glamorous role models that they once (either accurately or not) seemed to be. They are not, at least right now, capturing the world's imagination.

WORLD SKYLINES AND THE RACE FOR THE SKY

Over the past decade, there has been a renewed interest in skyscrapers and city skylines as symbols of urban dynamism. A large number of books, articles, and newspaper accounts have monitored the tallest buildings in the world as well as the "greenest" towers, most unusual towers, and residential and hotel towers. Famous "passport architects" have created stunning places in parts of the world that few had heard of a few years before. Dubai comes to mind. Whether one thinks of skyscrapers as good or bad, their distribution has changed dramatically. As recently as 1965, over half of the tallest buildings in the world (over 400 feet tall) outside of the United States were in Latin America. Some, like the Kavanagh Building in Buenos Aires or the Torre Latino America in Mexico City, were consciously modeled after the Empire State Building in New York and were meant to show that those towers could compete in the realm of famous buildings (although King Kong never climbed one). The twisting form of the Edificio Italia building in São Paulo made news as one of the most futuristic of the region's towers, and of course Brasilia contributed to the new look of "skyscrapers in a park" advocated by Le Corbusier and other modernists. Compared to Latin (and of course North) America, the rest of the world was far behind. Moscow, for example, could only offer outmoded, 1920s-style "wedding cake" towers, while East Asia contributed nothing. Things have changed.

Today, the tallest building in the world is in Taipei, with Dubai scheduled to take the lead in 2008. Hong Kong is tops in terms of total skyscrapers, even surpassing New York City. Meanwhile, some of the most interesting new towers are going up in Europe, with the "twisting tower" of Malmö and the "giant gherkin" of London among the most novel. While many Latin American cities, especially in Brazil, have large numbers of medium-tall business buildings and apartment blocks, there are few, if any, skyscrapers or skylines that are currently attracting world attention. Russia, Japan, Malaysia, Australia, and a variety of emirates are getting most of the recognition as centers for new types of urban icons. Of the 200 tallest skyscrapers in the world, none are in Latin America. Similarly, it is doubtful, although there are no rankings on this, that any of the top 200 most architecturally interesting or environmentally sustainable towers are in Latin America either.

Skyscrapers represent only the tip of the iceberg. While supertowers are likely to be the most visible and famous of new urban monuments, there are lots of other contenders for world fame. Books such as *Icons of Architecture: The Twentieth Century* (Thiel-Siling, 2005), for example, list a variety of structures that are currently viewed as innovative and seminal. They include factories, opera houses, libraries, airports, convention centers, stadiums, government complexes, housing tracts, churches, museums, and monuments. Only one of the eighty-seven structures discussed (the Congress Building in Brasilia) is in Latin America. How did this situation come to be, and why is it important? I will attempt to answer these questions in the following pages.

In addition, there is the matter of innovative urban form and new planning strategies for both new developments and the creative reuse of existing landscapes. Through the 1960s, at least, some of the best-designed urban contexts in the world were in Latin America. The monumental, tree-lined Paseo de la Reforma in Mexico City, the broad, multilane streets of Buenos Aires, and the central plaza of Lima, for example, were better spaces than most cities of the world could match. Most of these places evolved over several decades with each making a contribution to an urbane Latin American aesthetic. Once more, however, the region has seemed to fall behind, as these excellent places have neither been widely re-created nor surpassed.

Recent huge planned developments like La Defense in Paris, the Docklands in London, and the Yokohama waterfront have no equals in Latin America. Although there are nice, but somewhat derivative, waterfront rehabilitation projects such as that found in Buenos Aires, they are often exceeded by newcomers to the world urban hierarchy such as Capetown. As Brasilia has become somewhat disappointingly passé, and as much of its landscape has lapsed into a kind of mundane normality, even that city cannot automatically serve as a context for the future. Mind you, this is not always a bad thing. All across the region from Curitiba to Queretaro, many cities have turned to historic preservation and the celebration of past landscapes and to good design at the micro level.

LATIN AMERICA AS A MAUSOLEUM OF MODERNITIES

The phrase "mausoleum of modernities" does not originate with me. It comes from a book by Laurence Whitehead entitled, *Latin America: A New Interpretation*; but I like it enough to borrow it because it sums up one of my themes. Whitehead argues that Latin America is unique as a world region because it has always, or at least over the past two hundred years, sought the very latest in modernity that the Western world had to offer, but has at the same time been unable to fully absorb and incorporate these new ideas before the next wave of modernity came along and displaced them. The result is that the landscape of Latin America is "littered" with unfinished, unevenly accepted modern projects, thus the phrase "mausoleum of modernities." Whitehead includes in his list of modernities everything from political and economic theories such as socialism, nationalism, and free trade to housing policies and urban design. For my purposes, architecture and urban design are the topics of importance. In every case, waves of new ideas arrive and fade only to be replaced by the next wave of ideas.

There are several reasons that Latin America is unique, or at least highly unusual, in this regard compared to Asia, Africa, or the Middle East. First, Latin America experienced a demographic collapse with the arrival of Europeans, making continuity with precolonial pasts difficult if not impossible. The fact that much of the region was isolated and/or lightly inhabited also made cultural continuity problematic. These conditions set Latin America apart from, say, China or the Islamic world, where precolonial traditions loom larger.

Second, the elites of Latin America have for the most part been thoroughly Europeanized and have thus seen Western culture as the obvious, if not the only, thing to emulate. While this view may not have been widely shared by "the masses," the leaders have looked to the modern world for nearly everything. Indeed, the leadership normally saw the region as deficient and in need of a wide range of advice from the modern world. New ideas tend to come from "above and without" rather than from home. However, the vast size of the region coupled with extremely uneven levels of urbanization, economic development, and political integration has meant that modern ideas brought in by the elite have not always spread very far or very fast. Indeed, Whitehead terms many local responses to modernity as being a combination of defensive absorption and deflection. Thus, before one project is finished, new ones have arrived to replace them, at least in the capitals.

Third, the size and uneven development of the region coupled with relative economic weakness has meant that Latin America has only rarely risen to the forefront of any kind of modernism. While cities such as Buenos Aires and Brasilia have on occasion epitomized the very latest in architecture and urban design, they have tended not to have the staying power of, say, Paris or New York, in part because their modernist projects either became passé or were never completely carried out. Again, Oscar Niemeyer's Brasilia is a case in point. The core of Brasilia was completed in the late 1960s, just as the radically modern ideas of Le Corbusier and other "towers in a park" designers were beginning to lose favor. After all, Jane Jacobs published her widely read antimodernist book *The Death and Life of Great American Cities* in 1961. By the 1970s, many critics were viewing Brasilia as a sterile mistake. In addition, the ambitious comprehensive design of the city was never fully realized. Soon squatter settlements and nondescript satellite cities surrounded the monumental core, and much of the urban area came to look much like any large Latin American metropolis. Thus Brasilia became a prime example of a mausoleum of modernity.

Once more Latin America seems to contrast with most other regions of the world. Australia and New Zealand, for example, also looked exclusively to the "modern" Western world but, because they were small and relatively homogeneous and prosperous, they could better carry out the modernistic ideas they sought. While Canberra stands out as a project not completely different from Brasilia, in general, Australia and New Zealand have completed most of their modernist projects in areas as diverse as democracy and suburban development to a much greater degree than Latin America did. Their landscapes are thus not littered with half-finished imports. In recent years, relative prosperity has allowed both countries to get "on the map" architecturally with buildings such as the Sydney Opera House and the towering residential structures of Gold Coast City.

Finally, since most of Latin America emerged from colonialism much earlier than much of the rest of the less modern world, it was much freer to import a wide range of modernities from all around the world. In contrast to British, French, and continuing Iberian colonial contexts where the mother country called the shots, Latin America could borrow ideas from not only all of the countries of Europe but also the United States and the Soviet Union. Thus the landscape is littered not only with French Second Empire palaces, faux Swiss chalets, and American drive-ins but also with relics from a full range of ideologies including fascism, nationalism, communism, democracy, and various forms of liberal economic theory. Since at least the early nineteenth century, when the Napoleonic Wars facilitated an independence movement throughout the region, most of Latin America has been free to pick and choose the latest modernities from the latest trendy sources.

SOME MAJOR STAGES IN THE EVOLUTION OF MODERN ARCHITECTURE AND URBAN DESIGN IN LATIN AMERICA

The cities of Latin America were frozen in time for nearly two hundred years. In Spanish America, the Laws of the Indies mandated a plaza-centered, grid layout, with street width determined by such things as climate and topography. Architectural and morphological homogeneity was the rule from Argentina to Mexico. While the Portuguese colonies were not subject to the same regulations, the Roman-Iberian ideal dominated for civic, religious, and domestic architecture. Things slowly began to change only in the late 1700s, when the Bourbon rulers of Spain finally became involved with the Enlightenment. With independence and later the move toward secularization, Latin Americans became more open to ideas from the outside although, in reality, they were never completely isolated from non-Iberian influences.

In terms of architecture and urban form, the frozen cities of (Spanish) Latin America remained tied to the original plaza-centered grid plans mandated by the Laws of the Indies. Demographic and economic stagnation through much of the 1600s and early 1700s meant that there was little need or money for expansion. We could call these traditional town plans a kind of modern landscape from "above and beyond," in the sense that they were examples of the very latest in European ideal city design in the sixteenth century. As such, they could be called the first examples of relic landscapes in the regional mausoleum of modernity. But there are better examples, especially since it is possible that "checker-board" pre-Columbian cities such as Tenochtitlan reinforced the grid-plan idea.

Throughout the nineteenth century, new types of architecture and planning ideologies were exported to Latin America from a wide variety of sources. Indeed, some recent books such as Jeffrey Cody's *Exporting American Architecture: 1870–2000* (2003) demonstrate the aggressive role that many American architects and entrepreneurs played in this process. During the early decades of the century, however, most of the new ideas came from Europe, especially France. New types of landscapes were needed, since at least four cities—Rio de Janeiro, Buenos Aires, Caracas, and Mexico City, had over 50,000 people by 1810.

By the middle of the nineteenth century, grand tree-lined boulevards and monumental civic buildings were appearing in several Latin American capitals. New architectural icons were concentrated on these major spines of development. Mexico City's Paseo de la Reforma became the premier example, with the help of a brief period of actual French political control under Napoleon III, but other cities soon followed suit. Improvements in infrastructure came too, as the new boulevards were often the first places to have gaslight, horse-drawn trams, water and sewerage systems, and paved sidewalks. The model was the Champs Elysées and while few cities completed the idea, an elite spine became a prominent feature in many Latin American cities.

While Haussmann's boulevards in Paris were meant to open up and cleanse existing slums, in Latin America, the (usually single) boulevard typically extended into the countryside and thus played a major role in the first planned expansion of the compact grid. While Paris provided the major inspiration, the Latin American boulevards rarely looked French. The large apartment building was not yet the norm in most cities, and a variety of building types, including British Victorians and Germanic cottages, appeared in the new elite neighborhoods. These contrasted mightily with the Spanish courtyard house typical of the old grid. Again, the modernist projects were rarely completed, thus few homogeneously coherent "Western" communities were built.

By the late 1800s, the waves of modernization were speeding up. British-financed railroads helped to usher in early attempts at industrialization and port expansion, especially in Argentina and Brazil. For the first time (at least since plantations and slavery), not only were new types of landscapes created but also new types of people were actively sought to inhabit them and make them work. During the late nineteenth and early twentieth centuries, many Latin American governments sought to Europeanize (read "whiten") their countries by importing large numbers of immigrants from Italy, Germany, and Spain. Modern industrial landscapes could then be filled with modern industrial workers.

Like other waves of change before it, Latin America's industrial revolution failed to completely transform many cities. Unlike North American cities such as Cleveland and Pittsburgh, few Latin American cities created a "hell with the lid off" of massive industrial complexes, smokestacks, oil refineries, and rail yards. There were no Manchesters or Ruhr Valleys. Rather, industry usually came to the edge of preexisting cities (most often capitals) and tended to be focused on import substitution. Nevertheless, it is interesting that Buenos Aires, once known as "the Paris of South America," later came to be known as the "Chicago of South America" because of its dense rail net focusing on a busy industrial port.

Throughout the twentieth century, there were many additional attempts to bring to Latin America modern features from the cultural hearths of Western civilization. Without wishing to belabor the point, a few last examples can be made. Many Latin American countries, especially those with an important pre-Hispanic cultural identity, began to actively search for nationalistic landscapes that would confirm the importance of heritage and local tradition beyond the relics of colonialism. At first glance, this quest could be seen as a rejection of European emulation, but in reality the same quest was being undertaken in Europe as well. Many European countries, especially those that had recently created a new national state, such as Germany, Italy, or Finland, sought architecture, art, music, and even traditional clothing styles that could enhance national identity. Similarly, Latin American cities began to seek ways to incorporate Mayan, Incan, African, and other extracolonial influences into architecture and urban design. Some of these efforts resulted in remarkably stunning individual buildings in the form of university buildings, such as the mosaic-covered central library in Mexico City, museums, theaters, and monuments, but, to a very real degree, continuity with a precolonial urban tradition was too thin to contribute more than a veneer. There were few still-practicing Aztec architects and engineers.

In recent decades, of course, North American influences have become dominant, with strip malls, suburban housing tracts, shopping centers, and office towers sprouting up everywhere. As in the United States, auto-dependent landscapes are becoming the norm, and once tight-knit urban fabrics are being stretched and diluted by parking lots. The cities that have resulted from all of these eras and waves are surprisingly coherent and widespread. Indeed, I have tried to model what I view as typical Latin American cities.

A MODEL OF LATIN AMERICAN CITY STRUCTURE

I have previously published attempts at modeling the Latin American city. The above discussion of the evolution of ideal architectural and planning components is aimed at providing a better understanding of how the model, especially the latest version, was put together (see figure 4.1). The model postulates a strong, but very mixed, central business area focusing on the traditional plaza. Although the center may be divided into a modern office area and a more traditional market district, it tends to be relatively intact, with a church, government buildings, and retail occupying space on the original grid. Housing once occupied by the elite has been converted to commercial space. The strength of the area is partly due to tradition and partly due to a heavy reliance on public transit that comes together here.

Emanating outward from the central zone is an elite spine of varying monumentality depending on how much "Parisian" influence was absorbed. A large percentage of the upscale office and retail establishments not found in the center is located on or near this spine. There also may be expensive residential areas, including old mansions close in and newer condominium towers farther out. "Cafe districts" such as Mexico City's Zona Rosa are also found along the spine, and toward the suburban end new malls and office parks may be present. Many of the better residential districts are located in a sector focused on the spine, since access to nice restaurants and important social events is a high priority. Within this spine/sector, most of the buildings are architect-designed and professionally built and financed. Beyond the sector, things can be quite different.

Most of the traditional and self-built housing and commercial structures are located in a series of concentric zones of declining status around the plaza/core and spine/sector. One of the crises in Latin American architecture and development is the failure to provide adequate housing for low-income populations. Beyond the elite sector, most of the housing is self-built, often in what can be termed squatter settlements. Over time, according to most studies, this housing gradually improves and shacks become solid houses as people invest in materials and add their own sweat equity. This, combined with the fact that government is only able to upgrade the infrastructure very slowly, means that the inner rings are likely to be established neighborhoods with paved streets and water and electricity, while the outer rings are typically devoid of any municipal improvements.

In recent years, some middle-class, professionally built housing tracts have appeared close to the outer margins of the elite sector as economies have modernized. In addition, there may be historically designated, gen-

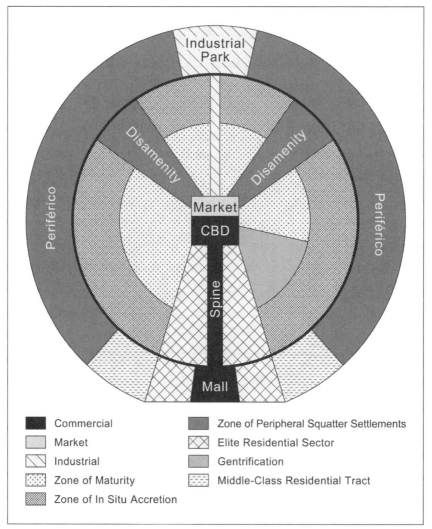

Industrial
Park

Disamenity

Disamenity

Periférico

Periférico

Market

CBD

Spine

Mall

◼ Commercial		◼ Zone of Peripheral Squatter Settlements	
▨ Market		⊠ Elite Residential Sector	
◺ Industrial		▦ Gentrification	
▦ Zone of Maturity		▨ Middle-Class Residential Tract	
▦ Zone of In Situ Accretion			

Figure 4.1. An improved model of Latin American city structure. Model created by Harry Johnson; first published in *Geographical Review* 86, no. 3 (July 1996). Reprinted by permission.

trifying neighborhoods close to the city center that are gradually attracting capital investment. Industrial zones, if they exist at all, are likely to be truck-oriented and near peripheral highways rather than in inner-city locations close to rail yards as was historically the case in much of the modern world. For a variety of reasons, this model describes a common form, albeit with many variations, throughout Latin America. It also describes how the emulation of modernity was written into the landscape there.

HOW DID EMULATION AND DIFFUSION OCCUR? GLOBAL ARCHITECTS AND URBAN CHANGE

Throughout the twentieth century new office buildings, transit systems, hotels, and apartment buildings have gone up in many Latin American cities. In some cases, the transfer of architecture from the more developed West was obvious and straightforward, as when a direct copy of the U.S. Capitol was designed and constructed for the National Capitol in Havana by the New York firm of Purdy and Henderson. In more cases than not, however, the transfers were more indirect and confusing. For example, often U.S. architects sought to create and/or introduce an architectural style that they thought was suitable for the region's existing sense of place, even when locals were seeking an imported new and modern look. When the U.S. architectural firm of Stone and Webster designed the Banco de Boston Building in Buenos Aires in 1921, they used a Spanish "Plateresque" detailing in an attempt to create a national style for the newly emerging office skyline of the city. Similarly, Havana's quintessentially Cuban waterfront malecon was designed by a U.S. company.

European influences are often convoluted as well. For example, Jean-Claude Forrestier is often credited with bringing modern (French) town planning to Buenos Aires during the 1920s, but since he had recently worked in cities such as Seville, Bilbao, and Marrakesh, it is difficult to say that his ideas were purely modern or even French. This confusion is not unique to Latin America. For example, much of the iconic architecture associated with Seville, Spain, resulted from the 1929 World's Fair, which was inspired by the buildings of the 1915 World's Fair in San Diego, California (which was earlier inspired by the buildings of Salamanca, Spain). Still, since the cities of Latin America borrowed so much, the circuitous paths of the imports are interesting to ponder. But, as I argued above, it is my contention that the architectural flows and interactions involving Latin America have slowed in recent years. There are few projects in Latin America that illustrate globalization to the degree that is evidenced by the Petronas Towers in Kuala Lumpur, where Cesar Pelli, an Argentine-born American architect, built Islamic-influenced skyscrapers using Japanese engineers, Malaysian foremen, Indonesian and Bangladeshi laborers, and materials from all over the world.

GLOBALIZATION, PRESERVATION, AND THE POWER OF PLACE IN LATIN AMERICA

Today, even the construction of place is subject to global trends. The local costs of steel, concrete, and energy are all affected by what is going on

Figure 4.2. Two architectural imports in Mexico City: The *Torre Latinoamericana* and the *Palacio de Bellas Artes.*

elsewhere in the world. When China uses up to one-third of the world's steel, the cost of building megaprojects is impacted everywhere. Latin America, for example, may well be less able to emulate modernity than it was in previous decades, but this may not be a bad thing.

Traditional and symbolic places at a variety of scales have always been important in Latin America. Symbolic places such as pyramids, central plazas, grand boulevards, and courtyard houses have played important roles in shaping behavior in Latin American towns and cities over the past 500 years. In recent years, globalization has also led to global heritage tourism and a greater respect for the past than previously existed. This is especially true in Latin America, where until recently the old was often marginalized in the quest for the new—that is, the latest version of the modern. In *Plazas and Barrios*, Joseph Scarpaci writes about the new appreciation for the *centros historicos* of Latin American cities and the increasingly successful attempts to preserve their architecture and sense of place. While these projects can sometimes lead to museumification and/or excessive gentrification, they can also demonstrate a new pride of place in the region.

Latin American cities are full of powerful architectural icons and grand spaces from a variety of eras. Although the importation and development of new types of icons has slowed in recent years, there is now a greater appreciation of the assemblages that have accreted over time. As has happened in many European cities, parts of Latin America may be putting all of their urban design eggs in a historical basket. Whether by choice or design, few Latin American cities are currently on the "main stage" or cutting edge of architectural innovation but the issues of globalization remain. The ideal of Brasilia may have been replaced by the ideal Taxco or other heritage tourism destinations. Nevertheless, the power of place remains important throughout the region.

SUGGESTED READINGS

Bayon, Damian, and Paolo Gasparini. *The Changing Shape of Latin American Architecture.* New York: John Wiley and Sons, 1979.

Blouet, Brian, and Olwyn Blouet. *Latin America and the Caribbean: A Systematic and Regional Survey.* New York: John Wiley and Sons, 1997.

Cody, Jeffrey. *Exporting American Architecture, 1870–2000.* London: Routledge, 2003.

Dupre, Judith. *Skyscrapers: A History of the World's Most Famous and Important Skyscrapers.* New York: Black Dog and Leventhal, 1996.

Herzog, Lawrence. *Return to the Center: Culture, Public Space, and City Building in a Global Era.* Austin: University of Texas Press, 2006.

Kusnetzoff, Fernando, ed. *Latin America in Its Architecture.* Translated by Edith Grossman. New York: Holmes and Meier Publishers, 1981.

Low, Setha. ed. *Theorizing the City.* New Brunswick, N.J.: Rutgers University Press, 1999.

Nasr, Joe, and Mercedes Volait. *Urbanism: Imported or Exported? Native Aspirations and Foreign Plans.* London: John Wiley and Sons, 2003.

Olds, Kris. *Globalization and Urban Change: Capital, Culture, and Pacific Rim Mega-Projects.* Oxford: Oxford University Press, 2001.

Scarpaci, Joseph. *Plazas and Barrios: Heritage Tourism and Globalization in the Latin American Centro Historico.* Tucson: University of Arizona Press, 2005.

Thiel-Siling, Sabine, ed. *Icons of Architecture: The Twentieth Century*. Munich: Prestel, 2005.

Whitehead, Laurence. *Latin America: A New Interpretation*. New York: Palgrave Macmillan, 2006.

SUGGESTED WEBSITE

"High Rise Buildings of the World," at www.emporis.com.

5

U.S.-Mexico Borderlands

Altha J. Cravey

> Every American city is now a border town. If you drive through the
> Arkansas hills, you will see a single-wide trailer church with a sign that
> reads Templo Evangélico. If you take Interstate 10 through Metairie,
> Louisiana, and exit north, you will find a Mexican barrio hidden behind
> a neighborhood of Cajuns. In Naperville, Illinois, Spanish-speaking men
> in work clothes peruse the abundant "Hispanic foods" aisle, buying corn
> husks to make their traditional Christmas meal of tamales, but Chicago
> style—with bratwurst instead of beef.
>
> —Luis Alberto Urrea, *New York Times*, December 24, 2004

Many people live and work in the U.S.-Mexico borderlands. Many others
travel north through the U.S.-Mexico borderlands en route to U.S. destinations, where they settle in with family members or friends (see chapter 13).
The southwestern portion of the United States and the northern portion of
Mexico form a coherent cultural region known as the U.S.-Mexico borderlands, in spite of distinct national influences. The border and the borderlands are harsh and treacherous in many ways, and have become markedly
more so in recent years because of contradictory and violent effects of
uneven development that are laid bare in this desolate region bisected by
a boundary line that migrant advocates sometimes refer to as the "wall of
death."

A line 2,000 miles long divides the sovereign national territory of Mexico
from that of the United States (figure 5.1). Thousands and thousands of
newly manufactured television sets, garage-door openers, trucks, bras, and
panties are allowed to move freely across the line, while humans are ever
more restricted from movement. Why has it become so risky and so costly

for human beings to cross this imaginary line in the soil, when regional and national policies increasingly encourage the "opening of the border" to the flows of goods, services, and capital investments? In posing this question, we can begin to see why this line in the soil is a potent symbol of conflict, of possible dreams and futures, and of relationships between intimates and strangers. As Gloria Anzaldúa famously wrote in the 1980s, the U.S.-Mexico border is an "open wound," where "the first world grates against the third world and bleeds" (1987).

The history of the line itself provides some insight into this complexity, and further insight is gained by considering a few of the many different official (and unofficial definitions) of the U.S.-Mexico "borderlands." The line resulted from a violent conflict, in which Mexico lost half its national territory (one million square miles of land) to the United States, and which Mexican schoolchildren learn about as the "U.S. Invasion." In the United States, the more neutral sounding "U.S.-Mexico War" is understood as part of the natural expansion westward of European settlers who undertook a "civilizing mission" in sparsely populated, "underutilized," and well-endowed western territories. Political leaders, as well as adventurers and entrepreneurs, used the idea of Manifest Destiny to legitimate such expansionary conquests to U.S. citizens. The Treaty of Guadalupe Hidalgo (1848) ended the war and marked out a radically distinct boundary line between the two countries. In doing so, the agreement allowed the United States to encompass some 100,000 Mexican and 200,000 Native Americans.

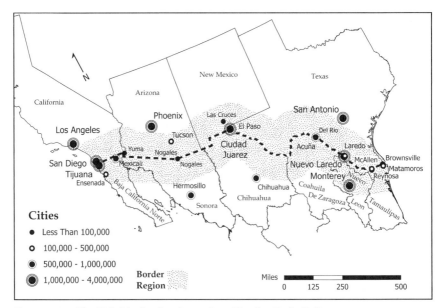

Figure 5.1.   The U.S.-Mexico border region. Map by Craig Dalton

The newly established U.S.-Mexico boundary line stretched along the Rio Grande in Texas and westward through the Sonoran Desert to include all or part of ten new states for the victors: Arizona, California, Colorado, Kansas, Nevada, New Mexico, Oklahoma, Texas, Utah, and Wyoming. A few years later, the Gadsden Treaty (1853) added a portion of southern Arizona and southern New Mexico to the United States and finalized the line we see on contemporary maps.

Specific questions raised in this chapter are: Why is the informal economy so dominant at the U.S.-Mexico border? Does it operate in different ways on the north and south sides of the border? Why is violence so prevalent at the border? Who is involved in trying to stem the violence and what is being done? Why does the violence persist?

To illustrate the contemporary reality of life in the U.S.-Mexico border region, two examples, the maquiladora program and migration, are presented in some detail. Gender dynamics are a key aspect of both of these examples. Gender issues are illustrated and connected to other concerns such as environmental, child-rearing, and neighborhood issues.

THE MEXICAN MAQUILA PROGRAM, NAFTA, AND SPACES OF NEOLIBERALISM

The Mexican maquila program (1965), officially known as the Border Industrialization Program, and the North American Free Trade Agreement (NAFTA, 1994) profoundly changed the character of the U.S.-Mexico borderlands. The maquila program began as a massive geographical experiment in which a strip of Mexican territory along the border was carved out as a growth zone, an "export processing zone." The rules of doing business were adapted in specific ways to encourage the expansion of global factories, sometimes referred to collectively as "the global assembly line." Mexico marked out and re-created a neoliberal space in an area that had been rather sparsely populated and poorly integrated with the rest of the country. By changing the rules of investment and the norms of labor and business regulation in this zone, Mexico succeeded in capturing a portion of United States' and global manufacturing investments flowing to the developing countries in the 1970s and 1980s, due to capitalist restructuring.[1] Industrial sectors that are especially prominent in Mexico's maquilas are textiles and apparel, electronics, and automotive parts.

By creating new factory jobs, the maquila program encouraged urbanization and migration in northern Mexico. Young people poured into the zone from nearby rural areas and from more distant locations in central and southern Mexico. During the 1960s, 1970s, 1980s, and 1990s, border cities in both countries grew faster than the national averages in their re-

spective countries. Mexican cities with maquila manufacturing grew especially quickly and in all cases except for Tijuana are larger, and grew faster,
than their U.S. counterparts due to Mexico's greater dependence on the
United States. Tijuana, and its U.S. counterpart San Diego, are exceptional
in this regard, because of San Diego's naval base, diverse economy, physical
amenities, and linkages to southern California. In his book *Where North
Meets South*, Lawrence A. Herzog provides an overview of the expansion
of an urban system in the late-twentieth-century borderlands (see Herzog,
1990:48–62). Migrants from the interior of Mexico seek jobs in the maquilas, as well as in the booming informal economy, retail establishments,
urban services, and elsewhere. Other migrants, sometimes members of the
same families, cross the international line and seek opportunities in the
United States. These transnational flows have had an indelible impact on
both countries; one of every seven Mexicans of working age is estimated to
be working in the United States.

The global assembly line in Mexico is known as the maquiladora industry, or simply maquila. The factories first emerged in 1965 as an ad hoc
experiment at isolated sites on the U.S.-Mexico border and expanded rapidly into a sophisticated comprehensive federal program to attract export
investment. Interestingly, before embracing maquila production, Mexico
was highly industrialized due to a long-term government project known as
import substitution industrialization (ISI), a centerpiece of Mexico's high-
growth "miracle" years of the 1940s, 1950s, and 1960s (see chapter 1).[2] In
the 1980s, Mexican industrial strategy was transformed and reoriented to
foreign investment for export production. Maquila production thus became
a symbol and a means of wider philosophical and political transformations
guided by neoliberal principles—principles that call for less state intervention and the expansion of the "free market" (see chapter 2). This shift
in industrial policy was marked by a geographic shift from a centralized
industrial core to dispersed northern sites, a transformation in the nature
of the state, and a corresponding reorientation of the state's productive
strategies. A range of inward-oriented industrialization policies was reversed
to encourage internationalization, liberalization, and privatization of the
economy. With the implementation of NAFTA in 1994, the neoliberal principles enshrined in maquila production were institutionalized and pushed
further along the same trajectory (Cravey, 1998).

These transformations did not occur in a vacuum: they influenced, and
were influenced by, Mexican social structure. Consideration of gender and
household relations helps to explain these wider transitions in Mexican history, geography, and development. Industrial workers in northern Mexican
factories tend to be young women rather than male breadwinners. They
typically pool several incomes and form extended households that reor-
ganize domestic tasks and incorporate new members as needed. As wage

earners, women maquila workers gain certain improvements in status. Still, this advance entails considerable contradictions and social costs. The gendered trade-offs are visible if one compares interior and border locations in Mexico that have been shaped by distinct factory regimes. Below, I compare the border city of Nogales, Sonora, with the interior city of Ciudad Madero, Tamaulipas, in order to better describe widespread social costs and contradictions in the U.S.-Mexico borderlands.

Nogales (population 300,000) sits across the border from Nogales, Arizona (population 22,000), and represents an entirely different production regime from the import substitution program that shaped Ciudad Madero. In comparing the two, the starkest difference is the lack of state public social programs for workers, families, and communities in Nogales. A casual visitor can observe the distinction in the dearth of clinics, schools, child-care centers, and other social goods in border locations. Political economic differences unsurprisingly shape distinct household forms in the two cities, as well as distinct channels of social access for urban residents.

The two cities reflect the urban social geographies of different factory regimes. That is, the regulatory role of the state between 1940 and 1976, which had nurtured domestic industrial capitalists and industrial workers in the old factory regime in Ciudad Madero, was completely revamped in favor of transnational capital accumulation in Nogales. Social policies in the new neoliberal spaces of Nogales support industrial investment rather than being aimed at workers and communities. Specifically, state policies and institutions in Nogales are geared toward providing transnational corporations with a dependent and relatively quiescent workforce by dismantling, deregulating, and privatizing social provision.

In short, the state emerged as a powerful ally of employers by dismantling traditional networks of social provision in new northern transnational production sites, making workers more dependent on their employers. Some necessary goods, such as health care, childcare, and housing were recommodified or became available only through the employment relationship. Goods considered social *rights* in Ciudad Madero became social *privileges* in Nogales and in the new factory regime. People who live in the borderlands resist, cope, negotiate, and reshape these processes in multiple and creative ways. Private provision of health care, childcare, and public housing undermined the system of public goods available to workers in the borderlands. In any case, there is also a qualitative difference in services provided in Nogales: In a variety of ways, social services that do exist have become more tightly bound to the employment relationship.

This makes workers far more vulnerable to the whims of their employers and renders access to social goods more insecure, as demonstrated by Ana's description of a harrowing experience involving emergency medical treatment for her daughter: "Ismelda was hurt at school and her ear was bleeding badly. She couldn't go to Social Security (IMSS) because she was born in the U.S. I ran to see the nurse (at the Avent maquiladora) and she called a private doctor who treated her for free." This mother's good record of maquila employment enabled her to secure the medical care her daughter urgently needed. Even though government help was unavailable, her long and close relationship with her employer helped her get assistance. The insecure nature of social goods and the way they are tied to the employment relationship is especially significant given the high turnover rates of maquiladora workers. On average, Nogales maquila workers last 15–16 months on a particular job.[3] By contrast, workers in Ciudad Madero in the old factory regime considered their jobs to be a lifelong arrangement. In turn, such changes in social provision weaken workers' positions when bargaining over conditions of employment. The geographically uneven nature of social provision reinforces differences in the development of the two industrial regions.

How does all this affect daily life? In what ways are gender and household dynamics caught up in larger globalization processes in northern Mexico? A gender and class perspective helps illuminate survival activities and how these daily struggles link to wider sets of relationships. In contrast to workers in earlier high-growth Mexican industrialization zones, maquila workers do not tend to form nuclear households, and those who prefer nuclear households find one factory wage to be insufficient. Instead, maquila workers often pool multiple factory incomes in various types of extended household arrangements, sometimes incorporating unrelated individuals and expanding and contracting the household as needed over time.

Domestic chores are particularly interesting to consider in these northern Mexican households. In talking with people, I found that mundane household work is a source of intense and on-going negotiation and conflict in maquila households in Nogales. In contrast to earlier industrial workers who relied almost exclusively on female domestic labor, these tasks are reorganized. Men in these maquila households contribute twice as often and in more significant ways to household labor. In fact, some men contribute in regular and systematic fashion. For example, a man who has small children may take the night shift and a woman the day shift, or vice versa, so that one or the other can be home to care for children at any hour of the day or night. Such sequential scheduling is an unusual and creative response to the changing conditions in the new economic areas. As one young mother explained, "My husband takes care of the children. He has to take care of them because I work (in the factory) at night. We take turns with it every day."

In these ways, both paid work and unpaid social reproductive work are reorganized in the context of rapidly globalizing labor markets. A relative dearth of public social programs (and a rapid retrenchment over time) has shifted a greater burden to individuals and households and in this way intensified conflicts over the division of domestic labor. Gendered negotiations over domestic work influence and are influenced by gendered negotiations in the (paid) workplace. As wage earners, women access a different source of power in northern households. Still, they are burdened by widespread shortages of social goods in their communities as well as insufficient and fluctuating incomes.

A severe housing shortage is also evident to a casual observer in Nogales. For this reason, many industrial workers live in rudimentary makeshift housing in squatter areas that are "regularized" over time. Organizing themselves in large groups and orchestrating "land invasions" is one direct means of providing shelter for one's self in a difficult environment. In the case of land invasions, women are frequently in the forefront of obtaining land and in the long process of gaining title and services (i.e., electricity, water, sewage disposal). In this way, a "politics of place" in Nogales is much more broadly focused than in the old factory regime: encompassing community and neighborhood concerns, issues of health and social reproduction, as well as identity, gender, and cultural politics. To be sure, politics suffuse factory work as well, yet in the formative years of the new factory regime Nogales workers consistently lost ground (as workers) while finding their neighborhoods and households were potential sites for organizing to improve their lives.

An examination of Mexico's transition to a new factory regime suggests that those very pressures that produced nuclear households in the old factory regime (Ciudad Madero) are causing further fragmentation of industrial households in the new deregulated northern industrial zones. Production in the new factory regime is far less protected from international competition than had been the case in the old factory regime. In the northern region, transnational employers lower the cost of doing business by including younger female and male workers in the labor market. In this way employers can lower the costs of social reproduction and retain more profit for themselves. Younger workers, in turn, find their wages to be insufficient for the nuclear family norm of industrial workers elsewhere and therefore develop other household forms. My research suggests that the same forces of fragmentation that created a nuclear family norm in central Mexico now threaten to further atomize the social fabric.

Building on the economic success of the maquila experiment, NAFTA locked in many specific maquila practices as well as broader neoliberal practices and "free trade" ideas that made northern Mexico a zone of economic expansion, rapid urbanization, and job growth in recent decades. The United States, Canada, and Mexico signed the treaty as a framework for regional economic cooperation. The agreement has some similarities to and some differences from the European Union project. Some of the immediate and visible social and cultural effects of NAFTA are in the U.S.-Mexico borderlands, where businesses sought to profit from increased cross-border trade and investments.

THE INFORMAL ECONOMY—DRUG SMUGGLING, PEOPLE SMUGGLING, AND MORE

Alongside the explosive growth of the maquila industry has been an expansion of informal economic activities in the borderlands, including drug-smuggling and people-smuggling operations that link suppliers in Mexico and Latin America with destinations, employers, and consumers in the United States. These transnational smuggling networks have dense connections to many border communities as well as many small towns and cities throughout the United States and Mexico (see also chapter 12). The human-smuggling networks are particularly interesting.

The U.S.-Mexico border is a key crossing point for unauthorized migrants to the United States. Human migration across the line, especially but not exclusively from Mexico, has been active since the line was established in the nineteenth century. These migrations have been more closely monitored in the twentieth century, especially after the establishment of a United States national police force, the Border Patrol, in 1924. In recent decades, border enforcement and militarization have become even more salient, particularly in the urban zones. In the two largest urban areas, San Diego/Tijuana and El Paso/Juarez, fences have been reinforced in the 1990s with triple layers of steel, high-tech sensors that can detect movement, and military drones. Border Patrol budgets have skyrocketed, and more Border Patrol officers have been hired to guard all sectors of the United States side of the line. While migration flows continue apace, these investments in border infrastructure create a highly visual and symbolic demonstration that the United States has "control" of its southern border (Nevins, 2002).

Migrants and migrant-smuggling networks that operate in the border have responded to these changes by developing migration pathways that wind through inhospitable rugged desert territory such as the "Devil's Highway" in the harsh Sonoran Desert of central Arizona. In this way, tiny border towns such as Sonoita have become busy staging areas and outposts for prospective migrants, *coyotes* (smugglers), and for those who provide rooms, meals, and services to migrants and their guides. Migrants thus face increased risk and higher fees in making the journey to interior U.S. locations.

The borderlands is a region of extreme violence, and this too provides a means of understanding the region. Violence on the north side of the line is largely directed against migrants from Mexico, Central America, and elsewhere who are trying to enter the United States. By contrast, violence in

Figure 5.2.   Checkpoint at El Tortugo, thirty miles south of the borderline at Sasabe, Sonora. Photo by Julian Cardona

northern Mexico is caught up with everyday traffic in drugs, prostitution, and myriad other informal economic activities. In recent years, the most well known victims of violence have been the young women of Ciudad Juarez whose desiccated (and sometimes mutilated) bodies provoke outrage, investigation, and protest. Hundreds of very young victims, often factory workers of humble origins, have died in the city Charles Bowden (1998) evocatively labeled "The laboratory of the future" for its single-minded focus on neoliberal policies and simultaneous neglect of social consequences. While the senseless deaths of so many young women are becoming widely known, journalists in Ciudad Juarez also suggest that countless young men die in the city as well, with mass graves unearthed from time to time in remote houses that serve as transportation nodes for powerful drug cartels that seek to move their merchandise across the line to the United States.

Violence on the U.S. side of the line takes many forms. Small-time bandits prey on migrants as they cross the border with perhaps a toothbrush and their life savings. Smugglers, their employees, and others take advantage of the vulnerability of women and commit rape and sexual abuse. Overshadowing these acts is the systemic violence of a contradictory arrangement that recruits workers for many economic sectors in the United States, while subjecting would-be applicants to a terrifying and deadly gauntlet in the borderlands. As I write this essay, Congress is considering legislation that would overhaul immigration law for the first time in twenty years. The proposals are quite complex, however, and include longer Berlin Wall–type installations at the border, guest-worker programs, lengthy paths to citizenship for "upstanding" migrants, and steep penalties for those who commit the "geographical crime" of crossing the border without a visa (Nevins, 2002). At this time, due to violent anti-immigrant rhetoric, it is unlikely that any comprehensive reform proposal will become law. At the same time, it is clear that many sectors of the U.S. economy would grind to a halt if cross-border migration were to slow down. Thus borderland violence, visited on families and children in the harsh and remote desert, is part and parcel of the dirty, dangerous, and difficult underside of the U.S. economy.

Demand for Mexican labor in the United States has a long history. In good times, immigrants are recruited for agricultural and other work, whereas in an economic downturn, immigrants are more likely to be deported. Thus the cycles of the U.S. economy correspond to increased and decreased flows of migrants. For example, while the Great Depression spurred dramatic mass deportations, World War II stimulated such a need for short-term workers that the United States and Mexico created the binational Bracero Program (1942–1965) in which prospective workers were matched with agricultural employers in the western and southwestern part of the United States. A contemporary program, dubbed H2A for the specific paragraph in the immigration law, matches Mexican workers with agricultural employers in the southeastern part of the United States. A region that previously had little Mexican settlement, these government-sanctioned programs have encouraged migration (both official and unofficial) and have deeply influenced the experience of migrants, creating racialized wage scales and distinctly racialized regional formations in the United States.

Another form of violence that illuminates the reality of the borderlands is *discursive violence*. This term refers to visual and rhetorical imagery that can be harmful, painful, and destructive. For example, the term "illegal immigrant" is dehumanizing and pejorative, yet commercial television, daily newspapers, and radio typically use this term to refer to Mexican migrants. In repeated usage, the term denigrates an entire social group regardless of actual immigration status or country of origin. Over time, the term has also become the norm in policy debates and everyday public discourse in the United States, as documented in Joseph Nevins's book *Operation Gatekeeper* (2002). The symbolic imagery of the border fence reinforces an invented notion that people of a certain color and cultural background belong on one side of the line, while people of another skin color and cultural background belong on the other side. Discursive violence and concrete manifestations of violence in the borderlands are destructive. Do you suppose people in the United States might keep building taller and more expensive border walls in the future?

HISTORICAL GEOGRAPHY OF THE BORDERLANDS

The borderlands region is a harsh natural environment that is extremely hot and arid. In both the United States and Mexico, the region was historically a marginal zone, isolated from centers of cultural, economic, and political influence. Vast open spaces, desert lands, rugged mountain terrain, and a few rivers and lakes characterized the physical environment. These conditions made effective colonization difficult for many years, and the region remained sparsely populated well into the twentieth century. The advent of modern transportation networks, including north-south railway lines, helped to link population centers in the region itself, as well as link these towns and cities with distant national capitals.

The experience of Native Americans in the borderlands is a complex and largely tragic narrative. Many different Indian groups inhabit the borderlands, which in the eighteenth and nineteenth centuries could be grouped in four categories. Those who had a settled way of life and farmed included the Tarahumaras, Yaquis, Mayos, and Pimas. Those who lived in pueblo-style compact villages used irrigation or dry farm agriculture. "Band" Indians such as the Apaches and Navajos mixed agriculture with hunting and gathering and did not live in permanent settlements. Finally a few thousand nonagricultural Seris formed roving bands that gathered wild foods and fished and hunted for a living. Their presence was seen as a "problem" by various interest groups in the United States and in Mexico. At the time of the U.S.-Mexican War,[4] James Polk used this to his advantage to argue that Mexico was incapable of controlling its territory and particularly the indigenous populations in the northern region. Of course, after the new boundary line was established after the war, the United States faced the challenge of establishing peaceful relationships with indigenous groups, maintaining order, and protecting its citizens. Indian raids into northern Mexico in the mid- to late nineteenth century wreaked death, destruction, and depopulation in northern Mexico. People on the north side of the line supported the system of raiding for some years and profited by buying goods and captives from the Indians (Martinez, 1988).

When the mid-nineteenth-century boundary line imposed new national divisions, this distinct cultural region was sparsely populated. By the late twentieth century, however, approximately ten million people lived in border cities and nearly 20 million lived within a 120-mile zone of either side of the line. One of the most dramatic changes, therefore, has been the very rapid urbanization of the borderlands and the acceleration of this trend in the second half of the twentieth century. Many factors influenced this process, including: international migration, expansion of U.S. military bases in the region, diversification of the region's economy, expansion of tourism and leisure activities in Mexico, regional restructuring in both the United

States and Mexico (the sunbelt phenomenon), Mexico's maquila program, expansion of informal economic activities, and transborder linkages of multiple kinds.

The border region today encompasses Texas, New Mexico, and Arizona, as well as southern California. In Mexico, it includes the states of Tamaulipas, Nuevo Leon, Coahuila, Chihuahua, Sonora, and Baja California. A jurisdictional line of nearly 2,000 miles runs through the middle of the region, from the Pacific Ocean to the Gulf of Mexico. On the eastern side, the line follows the Rio Grande River, while the western half of the line is purely geometric, cutting through the Sonoran and Mojave deserts and the coastal mountain range. As Herzog says: "In what was once an arid, resource-poor frontier at the edge of two nation states, a vital, dynamic economic base has emerged around the development of a regional system of cities, within which a subsystem of border cities has gained increasing importance" (1990:48).

The urban, economic, and demographic expansion of the borderlands has occurred in spurts that are associated with distinct economic activities. Early on, the international line itself provoked the establishment of small settlement nodes to handle cross-border traffic in the nineteenth century. Later, during the U.S. prohibition era, Mexican border settlements expanded tourism and entertainment industries for a predominantly North American clientele. Sex, liquor, drugs, gambling, and other vices were promoted in a variety of ways. A second growth phase followed the economic depression of the 1930s and "coincided with a US military buildup during the 1940s and 1950s" (Arreola and Curtis, 1993:26). Military bases were established and expanded in the United States Southwest during these years. On the other side of the line, border cities became increasingly important as staging areas for northbound migrants. A third phase of expansion began in the 1960s, tied to Mexico's maquila experiment. While maquilas quickly overshadowed other elements, the Mexican strategy actually began as a set of several different initiatives including border beautification and tourism promotion.

This last dramatic wave of expansion of the borderlands is thus a result of the expansion of assembly-plant manufacturing in Mexico and the explosion of formal and informal activities that are linked to this single sector. National and regional-scale restructuring (i.e., investment shifts to "sunbelt" locations in both countries) reinforced these trends. Urbanization and economic expansion are, of course, also tied to massive migration flows (discussed above), which is one of the key integrative processes that knit together places in northern Mexico and the U.S. Southwest, creating a region known as the borderlands. A proliferation of informal activities at the border (safe houses, false documents) provides assistance to undocumented border-crossers who want to join the ranks of ten million (or more!) unauthorized Mexican migrants currently working in the United States.

CONCLUSION

The U.S.-Mexico borderlands are immense and complex. The physical environment is spectacularly diverse and extremely rugged in places. The social and cultural geographies of the borderlands are equally complex and dynamic. In many ways, the region provides a window on the relationship between the United States and Mexico. Likewise, a close look at the region reveals some of the contradictory impulses of globalization, neoliberalism, and international development. As the opening quote from Urrea hints, the border has become something larger than life, penetrating deep into ordinary places in the United States (and Mexico), and transforming everyday activities and places. The U.S.-Mexico border symbolizes and embodies the inextricably close ties that knit together the histories and the future prospects of the two countries.

This chapter highlights some features of the U.S.-Mexico borderlands region, yet neglects other aspects. No matter what lessons we take from the borderlands, it is important to remember that for many people, the U.S.-Mexico border region is simply a place to live, work, and raise a family.[5]

NOTES

1. The central U.S. policy to encourage global manufacturing reorganization was the 1962 change in the Tariff Code Provisions 806.30 and 807.00.

2. Average annual growth rates of 8 percent.

3. These figures showing high turnover rates are consistent with other maquila research findings.

4. The war is known as the U.S. Invasion in Mexico.

5. The photo in this chapter is by Julian Cardona; Craig Dalton is the cartographer.

SUGGESTED READINGS

Bowden, Charles *Down by the River: Drugs, Money, Murder, and Family*. New York: Simon and Schuster, 2002.

Fox, Claire. *The Fence and the River: Culture and Politics at the US-Mexico Border*. Minneapolis: University of Minnesota Press, 1999.

Gómez-Pena, Guillermo. *The New World Border: Prophecies, Poems, and Loqueras for the End of the Century*. San Francisco: City Lights, 1996.

Maciel, David R., and Maria Herrera-Sobek, eds. *Culture across Borders: Mexican Immigration and Popular Culture*. Tucson: University of Arizona Press, 1998.

Stoddard, Ellwyn R. *Borderlands Sourcebook: A Guide to the Literature on Northern Mexico and the American Southwest*. Norman: University of Oklahoma Press. Published under the sponsorship of the Association of Borderlands Scholars, 1983.

Urrea, Luis Alberto. *By the Lake of Sleeping Children: The Secret Life of the Mexican Border*. New York: Anchor Books, 1996.

Urrea, Luis Alberto. *The Devil's Highway: A True Story*. New York: Little, Brown, 2004.

BIBLIOGRAPHY

Anzaldúa, Gloria. *Borderlands/La Frontera: The New Mestiza*. San Francisco: Spinsters/ Aunt Lute, 1987.

Arreola, Daniel D., and James R. Curtis. *The Mexican Border Cities: Landscape Anatomy and Place Personality*. Tucson: University of Arizona Press, 1993.

Bowden, Charles. *Juárez: The Laboratory of Our Future*. New York: Aperture, 1998.

Cravey, Altha J. *Women and Work in Mexico's Maquiladoras*. Lanham, Md.: Rowman & Littlefield, 1998.

Herzog, Lawrence A. *Where North Meets South: Cities, Space, and Politics on the U.S.-Mexico Border*. Austin: University of Texas Press, 1990.

Martinez, Oscar J. *Troublesome Border*. Tucson: University of Arizona Press, 1988.

Nevins, Joseph. *Operation Gatekeeper: The Rise of the "Illegal Alien" and the Making of the US-Mexico Boundary*. London: Routledge, 2002.

6

Spaces of Tourism

John Davenport and Edward L. Jackiewicz

Tourism has become one of the world's most important industries as many regions and countries are embracing it as a vehicle for development. The vast beauty of Latin America, a region naturally endowed with an abundance of biological and cultural resources, intrigued nonindigenous visitors who first set foot on its shores centuries ago. This wonderment instilled in past travelers is alive and well today. Nearly three decades of steady growth in Latin America's tourism industry attest to this ongoing love affair with the promise of a "New World." Yet, harnessing the beauty and diversity of the region, while minimizing the problems often associated with tourism development is no easy task. Indeed, the success of tourism in any given locale is contingent on the ability to lure people from beyond the area, with the "big catch" being those traveling from the global north. Moreover, tourism growth needs to be managed in such a way that most of the benefits circulate locally. The light of progress illuminates the potential of some destinations, while casting a shadow of uncertainty over others.

We frame this chapter on tourism in the region in terms of the "opportunities and constraints" associated with this type of development to discuss the industry's scope and scale. Opportunities to develop a tourism industry are presented in several ways, including: a rich, diverse natural environment such as rain forests, coastlines, mountains, and so forth; stable governments that support tourism development; and cultural amenities that appeal to a broad range of tourists, such as indigenous cultures and artifacts. Alternatively, the absence of one or more of these factors can pose constraints for successful tourism development. The scope of tourism development is defined as the diversification of tourist activities present throughout the region, and we use this as a way to highlight regional and spatial differentiation. By scale, we refer to the level of development within the tourism industry relative to other destinations in the region measured here by number of international arrivals (see table 6.1). The scope and scale of development in the tourism industry throughout Latin America is as widely varied as the human and physical environment of the region itself. The following synopsis serves to address some of the ways in which Latin America's distinct social, cultural, economic, political, and physiographic conditions influence intraregional variations in the tourism industry. A broad understanding of how the aforementioned conditions function in shaping spatial patterns in the tourism industry provides insight as to which obstacles, catalysts, limitations, and favorable conditions may influence intraregional inequities of involvement.

In recent decades the global economy has witnessed accelerated growth in its service sector (see chapters 2 and 3). Concurrent developments in the regional economy of Latin America have been no different. The advancement of tourism as a strategy for development remains a component of all Latin American countries' comprehensive plans to varying degrees. Some 8 percent of all visitor arrivals worldwide find their way to Latin America. In fact, Mexico ranks eighth among the world's top tourism destinations, and most countries in the region are experiencing an increase in the number

Table 6.1.   International Tourist Arrivals by Country of Destination (1000s)

	1995	2000	2001	2002	% Change*
Argentina	2,289	2,909	2,620	2,820	+23
Belize	131	196	196	200	+53
Bolivia	284	306	308	—	—
Brazil	1,991	5,313	4,773	3,783	+90
Chile	1,540	1,742	1,723	1,412	−8
Colombia	1,399	557	616	541	−61
Costa Rica	785	1,088	1,131	1,113	+42
Ecuador	440	627	641	654	+49
El Salvador	235	795	735	951	+305
French Guiana	—	65	65	—	
Guatemala	563	826	835	881	+56
Guyana	106	105	95	104	−2
Honduras	271	471	518	550	+103
Mexico	20,241	20,641	19,810	19,667	−3
Nicaragua	281	486	483	472	+68
Panama	345	484	519	534	+55
Paraguay	438	289	279	250	−43
Peru	444	797	789	846	+91
Suriname	43	58	—	—	—
Uruguay	2,022	1,968	1,892	1,258	−38
Venezuela	700	469	584	432	−38

Source: World Tourism Organization (WTO, 2005). Data as collected by WTO, Sept. 2003.
*From 1995 to 2002.

of international tourists (see table 6.1) (Meyer-Arendt, 2002). Developing countries increasingly rely on the service sector for employment and job growth (Harrison, 2001). Consequently, variations in the scope and scale of development in the tourism industry may frequently be viewed as a euphemism for the spatial patterns of "haves" and "have-nots." Citizens employed in Costa Rica's well-developed and managed ecotourism industry often enjoy the economic vitality of an industry that exhibits high multiplier effects and local participation (Weaver, 1999). In contrast, the often abhorrent living conditions of people residing outside the confines of Mexico's numerous coastal luxury resorts attest to pronounced inequities frequently associated with mass tourism and transnational investment (Brenner and Aguilar, 2002; Revilla, Dodd, and Hoover, 2001).

The range or scope of tourist activities in Latin America falls under at least one of four categories: beach or "3S" (sun, sea, and sand) tourism, nature-based tourism (including eco- and adventure tourism), cultural tourism, and urban tourism. Important to note are the varying opportunities and/or constraints generated by the synergistic association between economic, social, cultural, historical, political, and physiographic conditions in shaping the scope and scale of tourism in a given region. As with most phenomena deemed relevant to the body of geography, pulling one string of causation frequently results in corollary movement elsewhere. Underpinning the dynamic interplay of conditions exacerbating spatial variations in Latin American tourism is a useful starting point for prognosticating the economic vitality of this growing sector.

BEATEN PATHS: ON OR OFF?

Although intraregional travel accounts for the vast majority of international arrivals (Santana, 2001), it is highly desirable to lure foreign visitors who bring in outside currency and tend to spend more. As in other economic arenas, Latin America is highly dependent on the United States for tourism growth. The overwhelming purchasing power of the North American market underlies the region's fundamental dependence on the economic prosperity of its neighbor, giving Mexico a distinct geographical advantage over other Latin American countries. Many U.S. tourists are drawn to Mexico by the relatively inexpensive and short flights, but that is only one advantage Mexico possesses that contributes to its vast tourism industry. It also offers an array of cultural opportunities from museums to pyramids to indigenous cultures, beautiful beaches, diverse physiographic regions, and perhaps most importantly, it is perceived as a safe destination, even though this perception varies over time and locality (e.g., Mexico City is no longer considered a "safe destination" mostly as a result of the recent wave of kidnappings).

Tourism is an atypical export wherein the consumption of services rendered occurs simultaneously with their production and furthermore "on location"—tourism being the manufacturing of experience. Therefore, the fundamental task of the industry is to enable and ensure an adequate flow of customers to the point of consumption, that is, tourism sites. The development of these sites must appeal to a broad range of tourists, and a major obstacle to the development of tourism in many countries is fear, whether real or perceived by potential tourists. Many countries such as Nicaragua, Honduras, Guatemala, El Salvador, and Colombia have had recent episodes of violence that scar the images of these places in the minds of would-be tourists. All but Colombia seem to have at least partially shed that image, as the figures in table 6.1 indicate. Of course, Colombia is still in the midst of political turmoil and, at the time of this writing, the U.S. Department of State has a "travel warning" issued for Colombia, but nowhere else in the region.

Structural connectivity with the North American market is a luxury that not all Latin American countries enjoy, due in part to wide disparities in the level of development throughout the region. The majority of tourists only have a short time to vacation and accessibility is vital to the success of many potential tourism sites. Key cities of the region, such as Rio de Janeiro, São Paulo, Buenos Aires, and others, have frequent flights from the United States, but to extend trips from these destinations to more remote parts of the country is often difficult and time consuming due to limited infrastructure (roads, airports, etc.), and this limits the potential number of visitors. It is no surprise that the infrastructure that supports mass tourism shows a high degree of agglomeration in and around urban centers, which double as major transportation hubs.

In more developed tourism locales, current infrastructure needs center around the modernization of airline fleets, airport facilities expansion, and increases in flight frequency (Santana, 2001). In more isolated areas the needs are more basic and include such things as building roads and hotels, providing transportation, and promoting the area as a desirable tourism destination. Costa Rica, which is at the forefront of the ecotourism industry and boasts one of the region's highest standards of living, is in a unique position where it is poised to strengthen both its infrastructure and ties with regional markets abroad. Foreign investment in San Jose's infrastructure by the Marriott Corporation (albeit controversial) in the mid-1990s and the construction of a resort at Papaguayo both grew in concert with an increase of international flights arriving from Europe (Lumsdon and Swift, 2001). Consequently, the market swelled beyond the capacity of Costa Rica's infrastructure.

Not all countries are as fortunate as Costa Rica to have the demand in place as well as the ability to develop to accommodate the overflow. Quite often, attempts at developing infrastructure (hotels, roads, airports) are sought in an effort to elevate the status of remote locales to secondary, if not primary, transportation hubs and tourism destinations. Landing a location on the destinations list of international air carriers and/or popular travel guidebooks has the potential of launching a once remote location into the position of a lucrative enterprise. Although with any speculative venture there is risk involved. "If you build it they will come" remains a tenuous business plan, as more than one hastily built, underoccupied resort has shown.

Of course, certain types of tourism require more infrastructure than others. The development of large resorts requires that many amenities be in place to lure tourists seeking an experience where they can relax and be pampered. These destinations need to have an airport in close proximity and a fully developed infrastructure akin to resorts in North America or Europe. Other locations, especially those labeling themselves as natural or ecotourism destinations, pride themselves on their accurate portrayals of local livelihoods and seek an alternative type of traveler (see chapter 7). With relatively low levels of infrastructure, Guyana has opted to spur economic development through the growth of its ecotourism industry. This strategy seems well suited to Guyana's present condition, since ecotourism in general "needs less capital requirement in terms of infrastructure," as outlined by Lumsdon and Swift (1998:158). This is not to insinuate that a minimum number of transportation routes is not needed to grow a viable ecotourism economy. The isolated Chaco region of eastern Paraguay, for example, lacks a basic infrastructure around which nature-based tourism may grasp a foothold (Lumsdon and Swift, 2001). It appears roadways rather than hotel rooms should take priority in the pursuit of an evolving nature-based tourism sector in Paraguay. Gaining access to the backcountry, while certainly difficult, remains an unrealized precursor to further exploring Paraguayan ecotourism initiatives.

Mexico and Costa Rica are examples of Latin American countries that have taken a highly active role in developing and promoting their respective tourism industries. Such intensive state involvement has furthered the development of infrastructure at peripheral locations, thus attracting national and foreign investment (Brenner and Aguilar, 2002; Clancy, 2001). While Mexico's draw is not limited to "3S" mass tourism, such infrastructure-dependent activities have clearly benefited from the state's asserted efforts in making tourism a centerpiece of its overall development strategy. For all of Mexico's success, none of this would be possible if not for its positioning at the doorstep of the North American market. The Costa Rican experience contrasts slightly with that of Mexico because the government focused on promoting its natural amenities and, as mentioned earlier, has evolved into a world leader in ecotourism.

TOURISM AND THE ECONOMY

Economic trends throughout Latin America over the past several decades have been marked by escalating foreign debt, growing disparities between the rich and the poor, pronounced intraregional variations in the wealth of nations, high rates of inflation, high unemployment, low tax revenues, and general economic volatility (see chapters 1 and 2). As a result, investor confidence at home and abroad has been shaky. Securing capital investment for structural improvement projects remains a major obstacle for many nations seeking to develop their tourism industries. While addressing the role of economics in fostering or stunting the growth of Latin America's tourism industry, it is noteworthy to mention business travel. An increase in regional economic integration promises to generate a rise in inter- and intraregional business travel. Of course, this trend would accelerate if the pending Free Trade Area of the Americas (FTAA) legislation were to pass (Strizzi and Meis, 2004), although this seems to be increasingly unlikely. Certainly, all tourism activities located in and around urban areas would benefit by any such increases in business arrivals. As previously mentioned, the majority of international arrivals in Latin America originate from within the region itself. Thus, regional economic prosperity and cohesion, resulting in adequate levels of discretionary income by which Latin Americans may travel freely throughout the continent, appears instrumental in strengthening the industry as a whole. Research has shown that an increase in the number of tourists among *developing* countries correlates with strong opportunities for economic growth (Eugenio-Martin, Morales, and Scarpa, 2004). Along this line of thought, such findings suggest that reciprocal benefits might occur on a broader scale when citizens of developing countries achieve the opportunity to participate in intraregional travel, more equitable patterns of tourism development being one result. As we will see next, poor economic conditions are often accompanied by undesirable social consequences.

SAFETY, IMAGE, AND POLITICAL CONDITIONS

As previously mentioned, fear can be an overriding factor when tourists are seeking a potential vacation destination. It is also evident that safety significantly correlates with per capita gross domestic product (GDP) and general economic stability in Latin American countries (Eugenio-Martin, Morales, and Scarpa, 2004). Both Honduras and Nicaragua have low levels of income per capita and unfortunate histories of civil war, military conflict, and political instability. Such findings seek not to relegate the impoverished to deviancy, but to illustrate that deflating economies tend to foster inhospitable living conditions, such as high crime rates for permanent residents and visitors alike. Reputations such as these can often take a long time to be erased from the potential tourist's memory and detract from the ability of these places to develop a tourism industry. These images stunted tourism growth throughout the 1980s and 1990s, but recent tourism figures illustrate that many of these images have been erased.

Large-scale violence, including civil war and armed conflict associated with political unrest, is not the only deterrent of tourist arrivals in portions of Latin America. Street crime in Mexico City, illicit drug activity in Colombia, and thievery in Pelourinho, Brazil (TED Case Studies, 2004), which is a cultural and historic tourism district in the city of Salvador, undoubtedly put up red flags in the minds of potential visitors. In 1995, more than 66 percent (4,000 total) of all kidnappings in the region occurred in Colombia, and in 1994, Mexico saw 1,400 abductions (Macko, 1997). These numbers continue to increase and have even become popularized in such Hollywood movies as *Man on Fire*. The Latin American region and Colombia specifically continued to post the world's highest rates of kidnapping during the late 1990s; this figure adversely affects perceptions abroad concerning the safety and security of travel throughout Latin America.

Fledgling democracies often serve as the political backdrop for such volatile relations. Politically motivated violence has a long history in Latin America and casual observers of the region may view this problem as endemic and look elsewhere when it is time to book their next trip. As negative images of the region persist and intensify, some legitimate, others unwarranted, the reality of expanding the scope and scale of tourist activities throughout the region appears inexorably hindered by stereotype and stigma. Many of the countries with incipient tourism industries, such as Nicaragua, Guatemala, and El Salvador, are also relatively inexpensive to visit, luring in a growing number of budget travelers. It is important to remember, however, that this positive trend could turn on the next social or political upheaval, leaving the continued success of tourism in a precarious position, intimately tied in with the social, political, and economic futures of the countries.

Likewise, the security concerns of travelers extend beyond what potentially awaits them at their final destination, especially since the events of 9/11. Safe air travel en route to Latin America, or any region of the world for that matter, became a matter of increasing interest among both ailing air carriers and worried customers. Consequently, the airline industry incurred a rapid decline in sales and customer confidence. Such anomalous developments do much in the way of exposing the fickle nature of a service industry that is so tightly connected to the well-being of commercial air carriers. Discontinuing or limiting the number of flights connecting Latin America with the North American market quite literally puts a "kink in the hose" through which capital is gained and circulated throughout the region. The fallout after 9/11 included negative consequences concerning the structural connectivity of Latin America with its neighbors to the north. Ultimately, the region's number of international arrivals plummeted when the volatile conditions of 9/11 arose.

MORE ON THE SCOPE OF TOURISM

Ecotourism

Of the dominant forms of tourism present in the region we will first address ecotourism (see also chapter 7). It is widely held that ecotourism is the fastest growing sector of tourism worldwide (Campbell, 1999). The varied landscapes of Latin America, particularly the large tracts of rainforest, have placed the region among the world's top ecotourism destinations. Countries that possess rain forests or unique nature-based destinations, such as Brazil, Costa Rica, Ecuador, Peru, and Argentina (Schluter, 2001), have led the way in attracting arrivals interested in this increasingly popularized form of tourism. For a general definition of ecotourism we draw directly from Weaver's three core criteria (1999:793—see also chapter 12):

1. the primary attraction is nature, and culture is a secondary attraction
2. the study and/or appreciation for nature in its own right as opposed to its use for another purpose
3. the activities of tourists are benign to the local environment

Additionally, ecotourism is especially well suited for incorporation into areas on the global periphery (Weaver, 1999); a further extension of Turner and Ash's (1975) "periphery of pleasure" with perhaps a small measure of ecological conscience now incorporated. According to Brohman (1996:65), "proponents of alternative tourism [including ecotourism: words ours] argue that it provides scope for less negative impacts, yet retains, and in some cases enhances, the positive economic benefits of tourism, and contributes to a more appropriate form of development." Ideally, ecotourism incorporates community involvement and environmental sustainability with clearly defined development objectives.

Where, then, is ecotourism taking a foothold in local economies? In Ecuador's Galapagos Islands a preservation zone stands as one example of ecotourism activity. In fact, the Galapagos Islands are one of the world's top ecotourism destinations. As ecotourism has expanded both in scope and scale, Honey (2003) warns us that many places have co-opted and corrupted the term by labeling their experience "ecotourism" even when they fail to meet one or more of the core criteria.

Ecotourism destinations are now spread far and wide throughout the region in highly diverse geographic locales. For example, in Mexico ecotourism destinations include such diverse places and activities as: bird-watching in the Sierra Madre Mountains, observing whales off the coast of Baja California (Barkin, 1999; Pearson, 1999; Young, 1999), hiking through numerous rain forests, and a Monarch Butterfly Reserve located west of Mexico City among many others. As the demand for such experiences expands, places are more than willing to accommodate them, even if it requires bending the definition a bit.

The Amazon basin puts Brazil on the map as a primary ecotourism destination, although the basin's extension into several other countries has helped develop ecotourism industries in Ecuador, Peru, Colombia, and Venezuela. The city of Manaus serves as the main point of departure for ecotourism excursions in Brazil, but beyond there much of Brazil's Amazonian rain forest lacks a necessary infrastructure required for receiving the high volume of tourists it is projected to encounter in years to come. Manaus, like other tourism gateway cities, is illustrative of this symbiotic relationship between primary mass tourism markets and secondary ecotourism markets. As the infrastructure of Manaus continues to grow, parallel developments in human resources and surrounding park facilities needed to accommodate such an increase may lag behind (Lumsdon and Swift, 2001). Consequently, issues related to incremental and sustainable development of the ecotourism industry have become a pressing concern. The 1994 implementation of Brazil's Politica Nacional do Turismo (PNT, or National Tourism Policy) gives some cause for optimism, as the development of infrastructure, training of human resources, and decentralization and modernization of tourism administration are all key strategies of this plan (Santana, 2001:16). The stifling influence of bureaucratic affairs is often an obstacle to implementation in many Latin American countries, but hopefully Manaus's position as a detached metropole will not leave its surrounding habitat at risk of over- and improper use due to spatial inequities of political power.

Costa Rica is often considered an exemplar for other countries embarking on ecotourism initiatives. With 230 separate protected areas and an extensive national park system created in 1969, Costa Rica is well positioned to continue building its ecotourism industry (Honey, 2003:40). Costa Rica's one hundred years of democracy and fifty years without an organized military have helped foster a stable political and social climate. Thus, sound resource management, land use planning, and environmental concerns are well funded and tended to in a systematic and scientifically informed manner. Weaver (1999) adds that private reserves such as La Selva, Rara Avis, and Monteverde Cloud Forest Preserve have been established as a means of complementing the public system. The combined holdings of the private/

public preservation system and their immediately surrounding areas house the majority of ecotourism activity in Costa Rica. Following the spatial trends of ecotourism elsewhere, activities tend to agglomerate around San Jose, the country's hub for international travel, and its coastal resorts catering to "3S" tourism.

Fundamental to this trend is the tourists' apparent attraction to the "'front' country of relatively easily accessible natural settings with a good but unobtrusive infrastructure of basic facilities" (Kearsley, Hall, and Jenkins, 1997:71, from Weaver, 1999:794). Accordingly, a growth in mass tourism of perhaps any nature may indicate a precursor to possible market expansion into secondary ecotourism activities. Alternately, as seen in the development of Costa Rica's Papaguayo resort, established secondary ecotourism activities may experience an increase in volume of arrivals due to a spillover of tourists from burgeoning mass tourism markets. Concerning spatial patterns of tourism development in Latin America, such a finding does not infer a mutual dependence between the two forms of tourism, but rather reveals the gravity between economic activities despite their inherent differences in location. It is reasonable to expect an overlap in the spatial patterns of mass and ecotourism whenever possible.

Many Central American countries are trying to become the "new Costa Rica" in terms of its ecotourism development. Interesting in this regard is Belize, which, according to Weaver (2001), is probably the biggest competitor to Costa Rica for ecotourists and, like Costa Rica, Belize has experienced concurrent growth of mass tourism in its costal regions, aiding in the development of its ecotourism industry. Weaver adds that the close proximity of mass resorts in nearby Cancun generates valuable cross-border arrivals for Belize's growing ecotourism market. Other Central American countries such as Honduras, Nicaragua, and Guatemala have to date been less successful at developing an ecotourism industry, although it's not that they aren't trying. Ecotourism, however, will always need to confront its inherent paradox: what is the tipping point where too much (i.e., success) results in irreparable environmental damage and ultimately destroys itself?

"3S" Tourism

Another popular form of tourism in the region is "3S tourism"—shorthand for sun, sea, and sand. Beach vacations, all-inclusive coastal resorts, and waterfront island getaways all come to mind when speaking of 3S tourism. We have established that ecotourism and forms of mass tourism such as 3S tourism often work in concert with one another. That is, one person's vacation may combine an ecotour with equal time spent at a beachside resort. *Where*, then, do the coastal resorts so often associated with 3S tourism tend to be situated? Obviously, a coastal location is a start, but every country in

Latin America, sans Paraguay and Bolivia, has coastal access, so this is not the only criterion for success. Brazil and Mexico are both noteworthy for their relative success in this area. Mexico, with an abundance of integrated and enclave resorts, and access to the North American market, enjoys the most robust 3S tourism market in the region. Resorts at Acapulco, Los Cabos, Loreto, Puerto Vallarta, Huatulco, Cancún, Manzanillo, and others, welcome thousands of tourists each year to the warm waters, moderate climate, and sandy beaches along Mexico's Pacific and Gulf coasts. Thirty years ago Cancun was nothing more than a small isolated beach community, but then due to a coordinated government strategy it emerged as Mexico's primary beach resort, and in 1989 became *the* tourist destination most visited by international arrivals to Mexico, surpassing the top ranked Federal District surrounding Mexico City (SECTUR, 1991, from Clancy, 2001:59).

Coastal development in Brazil begins with Rio de Janeiro and its world-renowned beaches of Copacabana and Ipanema. The images of Rio are familiar around the world and the beaches have been luring visitors for decades. The successful tourism of the city and its beaches, enhanced by Rio's "party image," culminates every year in the Carnaval celebration. Further north, the Brazilian state of Bahia, a region of distinct Afro-Brazilian heritage, attracts millions of tourists each year; many of them travel to the region in pursuit of its coastal amenities and cultural attractions (TED Case Studies, 2004). Rio de Janeiro, with its 80 kilometers of beaches, has been one of the premier Latin American destinations for travelers from abroad for decades (Riotur, 2005). Intraregional arrivals support Brazil's 3S tourism industry too, as a considerable number of Argentines and Paraguayans contribute to the success of Brazilian beach resorts (Lumsdon and Swift, 2001).

It is important to note that 3S tourism has been transformed by the emergence of all-inclusive resorts such as Club Med. At this point, Club Med villages in Latin America have been limited to Brazil and Mexico (as well as throughout the Caribbean). These resorts make it convenient for the tourist by charging one price for accommodations, meals, and activities but tend to have limited multiplier effects in the local economies because little money is spent supporting local businesses outside of the resort.

Cultural and Urban Tourism

The last two forms of tourism addressed are cultural and urban. While many cultural tourism activities do occur in metropolitan centers, by no means do such forms take place exclusively within urban areas. An appreciation of cultural attractions extends beyond the confines of city life, as seen through travelers' interest in traditional ways of life and the heritage of mostly rural indigenous peoples. Developing countries in particular have utilized the cultural wealth of indigenous people in an effort to generate capital amid limited economic alternatives. Peruvian sites such as Machu Picchu point to local Incan heritage; the Mexican pyramids of Teotihuacan display the Aztec heritage so important to their cultural tourism industry. Indigenous cultures throughout the Andean countries as well as Central America's Mayan civilization are increasingly popular tourist attractions. The "Mundo Maya" project, encompassing five Central American countries, has received much attention from tourists and critics alike (Lumsdon and Swift, 1998).

Visitors are often attracted to Latin American cities to experience the colonial heritage signified through local architecture and museum pieces. Scarpaci's (2004) *Plazas and Barrios* explores the institutional, commercial, and residential uses of historic districts throughout Latin American cities such as Bogota, Colombia; Buenos Aires, Argentina; Cartagena, Colombia; Cuenca, Ecuador; Montevideo, Uruguay; Puebla, Mexico; and Quito, Ecuador. Scarpaci presents historic districts of the aforementioned urban environments as cultural landscapes from which social meanings (in the most humanistic of terms) may be derived; the reading of a "social document," as he so rightly puts it (2004:33). Scarpaci's reading of the urban text takes into account material and nonmaterial culture alike, both of which continue to lure tourists.

People are also drawn to the contemporary culture expressed most profoundly in urban areas. Festivals, sporting events, restaurants, and art galleries all bring in outsiders. The cultural affairs at home in some of Latin America's most cosmopolitan cities (Salvador and Rio de Janeiro, Brazil) are often mirrored by less publicized forms of tertiary activity, including the proliferation of sex tourism in many metropolitan centers. Historical inequities based on race and gender, gaping disparities of wealth, accepting social climates, lax legal codes, and reputation abroad have all contributed to a growing preponderance of prostitution within the economic sphere of urban tourism. Brazil is internationally renowned for its liberal sexual climate. Facing the beautiful backdrop of Copacabana beach in Rio de Janeiro is a vibrant nightlife area, where hundreds of prostitutes are present on any given night. Many young girls are drawn to the urban areas from poor rural areas with the hopes of earning the relatively large sums of money that are unattainable in their place of origin. Other women use prostitution as a means of supplementing the insufficient wages garnered in their "day jobs."

A more recent form of cultural tourism to take hold in Latin America is to gaze on the region's vast impoverishment. The Rio de Janeiro favela of Rocinha, Latin America's largest informal settlement, has recently begun to offer tours of the settlement. Tourists are met outside of the favela by a guide and two escorts (see figure 6.2), who lead the visitors through the community of 250,000, discussing the history, culture, economy, and environment. Without the guide and escorts, it would be impossible for an

Figure 6.1. An after-school job hawking handicrafts to tourists, Antigua, Guatemala.

Figure 6.2. Favela tour escorts, Rocinha, Rio de Janeiro. Photo by Ray Martin

outsider to navigate the labyrinthine streets of the favela. Moreover, they are evidence that these visitors are not intruders but rather paying customers.

The drive to incorporate tourism into the local economies of Latin American cities is just one of many globalizing forces that serve to rearrange both the built environment and social sphere of urban centers throughout the region. Urban tourism remains an integral part of the Latin American experience for nearly any variety of traveler, whether "in town" to visit a historic center, survey the shantytowns, or frequent the red light district.

CONCLUSION

Despite the growing popularity of tourism as a vehicle for development, it continues to be controversial and frequently criticized. The industry itself has proven to be fickle (see post-9/11 figures for just one example), highly competitive, and poorly managed. From a Latin American perspective, much of this development is dependent on investment from outside the region (not to mention the increasing reliance on visitors from these areas). Local businesses often struggle with the entrance of foreign hotels and restaurants catering to the tourist crowd leading to the "leakage" of much of the potential profit. If a traveler from the United States books her/his reservation at a U.S. travel agent, flies on a U.S. carrier, stays in a foreign-owned hotel, and eats most meals in nonlocal establishments, the bulk of those dollars spent do not circulate locally to promote local development (Mihalic, 2002:94).

Nonetheless, tourism remains popular because it is relatively easy to implement and can be an attractive option for financially strapped countries with little resources to invest. It often brings in money from outside of the region and can help foster the development of local industry, if managed properly. It creates much needed jobs, even if they are often low-wage and sometimes exploitative (e.g., prostitution). Tourism can also provide incentives to protect local environments and cultures, provided these incentives are strong enough to ward off the urge to exploit these resources for short-term gains.

This chapter has illustrated that tourism development is a slippery slope fraught with problems, yet can prove to be beneficial if it promotes local development and is managed in a way to benefit local and national economies and not solely foreign enterprises. This requires an active government policy as well as educated consumers (i.e., tourists) who are sensitive to local conditions and the implications of their actions. Furthermore, certain countries are well poised to take advantage of the growth in the tourism industry. Costa Rica and Mexico have already proven to be successful on many levels. (By no means does this suggest that tourism in these places is not problematic, indeed it is. This merely points out that through active government involvement and foreign investment these two places have developed their infrastructure and continue to draw in large numbers of visitors.) Certain intangibles like a poor public image or an unfavorable reputation can be a constraint and relegate specific destinations to "off limits" zones (e.g., Colombia) in the collective mind of would-be visitors. At other times, inadequate infrastructures and limited access to capital can pose seemingly insurmountable obstacles in the development of mass tourism markets (Guyana and Paraguay). Likewise, a prevalence or relative lack of natural resources can make ecotourism a viable option in one locale, while merely wishful thinking in another. A country's intraregional position and location relative to the North American market can have immense consequences on tourism development (Curtis and Arreola, 1991)—especially when accounting for 3S tourism activity. State involvement in tourism-centered development initiatives plays an undeniable role in fostering a political climate well suited to industry growth (as seen in Mexico and Costa Rica).

The varied successes and failures of tourism throughout the region are indicative of broader issues related to disparities in economic development, natural and monetary wealth, and standards of living. To view regional inequities through the prism of tourism should prove helpful in shedding new light on old problems within a land of vast potential.

SUGGESTED READINGS

Boniface, Brian, and Chris Cooper. *Worldwide Destinations: The Geography of Travel and Tourism.* 4th edition. San Francisco: Elsevier, 2005.

Pattullo, Polly. *Last Resorts: The Cost of Tourism in the Caribbean.* London: Cassell Books, 1996.

Shaw, Gareth, and Alan M. Williams. *Tourism and Tourism Spaces.* London: Sage Publications, 2004.

BIBLIOGRAPHY

Barkin, D. "The Economic Impacts of Ecotourism: Conflicts and Solutions in Highland Mexico." In *Tourism and Development in Mountain Areas,* edited by P. M. Godde, M. F. Price, and F. M. Zimmerman, pp. 157–172. London: CAB International, 1999.

Brenner, L., and A. G. Aguilar. "Luxury Tourism and Regional Economic Development in Mexico." *The Professional Geographer* 54, no. 4 (2002): 500–520.

Brohman, J. "New Directions in Tourism for Third World Development." *Annals of Tourism Research* 23, no. 1 (1996): 48–70.

Campbell, L. M. "Ecotourism in Rural Developing Communities." *Annals of Tourism Research* 26, no. 3 (1999): 534–553.

Clancy, M. *Exporting Paradise: Tourism and Development in Mexico.* Amsterdam: Pergamon, 2001.

Curtis, J. R., and D. D. Arreola. "Zonas de Tolerancia on the Mexican Border." *Geographical Review* 81, no. 3 (1991): 333–346.

Eugenio-Martin, J. L., N. M. Morales, and R. Scarpa. "Tourism and Economic Growth in Latin American Countries: A Panel Data Approach." *NRM–Natural Resources Management*, February 2004.

Harrison, D. "Tourism and Less Developed Countries: Key Issues." In *Tourism and the Less Developed World: Issues and Case Studies*, ed. D. Harrison, pp. 23–46. London: CAB International, 2001.

Honey, M. "Giving a Grade to Costa Rica's Green Tourism." *NACLA Reader* 36, no. 6 (2003): 39–46.

Kearsley, G., C. M. Hall, and J. Jenkins. "Tourism Planning and Policy in Natural Areas: Introductory Comments." In C. M. Hall, J. Jenkins, and G. Kearsley, *Tourism Planning and Policy in Australia and New Zealand: Cases, Issues and Practice*. Sydney: Irwin Press, 1997.

Lumsdon, L. M., and J. S. Swift. "Ecotourism at a Crossroads: The Case of Costa Rica." *Journal of Sustainable Tourism* 6, no. 2 (1998): 155–171.

Lumsdon, L. M., and J. S. Swift. *Tourism in Latin America*. London and New York: Continuum, 2001.

Macko, S. "Kidnapping: A Latin American Growth Industry." ENN Daily Intelligence Report-ERRI Risk Assessment Services, vol. 3-120 (Wednesday, April 30, 1997), http://www.emergency.com/latnkdnp.htm, 1–4.

Meyer-Arendt, K. J. "Commentary: Geographical Research on Tourism in Mexico." *Tourism Geographies* 4, no. 3 (2002): 255–260.

Mihalic, Tanja. "Tourism and Economic Development Issues." In *Tourism and Development: Concepts and Issues*, edited by R. Sharpley and D. J. Telfer, pp. 81–111. Buffalo, N.Y.: Channel View, 2002.

Pearson, K. "Gender and Ecotourism: The Case of Puerto San Carlos in Baja California Sur, Mexico." Master's thesis. Tucson: University of Arizona, 1999.

Revilla, G., T. H. Dodd, and L. C. Hoover. "Environmental Tactics Used by Hotel Companies in Mexico." In *Tourism in South America*, edited by G. Santana, pp. 111–127. New York, London, and Oxford: Haworth Hospitality Press, 2001.

Riotur. http://www.rio.rj.gov.br/riotur/en/(accessed January 24, 2005).

Santana, G. "Tourism in South America: A Brief Overview." In *Tourism in South America*, edited by G. Santana, pp. 1–22. New York, London, and Oxford: Haworth Hospitality Press, 2001.

Scarpaci, J. L. *Plazas and Barrios: Heritage Tourism and Globalization in the Latin American Centro Historico (Society, Environment, and Place)*. Tucson: University of Arizona Press, 2004.

Schluter, R. "The Impact of Tourism on the Patagonian Coast, Argentina." In *Tourism in South America*, edited by G. Santana, pp. 53–72. New York, London, and Oxford: Haworth Hospitality Press, 2001.

SECTUR. "Mexico's Tourism Sector: The Year in Review, 1990." Internal document. Mexico City: SECTUR, 1991.

Strizzi, N., and S. Meis. "Current and Future Developments in Tourism Markets in Latin America and Caribbean Region." 2004. www.hotel-online.com/Trends/PanAmerProceedingsMay99/DevelopMarketsLAC.

TED Case Studies. "Urban Tourism's Impact on Colonial Areas of Latin American

Cities: The Case of Salvador, Brazil." 2004, www.american.edu/TED/urbtour .htm.

Turner, L., and J. Ash. *The Golden Hordes: International Tourism and the Pleasure Periphery.* London: Constable, 1975.

Weaver, D. B. "Magnitude of Ecotourism in Costa Rica and Kenya." *Annals of Tourism Research* 26, no. 4 (1999): 792–816.

Weaver, D. B. "Latin America and the Caribbean." In *Encyclopedia of Ecotourism*, pp. 173–189. New York: CABI Publishers, 2001.

World Tourism Organization. *Compendium of Tourism Statistics.* WTO, 2005.

Young, E. "Balancing Conservation with Development in Small-Scale Fisheries: Is Ecotourism an Empty Promise?" *Human Ecology* 27 (1999): 581–620.

7

Sustainable Development and Ecotourism

General Principles and Eastern Caribbean Case Study

Thomas Klak and Ross Flynn

> We the people of Waitukubuli,[1] recognise Dominica's unique and fragile ecosystems as the basis for the development and advancement of our people and nation. As custodians of nature's biodiversity, we aspire to integrate the endowed gifts of our biotic wealth, with our cultural knowledge, to ensure economic, cultural and ecological integrity for the well being of present and future generations.
>
> —Dominica's Biodiversity Strategy and Action Plan (Ministry of Agriculture and the Environment, 2002)

This is a broad and powerful statement of national priorities. It goes well beyond what most governments have pledged toward ecological protection and cultural inclusion within a sustainable development agenda. Relatedly, Dominica was the world's first of only three Green Globe 21 benchmarked countries. This certification system annually reassesses practices and progress, and requires additional steps each year toward greater sustainability (Green Globe, 2006). This chapter explores the concepts of sustainable development and ecotourism in their Latin American and Caribbean contexts, and evaluates the extent to which commitments to sustainable ecotourism in Dominica are reflected in current practices and future direction.

WHAT IS SUSTAINABLE DEVELOPMENT?

Sustainable development became part of our popular lexicon after the World Commission on Environment and Development in its 1987 report *Our Common Future* defined it simply as "development that meets the needs of the present without compromising the ability of future generations to meet their own needs" (WCED, 1987). Sustainability was further advanced as a policy agenda by such United Nations efforts as the Rio Environmental Conference of 1992, its accompanying NGO Forum (nongovernmental organizations), the 1994 "Sustainable Development—Small Islands" conference in Barbados, and the Millennium Development Goals.

Sustainable development is now widely discussed but seldom defined. It means different things to different people, and is embraced by both ends of the political spectrum. (Can you imagine anyone advocating unsustainable development?) Its varied meanings and uses certainly qualify sustainable development as a "chaotic concept" (Lake and Hanson, 2000). One way to organize the competing views is to distinguish between weaker and stronger versions. The weaker version holds that improvements in the efficiency of resource use can allow continued economic growth. The stronger version maintains that humans must reduce their demands on a finite earth and appreciate the inherent value of other species (Williams and Millington, 2004).

In this chapter we take into account the various interpretations of sustainable development and explicitly link them to ecotourism. Sustainable development is defined in this chapter as that which simultaneously pursues the three complementary goals of ecological integrity, economic viability, and social justice. Sustainable development is secured by balancing on these goals as on a three-legged stool: relative weakness in any one of the legs and the stool topples over. Ecological integrity includes environmental health, protection, and stewardship. Economic viability refers to economic security, at the firm, community, and national levels. Social justice means social welfare and inclusion. When ecotourism is involved, it includes cultural interaction and mutual respect. The social dimension, even though it is probably the most nebulous, is crucial. Data analysis in one of the few comparative studies of ecotourism sustainability revealed that "local community participation is paramount for the success of an ecotourism project" (Kruger, 2005:596).

Sustainable development as defined here is a broadly encompassing concept that includes education, health care, secure and adequate local incomes, community empowerment to shape local economic opportunities, and support for cultural diversity. It requires a strong and secure economic base in communities that are not degrading the environment. Sustainable development has ecosystem health and the creative energies of local people at the center of any plans for resource use and investment.

Sustainability requires more than long-term employment prospects and environmental management. It also must include efforts to shift control and responsibility over development initiatives back to the communities and people whose lives depend on them (see Jackiewicz, 2006). Obviously this requires a shift away from top-down neoliberal development policies shaped by the interests of global investors and their allies (see chapter 2). Sustainable development is viewed here as an active and incremental process rather than an end state. The requirement of annual progress toward greater sustainability in the Green Globe 21 certification system is compatible with this definition (Green Globe, 2006).

Sustainable development as it has just been defined is clearly a challenging goal. In an era framed by U.S. hegemony, economic globalization, consumerism, advertising, and global aspirations for the "American Dream," sustainable development is difficult for any country, even the most wealthy ones, to embrace. What hopes are there for sustainability in Central America and the Caribbean, which are heavily trade dependent and indebted, economically desperate, and experiencing heightened vulnerabilities? Clearly one can expect that government pledges toward sustainability will not often be matched by firm commitments, and that pressures to choose unsustainable short-term solutions will abound.

MASS TOURISM VERSUS ECOTOURISM

Mass tourism is typically beach-focused, dominated by global hotel chains, and resource intensive and wasteful, and often centers on culturally isolated all-inclusive resorts (see chapter 6). It is therefore not a promising component of sustainable development. Nevertheless, the governments in the Caribbean, sooner or later, one by one (now including socialist Cuba), have come to rely on it. Central America has focused more on ecotourism, although its sustainability requires empirical assessment.

The growth of global tourism has been nothing short of spectacular, outpacing all other more conventional commercial sectors. The growth of Caribbean mass tourism has been led by North American and European hotel and cruise ship companies. By 2001, the Caribbean became the world's largest cruise destination, accounting for just under half of global cruise bed days (CTO, 2004). Major international chains such as Hilton, Hyatt, Marriott, Sheraton, Holiday Inn, Club Med, Cunard, Holland America Cruise, St. James Beach Hotels, Leisure Canada, and Delta Hotels have operated in the region since the early 1970s. Although there are transnational chains owned by regional companies such as SuperClubs and Sandals, the Caribbean tourist sector in general is highly globalized and depends on imports for food, beverages, and equipment, much of which comes from the United States or is manufactured by U.S. and European TNCs in the region (Momsen, 1998). Cruise ships too are not well integrated into regional economies. Cruise lines receive the vast majority of travelers' expenditures, with only a small portion distributed among the ports of call (Pattullo, 1996).

With regard to the Caribbean tourists, the United States is again the most important market, accounting for approximately half of all arrivals (CTO, 2004).

It is unlikely that sustainable development can be achieved through externally dominated mass tourism. Some Caribbean analysts maintain that neither mass nor ecotourism is sustainable, and neither is sufficient as the basis for development. One label, "plantation tourism," suggests the continuities of dependency from earlier economic priorities shaped by decisions abroad (Pattullo, 1996). Mass tourism's threats to culture and identity, and its lasting negative impacts on the environment, are notable. Most islands are unable to dispose of the massive waste produced by visitors. The pollution affects rivers, ground water, coastal zones, and offshore reefs (Potter et al., 2004). The environmental impacts of massive tourist influx are further multiplied by the fact that visitors overconsume resources such as food, water, and electricity. Insular ecosystems are among the world's most sensitive, and the negative effects on flora and fauna are often severe.

Policies that include ecotourism-related activities as a central component hold more promise. Ecotourism is the fastest growing sector of the world's largest industry. The International Ecotourism Society (TIES) defines ecotourism as "responsible travel to natural areas that conserves the environment and improves the well-being of local people." This means that those who implement and participate in ecotourism activities should follow the following principles:

Minimize impact
Build environmental and cultural awareness and respect

Figure 7.1. A cruise ship docks for the day at the port of St. John's, the capital of Antigua and Barbuda.

Provide positive experiences for both visitors and hosts

Provide direct financial benefits for conservation

Provide financial benefits and empowerment for local people

Raise sensitivity to the host countries' political, environmental, and social climate

Support international human rights and labor agreements (TIES, 2007)

This definition of ecotourism places priority on preserving the environment, developing rich interactions between visitors and locals, developing low-impact activities in natural contexts, and relying on local participation in the tourism industry that goes well beyond the low-level service sector employment of mass tourism.

An important component of ecotourism for the host communities is education concerning ecosystems and culture. This means developing the teaching capacity of local guides, and teaching visitors about nature and culture. It also includes creating the infrastructure to support educational workshops, service learning opportunities, and longer-term stays for foreign students, with a common thread being their commitment to building sustainable societies.

INTEGRATED SUSTAINABLE DEVELOPMENT

The priorities for ecotourism outlined above are laudable and challenging, but still they are not enough. They must be incorporated into a broader set of policies promoting integrated sustainable development. Components of this broader effort include progress toward agricultural self-sufficiency, selected agricultural export niche marketing including fair trade and organics, land tenure security, and strengthening community participation in NGOs, both local and international. Indeed, an underexplored and undervalued dimension of ecotourism is the industry's capacity to incubate and spawn wide multiplier effects. These need to go beyond the essential linkages that tourism must engender between local agriculture, microbusinesses (formal and informal), and producer services. They should also include local manufacturing of what are now extraregionally imported commodities and technologies; these need customizing for tropical/Caribbean island uses.

Perhaps the most crucial component of integrated sustainable development is a progressive and proactive state that fulfills a stewardship role of maintaining each country's landscapes, coastal zones, marine habitats, and cultural heritages. How can we move toward such a state? There must be "comanagement," in which authority and decision making is shared among several organizations, often operating at different geographical scales, in and out of the public sector. High priority must be placed on local democratic decision making on economic matters, involving not only those within the tourist sector, but also local communities, public-private coalitions of local authorities, NGOs, artisans, and citizens.

This vision sympathizes with a stronger version of sustainable development in that it can no longer mean economic growth. The region must begin living off the interest from its stock of ecological capital instead of running down its stock of natural resources. National development policies and projects must emanate from ecologically sound analyses of the natural resource base. Projects not meeting sustainability criteria must be rejected. This includes those that promise immediate foreign exchange earnings, are offered by international donors and investors, or are promoted by international financial institutions.

Taken together the form of ecotourism-related sustainable development outlined here is secured by balancing on the three legs of economic security, social justice, and environmental protection and stewardship. All this is obviously difficult to measure, and its progress is difficult to track. Most evaluations of the sustainability of ecotourism projects in Latin America focus either on the environmental impacts (e.g., Gayle, 1997; Kruger, 2005) or the local socioeconomic impacts (e.g., Stem et al., 2003; Carrier and MacLeod, 2005). However, measurement difficulties are not grounds for undermining a rich and important concept.

This robust vision of sustainability may seem idealistic but there are some hopeful signs that similar ideas are being pursued in various parts of the region (Cox and Embree, 1990; Berkes, 1999; Jackiewicz, 2006). In Dominica, the critical issues in ecotourism and sustainable development have been conceptualized in a way that parallels this three-legged framework (figure 7.2). Dominica therefore provides a useful case study that is explored below, following a brief discussion of some of the trends across Latin America.

ECOTOURISM-BASED SUSTAINABLE DEVELOPMENT IN LATIN AMERICA

Over the last decade, sustainable development and ecotourism have become principal policy themes throughout Latin America (Moreno, 2005). Despite the ubiquity of the rhetoric, however, the opportunities for truly sustainable ecotourism development are unevenly distributed. Locations and regions that have not already been developed for mass tourism hold more promise. This is because mass tourism tends to develop over time at any location through a series of sequential stages, beginning with small local proprietors and low-impact tourism and leading to large transnational

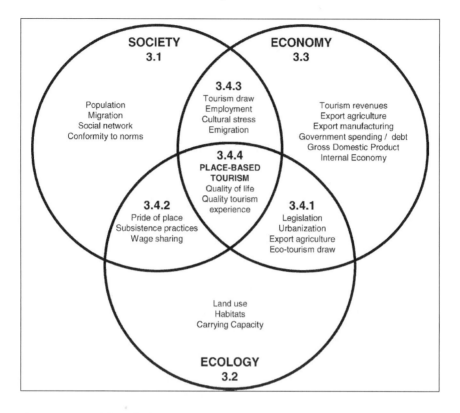

Figure 7.2.   Social, ecological, and economic issues influencing the quality of ecotourism in Dominica.

corporations and tourism on a grand scale. Each stage of tourism development is governed by a ratcheting effect, making it difficult to revert to an earlier form (Pattullo, 1996).

Consider the overdeveloped and environmentally degraded islands of Antigua and St. Maarten, or resort areas such as Cancún, Mexico, which alone drew 2.1 million guests, or 13 percent of all Caribbean visitors, in 2001. Such destinations have little hope of transitioning to sustainable ecotourism, even though places like St. Maarten offer "eco" resort settings that are advertised as "naturalistic," as opposed to "natural" (Henthorne and Miller, 2003). Many other Caribbean venues such as St. Croix, Puerto Rico, and Barbados are already in stage three, or what McElroy and de Albuquerque (1998) label "high density tourism styles." Of course sustainable ecotourism does not suit every visitor's tastes, and mass tourism, however locally unsustainable it is, will continue to dominate the market for some time.

Many less urbanized and developed parts of Latin America see great opportunities for ecotourism. For example, parts of Central America, particularly the Caribbean coastal zone and the Meso-American Caribbean Reef, and the northern coastal regions of South America have features with ecotourism potential. These features include relative isolation from wholesale development in the form of plantation economies, considerable areas of relatively pristine natural environments, and limited mass tourism to date (Moreno, 2005). Further, larger islands such as Cuba and the Dominican Republic, and larger South American countries such as Bolivia, Peru, and Brazil, have been setting aside blocks of remote or biologically significant territory for ecotourism (Cater, 1996; Weaver, 2001; Carrier and MacLeod, 2005). Even the smallest islands such as Saba and the Turks and Caicos are pursuing the economic and ecological benefits of protecting and featuring their coral reefs (Rembert, 1999).

Still, there is no guarantee that what is labeled "ecotourism" will contribute to local sustainable development. As we've seen, it is far too easy to attach "eco" to tourism as a "marketing ploy," which in reality amounts to no more than business-as-usual tweaked in the direction of nature (Kruger, 2005). But even recent tourism developments with an explicitly natural orientation often do not conform to the TIES standards listed above. For example, the *Sunday New York Times* recently allotted three full pages of text and photos to Francis Ford Coppola's three ecotourism lodges in Belize and Guatemala. Although these lodges do engage in an array of authentically ecotouristic practices, such as using renewable energy sources and harvesting from on-site organic gardens to feed visitors, the Guatemalan lodge also advertises that guests can rent ATVs (all terrain vehicles) to explore the surrounding landscape (Green, 2005).

Further obstacles to sustainable ecotourism result from the fact that development pressures are now virtually ubiquitous. Even more remote parts of Latin America are now witness to land-use conflicts, environmental deterioration, and foreign investment in tourism development that excludes locals from the benefits and threatens sustainability (Moreno, 2005). In the Caribbean region, where income-generating options are fewer than on the mainland, pressures are especially great to extract the maximum gain from tourism, despite the consequences. One observer flatly states:

> Across the Caribbean, the overriding concern of government and industry officials is to expand visitor arrivals, per capita expenditure and profit, taxation yield, and tourism-related employment. Neither governments nor advertisers take limits to growth—or sustainably developed tourism—into consideration. (Gayle, 1997)

Despite this bleak assessment, there are nonetheless some countertrends in the direction of sustainability, as the case of Dominica illustrates.

Figure 7.3. An image from a website advertising "ATV Jungle Rides" to cruise ship passengers docking in Dominica. Used by permission of High Ride Adventures

ECOTOURISM-BASED SUSTAINABLE DEVELOPMENT: THE CASE OF DOMINICA

As the previous section should make clear, ecotourism development in Dominica is not regionally unique, but rather representative of widespread efforts to attract ecotourists. In this section, we focus on one small island in order to examine crucial details associated with the successes and failures in the pursuit of ecotourism-related sustainable development.

Dominica has a population of 75,000, a territory of 290 square miles (750 sq. km), and a per capita gross domestic product (GDP) in 2005 of $3,800 (CIA, 2007). Owing to its rugged landscape, which was unconducive to sugar cane plantations (only 20 percent is arable), Dominica was historically more economically isolated and less developed during colonialism than most of its neighbors. Dominica's unsuitability for plantation agriculture, its fragile ruggedness, and relative isolation created an unfavorable context for its early experiments with mass tourism prior to the 1970s (Weaver, 2001). Dominica has few beaches by Caribbean standards, and certainly not the beach for each day of the year that neighboring Antigua boasts. Many of Dominica's beaches feature volcanic black sand and are littered with stones and boulders. These are certainly not the beaches of the

Caribbean tourism advertisements, perhaps best exemplified by Jamaica's six miles of white sand beach at Negril.

Further, due to the orographic uplift of tradewind air masses that reach this mountainous island, Dominica has the region's highest annual rainfall, averaging 175 inches and reaching 400 inches on the eastern windward slopes (Ministry of Agriculture and the Environment, 2002). This precipitation provides the island with hydroelectric power and ample water to export to cruise ships and its tourism-overdeveloped neighbors. But since most tourists dread rain during vacations, Dominica's status as the rainiest Caribbean island does not bode well for marketing. If mass tourism in the Caribbean revolves around "sun, sea, and sand," then Dominica has two strikes against it. However, as with many development prospects, this failure with respect to mass tourism also presents some other narrow possibilities.

Dominica's dramatic physical conditions provide the context for nature-based tourism today. More than 20 percent of the island is encompassed by three national parks and two forest reserves. Overall, about two-thirds of Dominica remains forested, ranging from tropical rain forest to dry scrub woodland in the northwest, where rainfall reaches only 50 inches per annum. The self-styled "Nature Island of the Caribbean" has made efforts to create sustainable ecotourism on the basis of its rich natural landscapes and engaging and receptive culture. Physical features include mountains with peaks over 4,700 feet, an advertised 365 rivers and waterfalls, tropical flora and fauna with considerable endemism, and active plate tectonic geology (Potter et al., 2004). The dynamic geology includes six active volcanoes and could be considered a nature tourism blessing or, in the longer run, more likely a curse. For example, in late 2004, north coast damage from an earthquake measuring 6.0 on the Richter scale was in the tens of millions of U.S. dollars. Hurricanes too have recurrently devastated the island's housing and agricultural sector.

Dominica is culturally unique by Caribbean island standards. There resides the largest continuing, culturally distinct settlement of Native Americans. The population includes 3,000 Caribs, the native residents of the Lesser Antilles until the arrival of Europeans, most of whom live in the 3,785-acre Carib Territory in the eastern portion of the island, which was established in 1903. Smaller numbers of Caribs today live in their ancestral locations in St. Vincent, Trinidad, and in mainland Suriname. Relocated populations live along the Caribbean coast of Central America and are generally referred to as Garifuna. There is also a Carib diaspora in North Atlantic countries. Although they have widely adopted the outsiders' label of "Carib," the native inhabitants refer to themselves as Kalinago (it literally refers to a man but is used gender inclusively).

Dominica's physical and cultural attractions have led to increases in stay-over visitors, from around 14,000 in 1980 and 40,000 in 1990, to

73,140 in 2003 and 79,964 in 2004 (Patterson et al., 2004; Buydominica. com, 2005a). But the figures for 2004 represent only about one-third the stay-over visitors to Antigua or St. Lucia. Tourism accounted for 18 percent of Dominica's GDP in 2000. While this is comparable to larger and more economically diversified countries like Jamaica and Belize, it is lower than neighboring Antigua (44 percent) and St. Lucia (39 percent; *Economist,* 2002).

Airline inaccessibility to Dominica is one key reason why it draws fewer stay-over visitors. Air service is restricted to regional flights from the larger airports such as San Juan, Antigua, St. Lucia, and Barbados. Dominica's short runways, lack of airstrip night lighting, and the hazardous approaches to its two airports make it impossible for the larger aircraft originating beyond the Caribbean to land. The IMF (International Monetary Fund) studied the prospects for significantly lengthening the runways and judged it cost prohibitive (Patterson and Rodriguez, 2003:65). Venezuelan workers and funds are currently expanding and upgrading the main airstrip at Melville Hall.

As with many issues related to sustainable development, that Dominica is inaccessible to direct flights from the North Atlantic has both positive

Figure 7.4. Irvin, an employee at Jungle Bay Resort in Dominica, demonstrates to a student group various foods and medicinal plants he grows in his backyard.

and negative dimensions. It certainly prohibits the delivery of larger numbers of tourists. Dominica's short runways also hinder economic diversification. For example, the additional leg of flying from Dominica to Antigua adds 50 percent to the cost of transporting cut flowers to Europe. This added time and cost has made competing for export niche markets difficult (Wiley, 1998). One bright spot in the export market niche sector is that the U.K. supermarket chain Tesco has been importing and selling Dominica's fair trade bananas since September 2002. All goods produced under the Fairtrade label must meet certain social and environmental criteria (http://www.caribbeannetnews.com). Overall, however, progress toward significant exportation of a range of organic or fair trade products from Dominica or other Eastern Caribbean countries has been slow (UNEP-UNCTAD, 2003), and does not approach the export earnings level from the Lomé/Cotonou arrangements (see chapter 2).

Dominica's inaccessibility helps to self-select visitors more appropriate for ecotourism. Its visitors are relatively motivated (willing to endure longer and more costly transportation) and seek an experience that is slower paced and off the beaten path. It has also kept away most of the components of global tourism such as hotel chains, although the Dominican government welcomes them so long as they are not out of character with the existing built environment (Pascal, 2006). This lack of hotel chains leaves more opportunities for locals and smaller-scale investors to capture a larger share of tourist spending. However, an additional challenge for Dominica is that nature tourism is often very small scale, not especially lucrative, and generates less spending per capita than mass tourism. Self-guided activities like hiking and bird watching may not involve any spending at all (Cater, 1996:130). Ecotourists are often experienced travelers who tend to vacation more simply, avoiding lavish accommodations, expensive shopping, and fancy meals. Therefore, while ecotourists have a low impact on their setting, their impact on the local economy can be similarly limited. Local ownership and management of hotels, restaurants, guide operations, and other services becomes an even higher priority for ecotourism than for mass tourism because the majority of revenue will accrue in these services. Minimizing the leakage rate, which is the share of tourist spending that accrues outside the host country, is particularly important for successful ecotourism. Good information and signage is also key. However, a recent analysis found that Dominica does not provide systematic information and signage about the range of its own attractions, thereby limiting ecotourist activities and potential spending (Tourtellot, 2003).

Dominica has a lower tourism leakage rate than most Caribbean islands (Wiley, 1998). In 1991, Dominicans owned 62 percent of all accommodations on the island, while another 19 percent were jointly owned. Many small foreign-owned accommodations have been built since, as models of tourism evolution predict (Potter et al., 2004). However, many of these new owners have taken citizenship and most live year-round on site. Dominica still has a relatively high rate of local ownership. This ownership ende-mism (whether from Dominican roots or adoption) is a key reason for Dominica's low leakage rate compared to neighboring islands that have been in the tourism business longer and feature more mass tourism. An-other reason for Dominica's lower leakage rate is that its small and locally owned accommodations and restaurants more often buy from local farmers than would large foreign-owned resorts (Wiley, 1998; Momsen, 1998). Still, there is much room for improvement. Many on the island believe that the agriculture and tourism sectors should be much better integrated. A recent Dominican editorial laments:

> It is saddening to speculate upon the bulk of money that could have been salvaged if we only could harness the prospective businesses that lay between the intersecting points of tourism and agriculture, by creating synergy and symbiosis, recognizing the intersectoral linkages between this bulwark pair of our economy. (BuyDominica.com, 2005a)

Besides the obvious tendency for at least some foreign investors to repatri-ate profits abroad, Dominica's increasing tourism leakage rate is also partly the result of the fact that locals are investing more of their profits abroad (Patterson and Rodriguez, 2003). Obviously local reinvestment would be more supportive of national sustainable development. It would be useful to know if capital flight is a reaction to Dominica's economic fragility or if other factors are involved that policy could more directly influence.

The need for Dominica's ecotourism to be more locally integrated ex-tends beyond lodging and agriculture, to society as a whole. Government proclamations about sustainable development and ecotourism claim that their legitimacy is based on a national consensus favoring environmental protection: "In Dominica the conservation and protection of natural eco-systems and species is deeply entrenched in national values" (Ministry of Agriculture and the Environment, 2002:3). However, based on interviews with a broad range of Dominicans concerning their views of local ecology and development, Thurlow found that ecotourism advocates have thus far failed to unite and incorporate average Dominicans into the project:

> The majority of local people have failed to find any personal benefit within the conservationist vision of Nature Island development. They do not see the connection between the conservation of natural resources and wildlife and the generation of financial capital and economic growth. [In their view,] "eco-tourism" or "nature tourism" serves as the primary tool used by conservation-ists to convert environmental interests into development interests. (Thurlow, 2002:16)

Comments like these suggest serious shortfalls in the sustainability of ecotourism. There is an urgent need for nationally coordinated efforts to promote local inclusion, empowerment, and ownership of ecotourism infrastructure.

Dominica's transportation constraints inhibit agricultural exports and place a greater share of the foreign exchange earning burden on tourism, including cruise tourism. Tourism revenues have generally increased (although they fell in 2005 owing to weather and the loss of a major cruise line), but gains have not been enough to offset Dominica's widening trade gap and growing foreign debt over recent years. Dominica's foreign debt now exceeds its GDP. It joins Antigua, which is on the other end of the tourism spectrum, by having the greatest debt burden by that standard among the two dozen Caribbean island countries (*Economist*, 2002). As in other seriously indebted countries, the IMF has been providing Dominica short-term debt relief in exchange for commitments to reduce government spending and increase exports (tourism is considered a service export). The IMF conditionalities include policies such as a tax holiday program to encourage foreign investment.

Additional aid comes from Asia. In exchange for Dominica's vote in favor of whale hunting comes Japanese aid, ironically for an island touting whale watching as a key ecotourism activity. And after many years of financial support from Taiwan, Dominica and other Eastern Caribbean countries have recently stated publicly that there is but one China and therefore Taiwan is part of the People's Republic of China (PRC). The government of Dominica argues in a recent IMF compliance letter that new levels of financial support from the PRC will help it to meet its IMF financial obligations. This seems a striking example of global economic convergence.

MASS ECOTOURISM?

A leading ecotourism scholar, David Weaver, recently argued that larger countries with less fragile ecosystems can use "soft" ecotourism (i.e., mass tourism with an ecological orientation) to complement and subsidize "hard" ecotourism. The larger-scale tourism can inject divertible money to protect and maintain more remote natural areas that hard ecotourism underfunds (Weaver, 2001). He suggests, however, that Dominica is probably among the locales that are too fragile and small for this type of coterminous tourism complementarity. With Dominica's fragility in mind, recent government efforts to encourage mass tourism (GOCD, 2006) raise concerns about its impacts on the ecosystems of the island and surrounding marine environments. Understandably, officials are attracted to immediate sources of foreign exchange earnings, but these efforts threaten to damage Dominica's sustainable value as a relatively pristine and culturally rich locale.

The growing number of cruise ships docking in Dominica raises such concerns. Dominica first expanded its terminal and received cruise ships in 1991. Cruise arrivals grew from 177,044 in 2003 to 380,608 in 2004 (Buy-dominica.com, 2005a). It is difficult to reconcile cruise line tourism with integrated sustainable development. The threats posed by unplanned and unmanaged cruise line–based tourism are considerable. It influences the types of tourism products offered, encourages a consumerism orientation, increases strip-mall development and urbanization, and negatively impacts the marine environment, particularly coral reefs. The Dominican government itself recognized the incompatibility of cruise and ecotourists in its 1991–1994 tourism sector plan, and proposed to geographically separate them (Gayle, 1997), however difficult that is on a small island with limited flagship attractions (Weaver, 2001).

Another critique of cruise tourism is its minor monetary contribution to the port of call. By one estimate, the average cruise visitor spent just U.S.$29 while on the island (Wiley, 1998:170). One reason is that the capital city of Roseau does not offer the name-brand and luxury-item shopping opportunities of other, more established Caribbean cruise stops. A recent study found that up to half of Dominica's cruise visitors never leave the ship (this in itself is a good thing for Dominica's fragile environment). Another quarter of passengers return to the ship by lunch without spending any money (Tourtellot, 2003). Overall, cruise visitors were more than twice as numerous as overnight guests in 2003, but cruise ships contributed just 5-12 percent of tourism income, depending on the source (Tourtellot, 2003; *Dominican Chronicle*, 2004).

There are other ecological concerns. Cruise ships—really floating towns averaging one thousand or more passengers each—dump their waste and bilge-water into the Caribbean Sea (figure 7.1). But islands are so dependent on cruise ship income that they have little capacity to negotiate the terms of dumping. Observers accuse cruise lines of playing islands off each other to reduce fees and favoring destinations with lax dumping regulations (Pattullo, 1996; Patterson and Rodriguez, 2003). Further, the accessibility of many of Dominica's pristine and fragile natural areas to volumes of cruise ship passengers has raised concerns about irreparable ecological damage and the need for higher user fees to offset the impacts (Goodbody and Smith, 2002). Also, cruise ship passengers inundate otherwise serene natural areas otherwise attractive to ecotourists. For these reasons, one observer likened Dominica's cruise visitors to "heavy-hoofed cows with no milk" (Tourtellot, 2003).

Tensions have flared between the providers of eco- and cruise tourism. In response the government has been trying to channel cruise ship tourists to the most easily accessible natural sites, while leaving most of the island for locals and the ecotourists (Wiley, 1998). As of 2006, however, government plans are to continue to increase the number of sites that are accessible to cruise tourists so as to further distribute the cruise tourist footprint. To provide cruise ship passengers better access to perhaps the most precious natural area, the government in 1997 endorsed a Canadian businessman's proposal to build an aerial tram to Boiling Lake. This was soon after UNESCO designated the Morne Trois Pitons National Park, which contains Boiling Lake, a World Heritage site. UNESCO threatened to withdraw the designation and so government officials restricted the one-mile tram, which opened in 2003, to the park's border (Tourtellot, 2003).

Based on examples such as the tram controversy, a team of tourism graduate students from George Washington University, who were conducting a ten-day "rapid assessment" of Dominica's tourism problems and opportunities, concluded that the island is ecologically unspoiled "by luck, not design" (Tourtellot, 2003). Another interpretation of these events is that it took pressure from a major global NGO to push government policy slightly in the direction of ecotourism relative to cruise tourism. This is hardly an endorsement of Dominica's ecotourism-centered sustainable development policy. But such are the tensions associated with nature tourism in the world's largest cruise tourism region, where foreign debt is high and foreign-exchange opportunities are limited. Mass tourism at all-inclusive beach resorts may not prioritize ecology, but its area of impact is for the most part "clearly defined and confined [to] resorts" (Cater, 1996:140). Ecotourism destinations in places such as Dominica are extensive but also remote and highly sensitive to human impacts. And the Dominican government is desperate to generate new revenue.

DISNEY'S CANNIBALS

Perhaps even more troubling is the fact that portions of two sequels to *Pirates of the Caribbean*, the 2003 Disney blockbuster that grossed $653 million worldwide, were filmed in April and May 2005 on Dominica and to a lesser extent the Bahamas and St. Vincent, the shooting location for the first film (*Indian Country Today*, 2005). Over 400 Dominicans, including about 100 Caribs, were hired as extras and service providers. Hotels, restaurants, bars, and suppliers of local produce experienced brisk business from the Disney film crew of over 600, who occupied nearly half of all rooms on the island (www.caribbeannetnews.com).

The films portray Caribs as cannibals. Carib Chief Charles Williams met with Disney's producers, who explained that there was "a strong element of cannibalism in the script which cannot be removed" (www.caribbeannetnews.com). Williams also said that Disney was insistent that Caribs be shown seminaked in the films (Richards, 2005). Note that the word "cannibal" originates in Christopher Columbus's accounts of the supposedly ferocious man-eating people whom he first encountered in 1493 and called Caniba (or Caribs; Meurens Yashar, 2005). European mythology then grew to produce historical depictions such as this: "The Caribs, it was thought, found Spaniards to be stringy and gristly, as opposed to the French who were rather delicious and the Dutch who tended to be fairly tasteless" (Johnson, 2007). However, neither Carib oral history nor archeological evidence supports the 500-year European characterization of them as cannibals. As Chief Williams explains, "Our ancestors stood up against early European conquerors and because they stood up . . . we were labeled savages and cannibals up to today" (www.caribbeannetnews.com).

This cannibalism controversy raises questions about the government of Dominica's approach to ecotourism-related sustainable development, particularly its crucial component of cultural education and social inclusiveness. Does the injection of short-term income and the global mainstream publicity outweigh yet another round of racist stereotyping? What will be the effects on young people, the films' target audience, of seeing Caribs as seminaked cannibals? And how does this tourism-inducing publicity mesh with the national priority placed on the cultural education of both locals and visitors?

It would be difficult for Dominican officials to reject or even to negotiate effectively with Disney, among the largest and most powerful of global media empires. Dominica's GDP was $380 million in 2002, of which the share accruing to the Caribs is a tiny fraction. Disney's revenues that year were $25.329 billion, or 66 times greater (CIA, 2003; Journalism.org, 2004). Disney's revenue from Winnie the Pooh merchandise alone was approximately $1 billion. This imbalance can help to explain why Dominica's tourism minister, Charles Savarin, has defended Disney's cinematic depiction of Caribs as cannibals on grounds that it is a "work of fiction." But the editors of *Indian Country Today*, a major news outlet of Native Americans in the United States, see it differently. They note that in the entertainment industry, fiction often trumps fact:

> Neither the wanton killing and rape by Spanish colonists of the first group of Caribs encountered—recorded during [Columbus's second voyage] by others on the ship—nor the Caribs' fierce, valiant defense of their territories and people are apparently proper subjects for a Disney movie. (*Indian Country Today*, 2005)

The editors of *Indian Country Today* join a growing number of U.S. and international Native American and human rights groups proposing a boycott of Disney. Here again, NGOs are more assertive than the desperate governments and the working poor of vulnerable states to challenge actions that violate the sustainable development criteria of ecological soundness, economic viability, and social justice. An obvious rebuttal is that international NGOs have the luxury of leveling critiques, while poor governments and people are preoccupied with earning money.

CONCLUSION

This case study of the self-styled "Nature Island of the Caribbean" reveals many challenges associated with the pursuit of sustainable development. Dominica has an amazing physical environment, a rich cultural heritage, and unusually friendly people, all of which provide an ideal base and great potential for ecotourism-related sustainable development. At the same time, its economic constraints and vulnerability are more severe than most countries' of the region. The Dominican government therefore finds itself under constant pressure to make policy decisions that have short-term financial payoffs and generate foreign exchange, but that are contrary to the vision of sustainable development as resting on a three-legged stool. For every positive feature or decision that looks to be in line with sustainability there seems to be at least as many that are questionable.

It would not be overstated to suggest that Dominica is at a crossroads. Conditions will likely get substantially better or worse over the next decade based on a variety of choices made unilaterally, or preferably in concert, by government officials, NGOs, and domestic and foreign private actors. Dominica can either fall in line as simply one more slight nature-oriented variant on dependent mass tourism, or it can continue to emerge as a model of ecotourism-related sustainable development.

Dominica is of course not alone in feeling pressures to choose short-term expedience over longer-term sustainable development. Over recent decades Central American and Caribbean countries have learned that U.S. economic and geopolitical dominance and its interventions make developing a diversified set of local and foreign investors, export sectors, markets, local interpretations of "democracy" and "development," and foreign policy relations extremely difficult. Because of these and other constraints, the region has generally converged on a set of neoliberal policies that pursues dependent capitalist development under U.S. guidance. But neoliberalism and economic globalization are primarily top-down systems that are foreign- and local-elite driven. Within this context of dependency and vulnerability, policy options are narrow and the path forward is littered with tempting short-term opportunities that are unsustainable, bankrupt, and/or damaging in the longer term.

The issues of ecotourism and sustainable development examined in this chapter have important ramifications for the United States. Should

Dominica and other countries of the region fail to generate good, long-term employment, the resulting social upheaval will undoubtedly be felt in the United States in at least four ways. First, additional political instability in Central America and the Caribbean will lead to greater emigration pressure on countries, including the United States, that already have communities of the various nationalities involved. Some, if not most, of that migration will be illegal, creating additional burdens in the United States. Second, illegal behavior will continue to expand into other sectors as well, particularly in agriculture, where increases in marijuana production for export can be anticipated as small-scale farmers seek a new cash crop as a replacement for bananas or other traditionals. The threat of this type of conversion was articulated by the Caribbean states during the protracted banana negotiations and helped gain greater U.S. understanding of their plight. Third, drug trafficking from South America and through Central America and the Caribbean will also increase. Fourth, tourism as a whole will be negatively affected by the social instability just when it is being called on to help fill the economic void created by the demise of traditional as well as neoliberal export sectors. Since Americans comprise the largest share of the region's tourists, increased threats to their security while traveling are likely under the failure scenario. In sum, regional stability rides strongly on the current efforts to generate new forms of sustainable livelihoods that do not degrade fragile tropical environments.

NOTE

1. The Carib name for Dominica, "Waitukubuli," means "tall is her body," in reference to the steep mountainous terrain; Caribs are now 4 percent of the national population.

BIBLIOGRAPHY

Berkes, Fikret. *Sacred Ecology: Traditional Ecological Knowledge and Resource Management*. Philadelphia: Taylor and Francis, 1999.

Buydominica.com. "The Necessity for Agro-Tourism in Dominica." April 10, 2005a, at http://buydominica.com/dominica/agrotourism.php (accessed May 14, 2007).

Buydominica.com. "Pirates of the Caribbean II—Dominica." May 6, 2005b, at http://buydominica.com/caribbean/pirates_caribbean.php (accessed May 14, 2007).

Carrier, James, and Donald MacLeod. "Bursting the Bubble: The Socio-Cultural Context of Ecotourism." *Journal of the Royal Anthropological Institute* 11 (2005): 315–334.

Cater, E. "Ecotourism in the Caribbean: A Sustainable Option for Belize and Dominica?" In *Sustainable Tourism in Islands and Small States: Case Studies*, edited by L. Briguglio, R. Butler, D. Harrison, and W. L. Filho, pp. 122–146. London: Pinter, 1996.

CIA. "The World Factbook." 2007, https://www.cia.gov/library/publications/the-world-factbook/geos/do.html (accessed May 15, 2007).

Cox, John, and C. Sid Embree. "Sustainable Development in the Caribbean." Nova Scotia, Canada: Institute for Research on Public Policy, 1990.

CTO. "Caribbean Tourism Performance 2003, Prospects for 2004." 2004, http://www.onecaribbean.org/information/documentview.php?rowid=2391 (accessed May 14, 2007).

Dominican Chronicle. "Let's Sell Dominica." October 4, 2004, http://buydominica.com/tourismnews.htm.

Economist. "Trouble in Paradise." November 21, 2002, www.economist.com.

Gayle, Dennis. "Ecotourism: Fad or Future?" *Hemisphere: A Magazine of the Americas* 8, no. 1 (1997): 20–24.

GOCD (Government of the Commonwealth of Dominica). "Medium-Term Growth and Social Production Strategy (GSPS)". Roseau: GOCD, 2006, http://siteresources.worldbank.org/INTPRS1/Resources/Dominica_PRSP(April2006).pdf (accessed March 23, 2007).

Goodbody, Ivan, and David Smith. "Recreational Use of Natural Resources." In *Natural Resource Management for Sustainable Development in the Caribbean*, edited by Mona Ivan Goodbody and Elizabeth Thomas-Hope, pp. 389–425. Kingston, Jamaica: Canoe Press, 2002.

Green, Michelle. "Eco-Tourism: The Director's Cut." *The Sunday New York Times*, April 3, 2005, http://travel2.nytimes.com/2005/04/03/travel/03coppola.html?ex=1116648000&en=5d41d918a2d2a429&ei=5070 (accessed May 14, 2007).

Green Globe. "Sustainable Travel and Tourism." 2006, at www.greenglobe21.com (accessed April 24, 2007).

Henthorne, Tony, and Mark Miller. "Cuban Tourism in the Caribbean Context: A Regional Impact Assessment." *Journal of Travel Research* 42 (2003): 84–93.

Indian Country Today. "Disney's Carib Indian Cannibals Deserve Boycott." April 14, 2005, http://www.indiancountry.com/content.cfm?id=1096410746 (accessed May 14, 2007).

Jackiewicz, Edward. "Community-Centered Globalization: Modernization under Control in Rural Costa Rica." *Latin American Perspectives* 33 (2006): 136–146.

Johnson, Kim. "The Story of the 'Caribs and Arawaks.'" *Race and History*, 2007, http://www.raceandhistory.com/Taino/ (accessed May 14, 2007).

Journalism.org. "The State of the News Media 2004." 2004, http://www.stateofthenewsmedia.org/narrative_networktv_ownership.asp?cat=5&media=4 (accessed May 14, 2007).

Klak, Thomas, and Raju Das. "The Underdevelopment of the Caribbean and Its Scholarship." *Latin American Research Review* 34 (1999): 209–224.

Kruger, Oliver. "The Role of Ecotourism in Conservation: Panacea or Pandora's Box?" *Biodiversity and Conservation* 14 (2005): 579–600.

Lake, Robert, and Susan Hanson. "Needed: Geographic Research on Urban Sustainability." *Urban Geography* 21 (2000): 1–4.

McElroy, J., and K. de Albuquerque. "Tourism Penetration Index in Small Caribbean Islands." *Annals of Tourism Research* 25 (1998): 145–168.

Meurens Yashar, Claire. "Cannibalism as Cultural Libel." *Caribbean Amerindian Centrelink Review*, 2005, http://cacreview.blogspot.com/2005/04/cannibalism-as-cultural-libel.html (accessed May 14, 2007).

Ministry of Agriculture and the Environment, Government of Dominica. "Dominica's First National Report to the Conference of Parties—Convention on Biological Diversity." 2002, http://www.biodiv.org/doc/world/dm/dm-nr-01-en.doc (accessed May 14, 2007).

Momsen, Janet H. "Caribbean Tourism and Agriculture: New Linkages in the Global Era?" In *Globalization and Neoliberalism: The Caribbean Context*, edited by T. Klak, pp. 15–34. Lanham, Md.: Rowman & Littlefield, 1998.

Moreno, Peter. "Ecotourism Along the Meso-American Caribbean Reef: The Impacts of Foreign Investment." *Human Ecology* 33 (2005): 217–244.

Pascal, Sharon (director of tourism, National Development Corporation of Dominica). Interview with author. Roseau. January 4, 2006.

Patterson, Trista, and L. Rodriguez. "The Political Ecology of Tourism in the Commonwealth of Dominica." In *Tourism and Development in Tropical Islands*, edited by S. Gossling, pp. 60–87. Northampton, Mass.: Edward Elgar Publishing, 2003.

Patterson, Trista, et al. "Integrating Environmental, Social and Economic Systems: A Dynamic Model of Tourism in Dominica." *Ecological Modelling* 175 (2004): 121–136.

Pattullo, Polly. *Last Resorts: The Cost of Tourism in the Caribbean*. New York: Monthly Review Press, 1996.

Potter, Robert, David Barker, Dennis Conway, and Thomas Klak. *The Contemporary Caribbean*. Essex, U.K.: Addison Wesley Longman and Prentice Hall, 2004.

Rembert, Tracey. "Protecting Paradise." *E: The Environmental Magazine* 10, no. 4 (1999): 46.

Richards, Peter. "Arrr, Matey! The Curse of the Racist Sequel?" Inter-Press Service News Agency, 2005, http://ipsnews.net/interna.asp?idnews=27663 (accessed May 14, 2007).

Richardson, C. (permanent secretary in the Ministry of Commerce, Industry, and Consumer Affairs, Government of St. Lucia). Interview with author. Castries. September 16, 1997.

Stem, Caroline, et al. "Community Participation in Ecotourism Benefits: The Link to Conservation Practices and Perspectives." *Society and Natural Resources* 16 (2003): 387–413.

The International Ecotourism Society (TIES). "Definitions and Principles." 2007, http://www.ecotourism.org/webmodules/webarticlesnet/templates/eco_template.aspx?articleid=95&zoneid=2) (accessed April 25, 2007).

Thurlow, Kim. "The Roseau Botanical Gardens and Peripheral Link Project." The Hixon Center for Urban Ecology, Yale University School of Forestry and Environmental Studies, 2002, http://www.yale.edu/hixon/research/pdf/KThurlow_Roseau.pdf (accessed May 14, 2007).

Tourtellot, Jonathan. "Can Unspoiled Dominica Keep Its Charm?" *National Geographic News*, November 7, 2003, http://news.nationalgeographic.com/news/2003/11/1107_031107_dominica.htm (accessed May 14, 2007).

UNEP-UNCTAD. "Environmentally Preferable Goods and Services: Opportunities and Challenges for Caribbean Countries." 2003, http://www.unep-unctad.org/cbtf/cbtf2/meetings/jamaica/conceptnote10.pdf (accessed May 14, 2007).

WCED (UN World Commission on Environment and Development). *Our Common Future*. Oxford: Oxford University Press, 1987.

Weaver, David. "Ecotourism as Mass Tourism: Contradiction or Reality?" *Cornell Hotel and Restaurant Administration Quarterly* 42 (2001): 104–112.

Wiley, James. "Dominica's Economic Diversification: Microstates in a Neoliberal Era?" in *Globalization and Neoliberalism: The Caribbean Context*, edited by T. Klak, pp. 155–178. Lanham, Md.: Rowman & Littlefield, 1998.

Williams, Colin C., and Andrew C. Millington. "The Diverse and Contested Meanings of Sustainable Development." *The Geographical Journal* 170 (2004): 99–104.

8

Drug Geographies

Kent Mathewson

Much has been written and depicted recently concerning the role of psychoactive substances (or what have been referred to as simply "drugs" for the past century or so) in the lives of Latin Americans, and especially in their societies and economies. Most of this reportage has appeared in the popular news media. The tenor and content of this publicity accentuates the lurid and negative dimensions of the drug commerce and trafficking of drugs, along with their consumption. Beyond the headlines there is also a rich repertoire of images, lyrics, and commentary woven into the cinematic, musical, and literary productions produced from within and without this geographical realm and its relations with drugs. Aside from these arenas of cultural production, there is a growing scholarly literature on the place of psychoactive agents in Latin America's varied geographies.

As in popular media, much of the recent scholarly research and writing on illicit drugs has focused on the economic and political aspects, especially international trafficking, and increasingly on their imbrication in political processes, from fueling armed insurgencies and feeding local practices to oiling the machinery of state in all of its branches (Bagley and Walker, 1994; Mabry, 1989; Thoumi, 2003; Walker, 1996). There is also an established literature that treats drugs and their geographies in a wider scope (Courtright, 2001; Mathewson, 1991, 2004). Here, the illicit or illegal cultivated substances such as cannabis, coca, and opium plus their derivatives, are joined by legal but regulated drugs such as alcohol and tobacco (Goodman, 1993; Porter and Teich, 1995), as well as an array of plant sources of mild psychoactives such as sugar, coffee, tea, and cacao directed to the world market (Anderson, 2003; Mathee, 1995; Sauer, 1993), along with more locally produced sources of stimulants, depressants, and hallucinogens. Any survey that fails to include these agents risks eliding whole chapters from the complex history of drugs in Latin America and their varied geographies. This expanded view of drugs reveals a historical and cultural record with millennial time depth and nearly universal importance in indigenous societies (Hobbs, 2004; Mathewson, 2004; Steinberg, Hobbs, and Mathewson, 2004). It also demonstrates the centrality of drug use, production, and commerce in the building and articulations of colonial economies and societies. As for modern times, drugs in all of their dimensions, at times for better but often for worse, constitute part of what Latin America has come to mean in the eyes of the world, and how it is located within various coordinates of our modern and postmodern worlds.

As both a force and factor in the production of Latin America's economic, political, and cultural conditions, drugs offer perhaps the best illustration of the workings of what has come to be called "globalization." Few would argue that the place of drugs in Latin America's economies has been insignificant (Jankowiak and Bradburd, 2003). At times, drugs have seemingly come to dominate a particular nation's economic rhythms and realities (Cambranes, 1985; Lee, 1989; Morales, 1989; Painter, 1994; Williams, 1994). For example, in Colombia during recent decades, the illicit drug cocaine has stormed the portals and taken over the palace—from currency exchanges and export earnings, to acts of corruption and military expenditures, to clandestine farm and laboratory productions and ultimately the infinite informal economics of street and backroom dealings (Camacho Guizado, 1994; McCoy, 2004; Reyes, 1994). No sector of the economy or polity is said to be immune. The metaphors of disease and contagion are often mobilized in the attempt to characterize the danger and dynamics of the drug trade. Like disease, one can identify the etiologies spawning the drug trade, and one can chart its traffic flows along paths or through networks. But little thought goes into uncovering the geographies the trade creates, or locating the geographies in which drug use, production, and commerce take place.

In this chapter, I will draw some of the contours, and provide a few datum points to show what a comprehensive geography of drug making, taking, and commerce for Latin America might entail. Not surprisingly, it is an uneven surface, with some places and regions registering intense nodes or zones of activity while other areas scarcely merit marks on the map. The history is not so uneven, but certain periods have pulsated with action, while other phases have been paced with only humdrum movement, involving mostly individuals or local groups pursuing quotidian routines punctuated with periodic celebrations. In addition, definitions need to be examined, and expanded (Lewin, 1964). "Drug" in its generic sense refers to: "any substance that in small amounts produces significant changes in the body, mind, or both" (Weil and Rosen, 1993:8). But foods and poisons can also fit this description. Sugar is both food and drug, and alcohol can be all three. On a continuum from food to poison, drugs can be described as agents of mind and/or body change that are primarily neither food nor poison. Here, we will limit the discussion to psychoactive substances. Moreover, most usage is outside formal or normal medicinal practice. Drugs such as quinine, derived from chinchona bark, or remedies from resinous trees such as liquidambar (sweet gum), precipitated intense regional export episodes and as such merit inclusion in any total drug trade geography. Space here does not permit this. Of course, "drug trade" in the Latin American context normally refers to the three classes of illicit substances already mentioned (cannabis, coca/cocaine, opium/heroin) plus much lesser quantities of bootlegged pharmaceuticals or confected synthetics such as amphetamines and tranquilizers. There are, however, several dozen other "drugs" that should be included in our discussion here, including a range of stimulants, stupeficients, and hallucinogens. In terms of their historical importance to Latin America's interactions with other world regions, and among its inhabitants on a quotidian level, the array and range of drugs that are produced, consumed, or marketed can be arranged hierarchically in five levels.

DEFINITION

Drug

"Any substance that in small amounts produces significant changes in the body, mind, or both" (Weil and Rosen, 1993). Foods and poisons also fit this description. Thus drugs can be defined as agents of body and/or mind change that are primarily neither food or poison, although some drugs such as alcohol can be all three depending on context and quantity consumed. In addition, drugs here refer to substances whose main usage is outside normal or formal medical practice.

HIERARCHIES OF IMPORT AND EXPORT

If judged on its historical importance, commercial export success to date, and range of geographical distribution, cane sugar (*Saccarum* sp.) should be considered Latin America's premier drug plant. It is much debated whether sugar should be seen as a primarily as a "food" or as a metabolic stimulant. Sidney Mintz's (1985) *Sweetness and Power*, a brilliant history of cane sugar as a co-stimulant of both New World slavery and early North Atlantic industrialism—at both societal and individual laborer levels—convincingly makes the case for both. When its derivative drugs, rum, *aguardiente,* and related distillations are added to the equation and conquest, it is no contest. Following sugar, the ordinal ranking of second-order substances such as tobacco (*Nicotiana* sp.), coffee (*Coffee* sp.), cacao (*Theobroma cacao*), and coca (*Erythroxylon* sp.)/cocaine (the latter a relatively recent entrant) is not so clear. Each has controlled the economies of single colonies and regions, and even whole nations at differing times. In aggregate they have engaged millions of workers and generated billions in revenues. Like sugar, their manufactured products have serviced the habits and provided the pleasures for many millions of consumers, at home but especially abroad. All are domesticated plants with several consumed species (save cacao), though each genus has a dominant commercial species, namely, *S. officinarum, N. tobacum, C. arabica, T. cacao,* and *E. coca,* with their own histories and geographies (Coe and Coe, 1996; Corti, 1996; Courtwright, 2001; Galloway, 1989; Goodman, 1993, 1995; Goodman, Lovejoy, and Sherratt, 1995; Gootenberg, 1999; Pendergrast, 1999; Young, 1994).

The third tier of drugs has a strong local base of consumers, but the drugs also find their way into national and international markets. They include both illicit and licit substances. Alcohol in all its exuberant varieties and cannabis (*Cannabis* sp.) in mainly its marijuana form are the main controlled or proscribed drugs at this level (Rubin, 1975). Native regional stimulants, such as mate (*Ilex paraguariensis*) and guarana (*Paullina cupana*), are culturally and economically important in parts of South America. Mate is the national drink of Argentina and is consumed in neighboring nations (Barretto, 1991). Guarana is consumed mostly in Brazil, but is expanding its range and markets (Spiller, 1984). Like sugar cane and the most common species of cannabis, tea (*Camellia sinensis*) and opium (*Papavera somniferum*) are Asian cultivars that were introduced in colonial times to Latin America (Booth, 1998). Both are produced for the export market and have localized distributions, though in some countries much of the tea is directed to the national market.

A fourth tier of drugs can be identified. This group comprises all of the other psychoactive substances collected or cultivated, prepared or manufactured, consumed in, or exported from, Latin America. Many of these drugs, especially the hallucinogenic plants and their preparations, are not part of normal commercial networks (Efron, Holmstedt, and Kline, 1967; Elferink, 1983; Emboden, 1979). Primarily embedded in indigenous cultural practices, or local rural and urban customs with strong links to indigenous folkways, these substances have only limited articulations with larger economic spheres (Feinberg, 2003; Kimber and McDonald, 2004). Most of the plant-derived drugs at this level are collected from undomesticated plants rather than cultivated ones (Furst, 1972; Schultes, 1972). The remaining drugs in this tier include refined forms of substances occurring in plants, such as morphine from opium, and mescaline from peyote and San Pedro cacti; semisynthetics, such as heroin made from morphine; and pure synthetics, made in laboratories from nonnaturally occurring chemicals. Whereas the first group in this tier—naturally occurring collected drugs—has long histories of use and cultural embeddedness, possibly predating agriculture in some cases (Dobkin de Rios, 1984), the others are artifacts of modernity, and have established geographies only in the past half-century or so.

DRUG GEOGRAPHIES IN HISTORICAL PERSPECTIVE

It is quite likely that knowledge of psychotropic drugs was part of the pharmacopoeia and skill-kits that Mesolithic hunters and gatherers brought with them from Asia, and possibly Europe, to the late Pleistocene New World some 20,000 or more years ago (La Barre, 1972). If so, once reaching the more temperate climes they found new plant sources for mind and body alteration. Their descendants, especially their Neolithic heirs, uncovered a cornucopia of psychoactive agents in settling the subtropics and tropics. One of the great distributional anomalies of global scale biogeography and culture history is that of the 120 or so identified hallucinogenic substances found in nature, fewer than two dozen occur in the Old World (La Barre, 1970; Davis, 1985). The rest are found in the New World, and the majority of these in subtropical and tropical environments. Other classes of New World drug plants and their preparations are similarly abundant. The discovery of drugs from natural sources is one of humanity's great empirical ventures. Whether or not New World shamans and other specialists in locating and learning how to use such substances were more proficient than their Old World counterparts is not known (or how many may have been sacrificed in the service of their science!). Or, it may be that the neoarctic and neotropical biogeographical realms, for whatever evolutionary reasons, simply developed more plants with psychotropic properties. Whatever the case, it has produced a complex set of geographies—cultural, sociopolitical, and economic, as well as biophysical. Space here does not allow for more than a brief overview. Some discussion of the pre-Columbian picture, however, is useful in setting the stage for the coming of Europeans and their world-system that launched a number of these drugs into global cultivation and commerce.

The degree to which neotropical hunter-gatherers were the discoverers and custodians of drug plants is not known. Today, it is primarily the remnant groups of Old World hunter-gatherers such as the Khoisan of southern Africa, or the Australian aborigines that exhibit knowledge and variety of indigenous psychoactive drugs (Balick and Cox, 1996). From ethnographic analogy and accounts, it seems safe to say their neotropical counterparts used members of the nightshade family such as wild tobaccos, daturas

(*Datura stramonium* and *D. meteloides*), and probably some of the wild precursors of the cultivated drug plants that became integral parts of virtually every pre-Columbian agricultural society from Mexico to the Southern Cone. While no theorist of agricultural origins has proposed a full-blown case for drug plants as the initial focus of the domestication process, tending wild forms of tobacco, coca, cacao, and the myriad fruits and other plant sources of fermentable beverages may have spurred early experiments in genetic modifications (Bruman, 2000). Carl Sauer (1952) suggested that it was the nonfood plants important to tropical Mesolithic fisherfolk, such as vines for cordage, gourds for floats, and fish poisons, that led to the first serious manipulations. Psychotropic drugs play roles in many tropical forest agriculturalists' hunting activities (La Barre, 1972). They may have played a role in the transition as well. Whether antecedent, or just part of the larger "Neolithic Revolution," drugs continued to play important roles as simple agricultural societies evolved into more complex sociopolitical structures—from tribes, to chiefdoms, to states and, in a few cases, empires (Rudgley, 1994).

The locus of power in neotropical chiefdoms from Mexico to subtropical South America was refracted and reflected through both material objects and symbolic spheres involving drugs and their ritual consumption. In Andean and Amazonian contexts, the shaman's stool was the literal seat of power. A range of powerful hallucinogens, including San Pedro cactus (*Trichocereus* sp.) (mescaline source), yage or ayahuasca (*Banisteriopsis* sp.) (harmaline source), and yopo or cohoba (*Anadenanthera* sp.) (tryptamine source) were associated with these objects (Harner, 1973). One of the diagnostic traits of a chiefdom level of complexity is the occurrence of large earthen mounds, usually at the center of villages or ceremonial precincts. These were often the sites of ritual celebrations involving beers, or *chicha*, made from root crops such as manioc (*Manihot esculenta*) or maize (*Zea mays*), and other drugs such as coca, tobacco, and hallucinogens. Chiefly power was in part demonstrated through such public gatherings. Drugs were a central component in the cultural and sociopolitical cement that went into constructing and maintaining chiefdoms. The geography of chiefdoms in pre-Columbian times varied over time, but the main areas included large parts of Central America, the Caribbean, and Northern South America, the so-called "Intermediate Area" in archaeological terms (Willey, 1971). To the north were the states and empires of Mesoamerica, and to the south the states and empires of the Andean realm.

EXPANDING POLITIES, EXPANDING TRADE

It was with the rise of states and empires in the pre-Columbian world that complex and accumulative trade networks and production and consumption regimes were developed. Cacao, a key component in ritual beverages (often mixed with other drugs and condiments), became the coin of the realm throughout Mesoamerica. Cacao beans were used as specie and were the standard medium of commerce (Coe and Coe, 1996). Accordingly, cacao plantations were prized possessions of various polities. Conflicts among states and empires in Mesoamerica were often over the control of resources and their places of extraction or production. Cacao territories were among the most contested (Bergmann, 1969). Tobacco, like cacao, was often state controlled and regulated and its consumption was associated with ritual practices but it also was used in quotidian ways (Robicsek, 1978; Wilbert, 1987). Other Mesoamerican substances with similar production and use patterns include alcoholic beverages made from *Agave* species, especially *pulque*, and chile peppers (*Capsicum* sp.) (Bruman, 2000). Today, chile peppers are seen as purely condiments, often the defining element of regional or national cuisines (Andrews, 1984). In pre-Columbian contexts, chile peppers were culinary staples, but also admixes for intoxicating and/or hallucinogenic drinks. As devotees will tell you, large doses of capsicum can bring on endorphin highs, and in combination with cacao, tobacco, and hallucinogens, the peppers presumably had psychoactive effects.

The production, consumption, and regulation of drugs in South American states and empires parallel and in some cases duplicate the patterns and practices of the Mesoamerican complex polities. The case of coca is best known and recorded. Even more than cacao in Mesoamerica, it assumed centrality in Andean culture, society, and in some regions, the economy (Allen, 1988; Plowman, 1984). It was at once a sacred substance, devotional object, trade item, quotidian staple, and stimulant aid to labor and transport throughout vast portions of western South America (Cassman, Cartmell, and Belmonte, 2003). Coca's domestication may have first occurred in the lowland fringes of the Andean realm, but its role as a force in the production of Andean states and empires was realized at higher altitudes. The main producing areas in pre-Columbian times, as they are today, lay along the eastern flanks of the Andean cordillera at intermediate elevations. The altitudinal and geographical differentials between zones of coca production and the main higher zones of coca consumption helped develop the vaunted Andean system of ecological and economic "verticality." From colonial times until quite recently, the cultivation and use of coca was largely eliminated from its northern and southern Andean districts. Coca's Peruvian and Bolivian hearth and homelands, though beleaguered, have persisted in the face of various campaigns of suppression (Gagliano, 1994). It is these famed eastern Andean valley regions, such as the Yungas in Bolivia and the Huallaga in Peru, that provided the geographical base for cocaine's emergence onto and into modern global drug scenes.

In pre-Columbian times, however, these prime producing areas fed a much less expansive trade. Even though Andean states and empires may have attempted to control the cultivation, trade, and consumption of coca, it was a far too important part of both the sacred and profane lives of Andean peoples to allow either local or imperial elites to overly circumscribe it or its use. There is some evidence, on the other hand, that elites had more success in controlling the production and use of maize for ritual *chicha* or "beer" making. The eminent Andean scholar, John Murra (1973) has argued that many of the finest stone-faced and irrigated terrace systems in Incaic landscapes were constructed for ritual maize cultivation. The geographical extent of these features is fairly well documented (Donkin, 1979), and many are on spectacular display at renowned ceremonial centers such as Machu Picchu. If Murra is correct about this, then this is an example of drug geography literally encoded in stone and distributed widely throughout the ancient Inca empire.

One of the universal traits of empires is the dynamics they set in motion with the "barbarians" on their peripheries (Teggart, 1939). Among the routine dynamics are circuits of trade that feed scarce or exotic products from less developed peripheries to civilizational cores. Among the more spectacular features are episodes of invasion and occasionally conquest of imperial centers by "barbarian hordes." A staple of Old World tales of civilizational collapse or capture, most notably involving the Roman Empire, but also some of the Near Eastern and Chinese dynastic regimes, the model also fits New World cases, particularly the rise and fall of complex Mesoamerican polities. The bands and tribes of Chichimeca roaming the arid lands north of the states and empires of Central Mexico are a classic example (Sauer, 1941). These "barbarians" gathered peyote (*Lophophora williamsii*) and other desert drugs and directed them to the imperial centers to the south. What began as simple trade relations periodically begat invasions. For the Incas, the tropical forest tribes at and beyond their imperial edges were a source of a number of exotic trade goods, including hallucinogenic drugs such as *yage* and *yopo*. From pre-Columbian times until the present, border zones along with remote peripheries have played important roles in the production and transshipment of drugs (Perramond, 2004). This is one of the geographical constants in the shifting theaters of drug production and trade throughout Latin America's history. Today, the New Barbarians at Empire's Gates are often said to be Latin America's footloose migrants, some serving as "drug mules," others following drug trafficking trails past porous borders, while still others find informal employment in the illegal drug business once they reach their destination.

EUROPE'S FORCED ENTRY

In a sense, the arrival of Europeans in the New World constitutes an extreme case of assault from a remote periphery—or in this case, from beyond either the real or imagined periphery (Galeano, 1973). To Moctezuma and his court at Tenochtitlán, or to Atahualpa and his court at Cuzco, the Spaniards seemed to be barbarians in the extreme (Pagden, 1993). The Spaniards, and laterally the Portuguese and slightly later the French, British, and Dutch, initially brought little for exchange save disease, against which the native pharmacoepias were largely ineffectual (Cook and Lovell, 1992). Beyond the precious metals, the Europeans found a secondary source of wealth in psychoactive drugs, with tobacco and cocoa heading up the list (Bradburd and Jankowiak, 2003). With their appropriation, many pre-Columbian patterns and practices of collection, production, and trade were disrupted or redirected (Wolf, 1982). Other patterns and processes were reconstituted with their incorporation into the European world imperial system (Wallerstein, 1974). Cacao was both desacralized and demonetized but never decommodified. It became the prime export commodity in the colonial economies of coastal Ecuador and Venezuela, and later in Bahia, Brazil. Tobacco was another drug that in pre-Columbian times was used mostly in ritual contexts, but under European commodity colonialism it became a staple crop in most of Europe's New World colonies. Cuba's prominence in the cultivation and later the production of tobacco products, especially cigars, did not develop until late in the colonial period. This illustrates yet another principle of the development of drug geographies in Latin America, that is, the uneven and shifting loci of cultivation and production centers over time.

Columbus was sailing, or so he said, for the "East Indies" when he undershot Asia and landed in the "West Indies" (Sauer, 1966). Spices, even more than precious metals or fine manufactures of silk and porcelain, were the main objective. Spices common in the West today such as pepper, cinnamon, cloves, nutmeg, mace, ginger, and other, less well known spices such as cardamom, zedoary, and star anise, were highly valued in Europe during the Middle Ages (Dalby, 2000). Initially, cane sugar, because of its cost and scarcity, fitted more the spice mold than its later role as a food and drink additive. The much-repeated notion that Asian spices were sought as the preservatives of European meats has been debunked (Schivelbush, 1992). Salting and smoking would, and did, serve that purpose well. Instead, European elites desired Asian spices as luxury commodities not so much as food condiments, but as substances in their own right to be bought, sold, and consumed. Their cultivation and production was often in clandestine or closely guarded locations. They generated complex trade circuits and immense profits. Their consumption was often ritualized and fetishized. In all of these aspects, spice use and trade in Europe's late Middle Ages anticipated the future waves of drugs to come. In addition, some of the spices (such as nutmeg and mace), if ingested by the spoonful as they were, could have psychoactive effects. Thus Columbus was primed for what he thought would be an end run around both Islamic traders and Portuguese rivals, and in through the backdoor to the Spice Lands. Of spices, he returned with few. Of lands, he returned with claims to whole continents.

COLONIAL PATTERNS

While the roots of the modern drug trade in Latin America may lie with Europe's quest for exotic spices in Asia, the base was laid with Europe's occupation of the Americas (Wolf, 1982). This history is broad and also deep, and it includes some of the key moments and movements within colonial Latin America's economic, but also social and cultural, histories. Although Columbus failed to find the fabled spices of the Orient in the Caribbean, he did find conditions suitable for sugar production. He brought sugar from the Canaries to Santo Domingo on his second voyage, in 1493 (Galloway, 1989). African slaves quickly followed. The sugar complex was largely imported intact from its Mediterranean and Atlantic island staging areas. From Hispaniola, sugar was diffused to all of Spain's New World colonies. By the 1520s the Portuguese had independently introduced sugar to Brazil from their successful plantations on Madeira and São Tomé.

For the first century and a half, the Iberians had a near monopoly on the New World sugar business. Brazil's northeastern coastal zone was by all measures the central arena, with lesser nodes spread throughout the Spanish colonies from Hispaniola to Mexico to Argentina. Sugar production produced significant landscape change in the regions wherein it prospered (Watts, 1987). Not only was it land extensive in its soil needs, but often required water for irrigation. Processing required abundant power (draft animal or wind) for grinding, and fuel (usually wood) for boiling. Landscapes were simultaneously degraded (deforested and soil depleted) and "improved" (plots mounded and/or terraced, irrigation works constructed). Perhaps the single most enduring impact of sugar production on Latin America geographies was the associated implantation of millions of enslaved African laborers. With few exceptions, the regions with the largest African-descended populations even today are those where sugar plantations held sway. Starting in the seventeenth century, northern European powers in-filled areas in the circum-Caribbean basin seized from, abandoned, or never settled by the Spanish (Richardson, 1992). The British, French, and Dutch each occupied a wedge of the Guianas and ultimately all the Lesser Antilles, along with Jamaica and Hispaniola (Saint Domingue). The Dutch also occupied prime portions of northeast Brazil between 1630 and 1654. Like the Iberians before them, they came with multiple motives, but quickly narrowed their preoccupations to mostly sugar monoculture. During the eighteenth century British Barbados and Jamaica and French Saint Domingue became crown jewels in their respective empires (Stinchcombe, 1995). Sugar (complemented with coffee and tobacco in Jamaica and Saint Domingue) provided the lustre and lucre; African slaves the labor. The flows of capital and commodities set in motion by these occupations (of land *and* labor) gave rise to the infamous "Triangular Trade," wherein Caribbean sugar and molasses were shipped to New England or England and distilled into rum, which was then traded for slaves in West Africa directed back to the Caribbean (Ambler, 2003). The French and Dutch performed comparable triangulations between their colonies, metropoles, and Africa. On lesser scales and intensities, tobacco, coffee, and cacao followed these geometrics. In more than metaphorical ways, the drug trade circuits established in colonial times between Latin America and the North Atlantic realm pointed the way for new drug commodity flows in postcolonial times.

Most of the formal colonial rule in Latin America ended during the nineteenth century, starting with the slave-led liberation of Saint Domingue (Haiti and Santo Domingo) in 1804 and ending with the U.S. occupation of Cuba and Puerto Rico in 1898. European dominion continued over the remaining British, French, Dutch, and Danish Caribbean islands, and the mainland Guianas and British Honduras (Belize). Between 1804 and the late 1880s formal slavery was abolished throughout Latin America. Despite political and socioeconomic reordering within much of the realm, many of the patterns of colonial drug production and commerce persisted. At the same time, new patterns emerged. For example, Barbados and northeast Brazil continued to be sugar centers, but in the wake of the collapse of Saint Domingue's plantation system, Cuba emerged as a major sugar center. Similarly, the new nations of mainland Central America and South America became important coffee producers. And within new nations, regional shifts in production geographies occurred. Although coffee had been cultivated around Rio de Janeiro since the 1770s, by the mid-nineteenth century São Paulo and its hinterlands were to become the unrivaled center of Brazilian coffee production (Pendergrast, 1999). Comparable cases could be cited for each nation and each of the major licit drug commodities that underwrote both the colonial and new national economies. These are well-known histories with clear cartographies. What is less known, and even less well mapped, is the historical geography of the emergence of the future illicit drugs that began to enter regional, national, and international commerce beginning in the nineteenth century.

MODERNITY'S DIFFUSIONS AND SUFFUSIONS

The geographic patterns of precolonial and colonial drug production, trade, and use in Latin America, while not static, generally formed and unfolded at tempos befitting premodern economies and societies. From the mid-nineteenth century onward, nation formation, industrialization, and liberal economics accelerated the circuits of exchange and pathways of change. New demand and supply regimes developed in both the realm and its North Atlantic extensions. Swiss perfections of chocolate confection led to mass marketing and consumption in the global North (Coe and Coe, 1996). Tobacco cigars became an emblem of Victorian sophistication (Corti, 1996), while coffee and cane sugar became quotidian necessities of all classes (Mintz, 1985; Pendergrast, 1999; Roseberry, Gudmundson, and Kutschbach, 1995). At the same time new psychoactive agents—ones that a century or so later would come to both symbolize and constitute the modern drug trade—began to enter the mix. The first was cannabis.

An ancient Old World cultigen of probable Central Asian provenance, *Cannabis sativa* used as a drug probably first reached the New World as part of the African diaspora (Rubin, 1975). An element of slave society in disparate locales throughout Latin America, it apparently diffused selectively into indigenous and local folk usage (namely, *maconha* in Brazil and *marijuana* in Mexico), though it largely escaped general notice. A second diaspora brought to it Euro-American attention. South Asian ("East Indian") indentured laborers in the Caribbean, especially Jamaica, are credited with "introducing" *ganja,* long a popular medicinal and recreational drug in India, to the Caribbean (Rubin and Comitas, 1976; Angrosino, 2003). From there, Afro-Caribbean Creoles are said to have introduced it to portions of the Central and South American rimland (Goode, 1969; Mahabir, 1994). Whatever the precise origins and processes of diffusion, by the mid-twentieth century potent strains of cannabis (e.g., "Panama Red," Colombian and Acapulco "Gold") were being widely consumed locally and increasingly trafficked to markets in North America and beyond. International proscriptions and prohibitions of cannabis did not take hold until the late 1930s. With usage mostly confined to the rural poor or marginalized urban sectors throughout much of its history, cannabis was largely a local affair. As part of the countercultural currents of the 1960s, vast new transclass markets were opened up first in the North Atlantic realm and then in Latin America. Various producer regions and districts—especially mountainous zones of difficult access—in a number of countries experienced boom times as a result of the cannabis craze. Mexico's Sierra Madre Occidental, Colombia's Santa Marta, and Jamaica's Blue Mountains all developed into major cannabis-producing areas. During the 1970s national authorities in these countries were prompted and aided by U.S. antidrug policies to launch campaigns of repression and eradication in these and other districts. The effect of this was at least twofold. First, new growing areas were developed within these countries and beyond. For example, Belize became a secondary center for a time in the 1980s with the help of foreign traffickers (Steinberg, 2004). These spatial displacements have been characterized as "the balloon effect": put the squeeze on one region and the activity balloons up in another region. Second, many of the trafficking networks formed during the heyday of the cannabis boom—the 1960s and early 1970s—were converted to cocaine networks from the mid-1970s on (Walker, 1989).

Like cannabis, the origins of cocaine commerce can be traced to nineteenth-century developments, but its mature articulations were a century in the making. As already mentioned, coca leaf mastication was an ancient and widespread practice in South America (Mortimer, 1974). Colonial prohibitions reduced its main range to the central Andean highlands and lowland Amazonia. The North Atlantic world discovered coca's stimulating elixir properties in the mid-nineteenth century, and refined cocaine became widely available by the 1880s in tonics, beverages (such as Coca-Cola), and as a powder for ingesting, inhaling, or injecting (Courtwright, 2001; Pendergrast, 1993). This initial cocaine boom was brought to a halt by legislation and suppression starting in the early 1900s. The second cocaine boom, which began in the 1970s, drew on traditional source areas such as Bolivia's Chapare region (Sanabria, 1993) and Peru's Huallaga Valley (Morales, 1989) for the raw coca, but increasingly Colombia, particularly Medellin, became the center for processing the finished product. The capital quickly amassed by Colombia's notorious regionally based cocaine cartels variously rippled and rushed out across Latin America, creating an increasingly vertically integrated enterprise. The infrastructure included transportation fleets (vehicles, water- and aircraft), refineries and factories, banks and commercial houses, archipelagos of producing areas in traditional zones, or clandestine narcoplantations in new cultivation territories, chiefly in Colombia's upper Amazonian districts (Thoumi, 2003). In some cases the cartels sponsored coca plantations in "liberated" territory in guerrilla zones operated by the Maoist Sendero Luminoso in Peru or the Marxist FARC (Fuerzas Armadas Revolucionarias de Colombia) and ELN (Ejército de Liberación Nacional) in Colombia (Palmer, 1994; Tarazona-Sevillano and Reuter, 1990). In addition to the territorial and material manifestations the cocaine trade registered in landscapes from northern Mexico to the Southern Cone, armies of workers to grow, process, transport, market, distribute, and protect the product were enlisted (Young, 2004). No nation or dependency and few regions in Latin America or the Caribbean have escaped cocaine's entanglements (Pacini and Franquemont, 1986). Since the 1970s dozens of Latin American governments have fallen, either directly or indirectly, to "cocaine coups" or scandals involving drug corruption (Cockburn and St. Clair, 1998; Eddy, Sabogal, and Walden, 1988; Lee, 1989; Steinberg and Mathewson, 2005). Yet in an age when neoliberal solutions to Latin America's persistent problems of dependency and underdevelopment have been forced on the region by national elites in concert with international agencies, cocaine's short-cut receipts for privatized prosperity and entrepreneurial success are hard to refute (Sanabria, 2004).

Within the overlapping spaces of cannabis and cocaine trafficking, there are other illicit drugs that have more restricted histories and geographies (Smith, 1992). Opium poppies came to the New World as part of the colonial pharmacopoeia, but enjoyed some recreational usage from place to place and time to time. Like *ganja* and South Asian laborers, opium use was part of the baggage that Chinese coolies brought to Western South America and the Caribbean. Since at least the 1960s opium cultivation for heroin production in Mexico and later in Colombia and Guatemala has been the agency of criminal syndicates often in collusion with local and sometimes national authorities. The opium business generally enjoys the preexisting networks and infrastructure established by the cocaine and/or cannabis trades. Since the 1920s there have been minor currents in the traffic of psychoactive pharmaceuticals diverted from legitimate channels. One of the most widely cited examples involved Honduras. During the 1930s large quantities of pharmaceutical morphine and cocaine purchased in Europe for putative medical use in Honduras were diverted to New Orleans for illegal distribution (Scott and Marshall, 1991; U.S. State Department General Reports, n.d.). Similar schemes seem to have been a common feature of loose regulation and control in many circum-Caribbean countries. After World War II and continuing to the present, various commercially produced drugs (particularly amphetamines, barbiturates, and tranquilizers) have made their way from legitimate channels into the Latin American drug networks. Trafficking scales range from freelance tourists bringing home more than "just for personal use," to truck, boat, and planeloads smuggled across borders. Methaqualone, an inebriant/tranquilizer known by its main brand name, Quaalude, enjoyed great popularity in the 1970s as a recreational drug and sexual stimulant. Organized drug networks in Colombia and elsewhere manufactured and trafficked in this substance as long as it was profitable.

PRESENT AND FUTURE TRENDS

Whereas once regions of Latin America would specialize in the production and distribution of one or two illicit drugs (cannabis or cocaine or heroin) increasingly there is diversification of products. This is most evident in the case of methamphetamine. Starting in the 1980s, major cocaine traffickers such as the Mexican Amezcua cartel began to dabble in the "meth" market as a sideline. They sold the precursor chemical ephedrine to California motorcycle gangs who controlled much of the manufacture and distribution of meth in the United States at that time. By the 1990s the Mexican syndicates realized that manufacture and distribution of meth could be profitable in and of itself. To counter border problems, Mexican cartels set up "superlabs" (capable of producing 10 pounds or more of meth in a single production run) in California. At the same time, small-scale (home or backyard) meth labs experienced explosive growth on the West Coast. In classic innovation diffusion style, the trend spread east, becoming most widely established in the Midwest. In the past few years, official reaction to the epidemic of meth abuse has managed to curb much of the local production in the U.S. heartland. Picking up market slack, the Mexican cartels simply took their operations back across the border. They have greatly increased both the purity and potency of the product in the process. As of 2005, it was estimated that Mexican superlabs were supplying 60 percent or more of the illegal amphetamine consumed in the United States. Mexican cartels were directly importing tons of ephedrine from the main producers, India and China, to supply their labs.

Following these Mexican innovations, other areas of Latin America are likely to see growth in illegal amphetamine production and use. In 2005 the importation of ephredine and pseudoephedrine (medicinally used in cold and allergy remedies) in Colombia and Argentina rose sharply. The United Nations Office on Drugs and Crime (UNODC) now considers methamphetamine to be the most widely abused addictive and illegally produced drug in the world. It estimates that there are some 25 million people addicted to methamphetamine, more than cocaine and heroin combined, with the majority in Southeast Asia. But given many Latin American cultural, social, and economic similarities to the Asian contexts, it is reasonable to assume that new amphetamine geographies will develop in Latin America.

Another example of this process involves a potent painkiller that until recently was only available through legitimate pharmaceutical channels. In the spring and summer of 2006 cities in the Midwest and eastern United States reported an "epidemic" of fatal drug overdoses (several hundred deaths). Upon investigation it was discovered that heroin had been mixed with fentanyl, a synthetic opiate (about 50 times stronger than heroin). In May 2006, authorities raided a clandestine lab producing fentanyl in Toluca, Mexico. In January 2006, U.S. drug agents intercepted a shipment of fentanyl along with "meth ice" (methamphetamine in reconstituted crystalline "rock" form) just north of the Mexican border in California. Prior to this, only a few illicit fentanyl operations had been uncovered in either the United States or Mexico. Whether this signals a new dimension in organized crime's geographical and product expansion within Latin America is unclear.

Each of these two newer products, and dozens of other different commercially or clandestinely produced synthetic drugs, have their own shifting trafficking histories and geographies. These geographies and the drugs that generate them will continue to be constructed and shaped by historical contexts, regional laws, consumer preferences, and the entrepreneurial drive of an important segment of Latin America's informal economic actors.

CONCLUSION

From the initial sedentarism of post-Pleistocene settlers, if not earlier, to the hyperconnectivity and mobility of postmodernity, the procurement and/or production, exchange, and consumption of psychoactive drugs in Latin America has been a constant feature of daily life as well as providing the material substance for much ceremonialism and significant portions of the realm's economic vitality. Entire landscapes have been made and remade in the service of sugar, tobacco, coffee, cacao, coca, cannabis, and opium cultivation. Entire local, regional, and national economies have been created and directed by the imperatives of both licit and illicit drug commerce. Entire communities, ethnic groups, and class strata have been brought into being and organized around the production, circulation, and consumption of psychoactive substances. Each of these patterns and processes is reflected in distinct geographies manifested at differing scales—from the bodies of individuals and their households, to localities and regions, to national states and global transactions. In this chapter I have not attempted to chart the particulars of the drug trade per se. Nor have I mapped the different drugs' distribution areas or trafficking paths. This information is generally available in the extensive literature, both scholarly and popular, on the topics of both licit and illicit drugs in Latin America. I have included a selection of this literature in the bibliography. Despite the extant scholarship with its voluminous coverage on some topics such as sugar or coca and cocaine, the general topic and most of its particulars have barely been explored from the perspective of geographers and geography. It is a wide-open research frontier that awaits both the curious student and the committed scholar.

SUGGESTED READINGS

Courtwright, D. T. *Forces of Habit: Drugs and the Making of the Modern World.* Cambridge, Mass.: Harvard University Press, 2001.

Jankowiak, W., and D. Bradburd. *Drugs, Labor, and Colonial Expansion.* Tucson: University of Arizona Press, 2003.

Mintz, S. W. *Sweetness and Power: The Place of Sugar in Modern History.* New York: Viking, 1985.

Steinberg, M. K., J. J. Hobbs, and K. Mathewson, eds. *Dangerous Harvest: Drug Plants and the Transformation of Indigenous Landscapes.* New York: Oxford University Press, 2004.

BIBLIOGRAPHY

Allen, C. *The Hold Life Has: Coca and Cultural Identity in an Andean Community.* Washington, D.C.: Smithsonian Institution Press, 1988.

Ambler, C. "Alcohol and Slave Trade in West Africa, 1400–1850." In *Drugs, Labor, and Colonial Expansion*, edited by W. Jankowiak and D. Bradburd, pp. 73–87. Tucson: University of Arizona Press, 2003.

Anderson, E. N. "Caffeine Culture." In *Drugs, Labor, and Colonial Expansion*, edited by W. Jankowiak and D. Bradburd, pp. 159–176. Tucson: University of Arizona Press, 2003.

Andrews, J. *Peppers: The Domesticated Capsicums.* Austin: University of Texas Press, 1984.

Angrosino, M. V. "Rum and Ganja: Indenture, Drug Foods, Labor Motivation, and the Evolution of the Modern Sugar Industry on Trinidad." In *Drugs, Labor, and Colonial Expansion*, edited by W. Jankowiak and D. Bradburd, pp. 101–116. Tucson: University of Arizona Press, 2003.

Bagley, B. M., and W. O. Walker III, eds. *Drug Trafficking in the Americas.* New Brunswick, N.J.: Transaction Publishers, 1994.

Balick, M. J., and P. A. Cox. *Plants, People, and Culture: The Science of Ethnobotany.* New York: Scientific American Library, 1996.

Barretto, M. *El mate: Su historia y cultura.* Buenos Aires: Ediciones del Sol, 1991.

Bergmann, J. F. "The Distribution of Cacao Cultivation in Pre-Columbian America." *Annals of the Association of American Geographers* 59 (1969): 85–96.

Booth, M. *Opium: A History.* New York: St. Martin's Press, 1998.

Bradburd, D., and W. Jankowiak. "Drugs, Desire, and European Expansion." In *Drugs, Labor, and Colonial Expansion*, edited by W. Jankowiak and D. Bradburd, pp. 3–29. Tucson: University of Arizona Press, 2003.

Bruman, H. J. *Alcohol in Ancient Mexico.* Salt Lake City: University of Utah Press, 2000.

Camacho Guizado, A. L. "Drug Trafficking and Society in Columbia." In *Drug Trafficking in the Americas*, edited by B. M. Bagley and W. O. Walker III, pp. 97–120. New Brunswick, N.J.: Transaction Publishers, 1994.

Cambranes, J. C. *Coffee and Peasants: The Origins of the Modern Plantation Economy in Guatemala, 1853–1897.* South Woodstock, Vt.: CIRMA, 1985.

Cassman, V., L. Cartmell, and E. Belmonte. "Coca as Symbol and Labor Enhancer in the Andes: A Historical Overview." In *Drugs, Labor, and Colonial Expansion*, edited by W. Jankowiak and D. Bradburd, pp. 149–158. Tucson: University of Arizona Press, 2003.

Cockburn, A., and J. St. Clair. *White Out: The CIA, Drugs, and the Press.* London: Verso, 1998.

Coe, S. D., and M. D. Coe. *The True History of Chocolate.* London: Thames and Hudson, 1996.

Cook, N. D., and W. G. Lovell, eds. "'Secret Judgments of God': Old World Disease in Colonial Spanish America." Norman: University of Oklahoma Press, 1992.

Corti, C. *A History of Smoking*. London: Bracken Books, 1996.

Courtwright, D. T. *Forces of Habit: Drugs and the Making of the Modern World*. Cambridge, Mass.: Harvard University Press, 2001.

Dalby, A. *Dangerous Tastes: The Story of Spices*. Berkeley: University of California Press, 2000.

Davis, W. "Hallucinogen Plants and Their Use in Traditional Societies: An Overview." *Cultural Survival Quarterly* 9, no. 4 (1985): 2–5.

Dobkin de Rios, M. *Hallucinogens: Cross-Cultural Perspectives*. Albuquerque: University of New Mexico Press, 1984.

Donkin, R. A. *Agricultural Terracing in the Aboriginal New World*. Viking Fund Publications in Anthropology, no. 56. Tucson: University of Arizona Press, 1979.

Eddy, P., H. Sabogal, and S. Walden. *The Cocaine Wars*. New York: W. W. Norton, 1988.

Efron, D. H., B. Holmstedt, and N. S. Kline, eds. *Ethnopharmacologic Search for Psychoactive Drugs*. Washington, D.C.: U.S. Department of Health, Education, and Welfare, 1967.

Elferink, J. G. "The Narcotic and Hallucinogenic Use of Tobacco in Pre-Columbian Central America." *Journal of Ethnopharmacology* 7 (1983): 111–122.

Emboden, W. *Narcotic Plants: Hallucinogens, Stimulants, Inebriants, and Hypnotics: Their Origins and Uses*. London: Studio Vista, 1979.

Feinberg, B. *The Devil's Book of Culture: History, Mushrooms, and Caves in Southern Mexico*. Austin: University of Texas Press, 2003.

Furst, P. T., ed. *Flesh of the Gods: The Ritual Use of Hallucinogens*. London: Allen & Unwin, 1972.

Gagliano, J. *Coca Prohibition in Peru: The Historical Debates*. Tucson: University of Arizona Press, 1994.

Galeano, E. *Open Veins of Latin America: Five Centuries of the Pillage of a Continent*. New York: Monthly Review Press, 1973.

Galloway, J. H. *The Sugar Cane Industry: An Historical Geography from Its Origins to 1914*. Cambridge: Cambridge University Press, 1989.

Goode, E. *Marijuana*. New York: Aldine, 1969.

Goodman, J. *Tobacco in History: The Cultures of Dependence*. London: Routledge, 1993.

Goodman, J. "Excitantia: or, How Enlightenment Europe Took to Soft Drugs." In *Consuming Habits: Drugs in History and Anthropology*, edited by J. Goodman, P. E. Lovejoy, and A. Sherratt, pp. 126–147. New York: Routledge, 1995.

Goodman, J., P. E. Lovejoy, and A. Sherratt, eds. *Consuming Habits: Drugs in History and Anthropology*. New York: Routledge, 1995.

Gootenberg, P., ed. *Cocaine: Global Histories*. London: Routledge, 1999.

Harner, M. *Hallucinogens and Shamanisms*. New York: Oxford University Press, 1973.

Hobbs, J. J. "The Global Nexus of Drug Cultivation." In *Dangerous Harvest: Drug Plants and the Transformation of Indigenous Landscapes*, edited by M. K. Steinberg, J. J. Hobbs, and K. Mathewson, pp. 294–311. New York: Oxford University Press, 2004.

Jankowiak, W., and D. Bradburd. *Drugs, Labor, and Colonial Expansion.* Tucson: University of Arizona Press, 2003.

Kimber, C. T., and D. McDonald. "Sacred and Profane Uses of the Cactus *Lophophora Williamsii* from the South Texas Peyote Garden." In *Dangerous Harvest: Drug Plants and the Transformation of Indigenous Landscapes,* edited by M. K. Steinberg, J. J. Hobbs, and K. Mathewson, pp. 182–208. New York: Oxford University Press, 2004.

La Barre, W. "Old and New World Narcotics: A Statistical Question and an Ethnological Reply." *Economic Botany* 24 (1970): 73–80.

La Barre, W. "Hallucinogens and the Shamanic Origins of Religion." In *Flesh of the Gods: The Ritual Use of Hallucinogens,* edited by P. T. Furst, pp. 261–278. London: Allen & Unwin, 1972.

Lee, R. W., III. *The White Labyrinth: Cocaine and Political Power.* New Brunswick, N.J.: Transaction Publishers, 1989.

Lewin, L. *Phantastica: Narcotic and Stimulating Drugs, Their Use and Abuse.* London: Routledge and Kegan Paul, 1964.

Mabry, D. J., ed. *The Latin American Narcotics Trade and U.S. Security.* Westport, Conn.: Greenwood Press, 1989.

Mahabir, N. K. "Marijuana in the Caribbean." *Caribbean Affairs* 7, no. 4 (1994): 28–40.

Mathee, R. "Exotic Substances: The Introduction and Global Spread of Tobacco, Coffee, Cocoa, Tea and Distilled Liquor, Sixteenth to Eighteenth Centuries." In *Drugs and Narcotics in History,* edited by R. Porter and M. Teich, pp. 24–51. Cambridge: Cambridge University Press, 1995.

Mathewson, K. "Plantations and Dependencies: Notes on the 'Moral Geography' of Global Stimulant Production." In *Ethics and Agriculture: An Anthology on Current Issues in World Context,* edited by C. V. Blatz, pp. 559–567. Moscow: University of Idaho Press, 1991.

Mathewson, K. "Drugs, Moral Geographies, and Indigenous Peoples: Some Initial Mappings and Central Issues." In *Dangerous Harvest: Drug Plants and the Transformation of Indigenous Landscapes,* edited by M. K. Steinberg, J. J. Hobbs, and K. Mathewson, pp. 11–23. New York: Oxford University Press, 2004.

McCoy, A. W. "The Stimulus of Prohibition: A Critical History of the Global Narcotics Trade." In *Dangerous Harvest: Drug Plants and the Transformation of Indigenous Landscapes,* edited by M. K. Steinberg, J. J. Hobbs, and K. Mathewson, pp. 24–111. New York: Oxford University Press, 2004.

Mintz, S. W. *Sweetness and Power: The Place of Sugar in Modern History.* New York: Viking, 1985.

Morales, E. *Cocaine: White Gold Rush in Peru.* Tucson: University of Arizona Press, 1989.

Mortimer, W. G. *History of Coca: "The Divine Plant" of the Incas.* San Francisco: And/Or Press, 1974 [1901].

Murra, J. V. "Rite and Crop in the Inca State." In *Peoples and Cultures of Native South America,* edited by D. R. Gross, pp. 377–389. Garden City, N.Y.: Doubleday, 1973.

Pacini, D., and C. Franquemont, eds. *Coca and Cocaine: Effects on People and Policy in Latin America.* Cultural Survival Report No. 23. Cambridge: Cultural Survival, 1986.

Pagden, A. *European Encounters with the New World*. New Haven, Conn.: Yale University Press, 1993.

Painter, J. *Bolivia and Coca: A Study in Depending*. Boulder, Colo.: Lynne Rienner, 1994.

Palmer, D. S. "Peru, Drugs, and Shining Path." In *Drug Trafficking in the Americas*, edited by B. M. Bagley and W. O. Walker III, pp. 179–197. New Brunswick, N.J.: Transaction Publishers, 1994.

Pendergrast, M. *For God, Country, and Coca-Cola*. New York: Charles Scribner's Sons, 1993.

Pendergrast, M. *Uncommon Grounds: The History of Coffee and How It Transformed Our World*. New York: Basic Books, 1999.

Perramond, E. P. "Desert Traffic: The Dynamics of the Drug Trade in Northwestern Mexico." In *Dangerous Harvest: Drug Plants and the Transformation of Indigenous Landscapes*, edited by M. K. Steinberg, J. J. Hobbs, and K. Mathewson, pp. 209–217. New York: Oxford University Press, 2004.

Plowman, T. "The Origin, Evolution and Diffusion of Cocoa, *Erythroxylum* spp., in South and Central America." In *Pre-Columbian Plant Migration*, edited by D. Stone, pp. 146–156. Papers of the Peabody Museum of Archaeology and Ethnology, vol. 76. Cambridge, Mass.: Harvard University Press, 1984.

Porter, R., and M. Teich, eds. *Drugs and Narcotics in History*. Cambridge: Cambridge University Press, 1995.

Reyes, A. "Drug Trafficking and the Guerilla Movement in Colombia." In *Drug Trafficking in the Americas*, edited by B. M. Bagley and W. O. Walker III, pp. 121–130. New Brunswick, N.J.: Transaction Publishers, 1994.

Richardson, B. C. *The Caribbean in the Wider World, 1492–1992: A Regional Geography*. Cambridge: Cambridge University Press, 1992.

Robicsek, F. *The Smoking Gods: Tobacco in Maya Art, History, and Religion*. Norman: University of Oklahoma Press, 1978.

Roseberry, W., L. Gudmundson, and M. S. Kutschbach. *Coffee, Society and Power in Latin America*. Baltimore: Johns Hopkins University Press, 1995.

Rubin, V., ed. *Cannabis and Culture*. The Hague: Mouton, 1975.

Rubin, V., and L. Comitas. *Ganja in Jamaica: The Effects of Marijuana Use*. Garden City, N.Y.: Anchor Books, 1976.

Rudgley, R. *Essential Substances: A Cultural History of Intoxicants in Society*. New York: Kodansha America, 1994.

Sanabria, H. *The Coca Boom and Rural Social Change in Bolivia*. Ann Arbor: University of Michigan Press, 1993.

Sanabria, H. "The State and the Ongoing Struggle Over Coca in Bolivia: Legitimacy, Hegemony, and the Exercise of Power." In *Dangerous Harvest: Drug Plants and the Transformation of Indigenous Landscapes*, edited by M. K. Steinberg, J. J. Hobbs, and K. Mathewson, pp. 153–166. New York: Oxford University Press, 2004.

Sauer, C. O. "The Personality of Mexico." *Geographical Review* 31 (1941): 353–364.

Sauer, C. O. *Agricultural Origins and Dispersals*. New York: American Geographical Society, 1952.

Sauer, C. O. *The Early Spanish Main*. Berkeley: University of California Press, 1966.

Sauer, J. *Historical Geography of Crop Plants: A Select Roster*. Boca Raton, Fla.: Lewis Publishers, 1993.

Schivelbush, W. *Tastes of Paradise: A Social History of Spices, Stimulants, and Intoxicants.* New York: Pantheon, 1992.

Schultes, R. E. "An Overview of Hallucinogens in the Western Hemisphere." In *Flesh of the Gods: The Ritual Use of Hallucinogens,* edited by P. T. Furst, pp. 3–54. London: Allen & Unwin, 1972.

Scott, P. D., and J. Marshall. *Cocaine Politics: Drugs Armies, and the CIA in Central America.* Berkeley: University of California Press, 1991.

Smith, P. H., ed. *Drug Policy in the Americas.* Boulder, Colo.: Westview Press, 1992.

Spiller, G. A., ed. *The Methylxanthine Beverages and Foods.* New York: Alan R. Liss, 1984.

Steinberg, M. K. "The Marijuana Milpa: Agricultural Adaptations in a Postsubsistence Maya Landscape in Southern Belize." In *Dangerous Harvest: Drug Plants and the Transformation of Indigenous Landscapes,* edited by M. K. Steinberg, J. J. Hobbs, and K. Mathewson, pp. 167–181. New York: Oxford University Press, 2004.

Steinberg, M. K., J. J. Hobbs, and K. Mathewson, eds. *Dangerous Harvest: Drug Plants and the Transformation of Indigenous Landscapes.* New York: Oxford University Press, 2004.

Steinberg, M. K., and K. Mathewson. "Landscapes of Drugs and War: Intersections of Political Ecology and Global Conflict." In *The Geography of War and Peace,* pp. 242–258. Oxford: Oxford University Press, 2005.

Stinchcombe, A. L. *Sugar Island Slavery in the Age of Enlightenment: The Political Economy of the Caribbean World.* Princeton, N.J.: Princeton University Press, 1995.

Tarazona-Sevillano, G., and J. B. Reuter. *Sendero Luminoso and the Threat of Narcoterrorism.* New York: Praeger, 1990.

Teggart, F. *Rome and China: A Study of Correlations in Historical Events.* Berkeley: University of California Press, 1939.

Thoumi, F. E. *Illegal Drugs, Economy, and Society in the Andes.* Baltimore: Johns Hopkins University Press, 2003.

U.S. State Department General Reports, n.d. "Drugs and Honduran Politics." In *Drugs in the Western Hemisphere: An Odyssey of Culture in Conflict,* edited by W. O. Walker III, pp. 80–81. Wilmington, Del.: Scholarly Resource, 1996.

Walker, W. O., III, ed. *Drug Control in the Americas.* Albuquerque: University of New Mexico Press, 1989.

Walker, W. O., III, ed. *Drugs in the Western Hemisphere: An Odyssey of Cultures in Conflict.* Wilmington, Del.: Scholarly Resources, 1996.

Wallerstein, I. *The Modern World-System: Capitalist Agriculture and the Origins of the World-Economy in the Sixteenth Century.* New York: Academic Press, 1974.

Watts, D. *The West Indies: Patterns of Development, Culture and Environmental Change since 1492.* Cambridge: Cambridge University Press, 1987.

Weil, A., and W. Rosen. *From Chocolate to Morphine: Everything You Need to Know about Mind-Altering Drugs.* New York: Houghton Mifflin Company, 1993.

Wilbert, J. *Tobacco and Shamanism.* New Haven, Conn.: Yale University Press, 1987.

Williams, R. G. *States and Social Evolution: Coffee and the Rise of National Governments in Central America.* Chapel Hill: University of North Carolina Press, 1994.

Willey, G. R. *An Introduction to American Archaeology.* Vol. 2, *South America.* Englewood Cliffs, N.J.: Prentice Hall, 1971.

Wolf, E. R. *Europe and the People without History.* Berkeley: University of California Press, 1982.

Young, A. M. *The Chocolate Tree: A Natural History of Cacao.* Washington, D.C.: Smithsonian Institution Press, 1994.

Young, K. R. "Environmental and Social Consequences of Coca/Cocaine in Peru: Policy Alternatives and a Research Agenda." In *Dangerous Harvest: Drug Plants and the Transformation of Indigenous Landscapes,* edited by M. K. Steinberg, J. J. Hobbs, and K. Mathewson, pp. 249–273. New York: Oxford University Press, 2004.

9

NGOs and Ongoing Changes in Latin American Society

J. Christopher Brown

This chapter is about NGOs, short for "nongovernmental organizations," in Latin America. So, what are NGOs? As academics tend to do with seemingly simple questions, many have written entire books and articles to answer that very question. For the purposes of this chapter, NGOs are a whole range of organizations, from an agricultural cooperative of family farmers similar to what you'd find in Kansas, to a not-for-profit urban health clinic similar to what one would find in Los Angeles, to a group of environmentalists similar to what one would find lobbying Congress in Washington, D.C. These organizations are ordinary to many of us in the United States. In Latin America, however, they have grown in number and importance only over the last few decades. Understanding NGOs in Latin America, and NGOs throughout the world for that matter, is important because they signal some major societal and even environmental changes in the region, which is why so many scholars study, track, and theorize about them.

The growth of NGOs and their importance in society is something that has been occurring in Latin America and throughout the world. Explaining what is happening in Latin America, then, must involve an understanding of international political, economic, and even environmental events over the last few decades that have set the stage for the growth and development of NGOs in our region of interest and around the world. One major author has identified this worldwide phenomenon as an "associational revolution" (Salamon, 1994). "Revolutionary" means something that is new and that challenges the predominance of what existed before. Up until the advent of NGO growth and influence, most people around the world tended to rely on two major "institutions" to organize, to get things done, to provide for the needs of themselves and their communities. Those institutions were the

market (the economy) and the state (governments). NGOs, then, are institutions that have entered the stage as both an alternative to and a challenger
of the predominance of the market and the state in people's lives.

The "associational" part of this revolution refers to the kind of human
organization that NGOs represent. The dominant institutions of the market
and the state are often talked about as fairly anonymous entities. Ordinary
people often view these institutions as impersonal, indifferent, cold, even
abusive. It is no wonder why, considering the market is often likened to "an
invisible hand," and considering many in charge of government in Latin
America have often abused their power to the detriment of people and the
environment. NGOs, then, are novel associations of people, often from the
lower and middle classes, who believe the state and market are incapable
of providing certain things that people need. So, people have organized
themselves into NGOs as a way to meet their own goals.

How significant is this associational revolution, and what general types
of associations make up this revolution in Latin America in particular?
One way to express the global significance of the revolution is to take note
of how powerful international organizations like the United Nations, the
World Bank, or the European Union (EU), all important forces in development, interact with NGOs. All these organizations now often channel funds
through NGOs to carry out development projects. For example, between
1990 and 1994, the EU increased greatly the amount of foreign aid it gives
through NGOs, from 47 to 67 percent of total aid (*Economist*, 2000). More
than 70 percent of World Bank–supported projects approved in 1999 involved NGOs in some way (World Bank, 2000). In one study, scholars estimate that in a sample of 22 countries, the NGO sector represents 4.6 percent of GDP and employs 5 percent of the total nonagricultural workforce
(Salamon and Anheier, 1999). Also, NGOs are organized not only at local
and regional scales. International NGOs dealing with social issues increased
in number fivefold between 1953 and 1993 (Keck and Sikkink, 1998). In
Latin America, the NGO sector can be divided into sectors depending on
what types of efforts the NGOs focus on. Forty-four percent of the NGO
sector in Latin America (termed "nonprofit") is involved in education.
Health, social services, cultural affairs, and professional associations are all
similar, from 10 to 12 percent of all NGOs. Finally, those NGOs focusing
on development, environmental advocacy, and other fields are all less than
10 percent of the composition of the nonprofit sector in Latin America
(Salamon, et al., 1999).

This chapter aims to give a better idea of how the associational revolution
occurred in Latin America. The chapter will give a greater understanding of
the diversity of NGOs, how they function, how they are funded, and what
they do. After a theoretical introduction based on the ideas of the social
construction of scale (translating a vibrant, yet difficult literature in geog-

raphy into accessible language and ideas), the chapter explains how NGOs arose within a global political and economic context of democratization and the rise of neoliberalism, both extremely important processes shaping the structure of social life in Latin America. NGOs are complex new political and economic actors. Like all forms of human organization, NGOs both shape and are shaped by the constraints and opportunities presented by globalization. The chapter ends with a case study of water resource governance and NGOs in Bolivia to give you a clear example of the circumstances under which NGOs formed around the desire to deal with a particular problem and how they are attempting to solve it.

NGOs AND ALPHABET SOUP

Back to the earlier question, what are NGOs? The way NGOs have been classified has changed greatly over the years as more and more people study them and as international political, economic, and ecological events have changed. In the 1980s, most people thought of NGOs as private, tax-exempt, nonprofit agencies that worked to provide overseas relief and development services. Such a view is insufficient for our purposes here because it completely ignores NGO activity in the developing world. Researchers also used the term PVO (private voluntary organizations) and began to include organizations based in the developing world that served their own communities under this term. As the associational revolution began to take hold, researchers began using the term NPO (nonprofit organization) and used it interchangeably with NGO. By the early 1990s, researchers Salamon and Anheier theorized that an organization's NPO status could be determined by considering characteristics such as legal status (how it is recognized by the state), origin of income (dues and contributions? or selling goods and services?), role or function, and structural/operational characteristics.

Salamon and Anheier eventually decided that the structural/operational characteristics of NPOs were the most useful in classifying them, and they came up with five major features that make NPOs stand out from other forms of human organization. First, NPOs are formal organizations—they are not based solely on family or kinship ties between people or geographic proximity, for instance. There is some officially stated reason why they exist, who can become members, and so forth. Second, they are private, as opposed to government-sponsored, organizations. Third, they do not operate with the goal of making profits. Fourth, they are autonomous. And fifth, they are voluntary. Even as others started treating NPOs and NGOs as synonymous, Salamon and Anheier stuck to their definition of NPOs, because they felt that NGOs were mainly groups whose function was to deal with social and economic development issues.

Other researchers felt that NGOs should be categorized by the relationship they have with civil society and the state in general. This was especially important to researchers seeking to understand the role the organizations played in checking the power of what were, at times, brutal authoritarian regimes. In some cases, NGOs grew out of broader social movements that first defined themselves as they protested the policies of authoritarian governments of the 1960s and 1970s in Latin America and elsewhere. With respect to the question of the relationship to the state, the picture of who is or is not an NGO is complicated further. That's because the state has often involved itself in NGO activity by creating the NGOs themselves (GONGOs, or government-organized NGOs). The state's strategy here is as follows: state officials realize that more and more foreign aid is being channeled through NGOs, and so to try to gain control over this significant amount of capital, state governments form their own NGOs. In similar fashion, certain donors want to channel their funds through an NGO, and so to have more control of exactly where donor funds go and how they are used, donors may create an NGO as well. Technically, such organizations meet the criteria of being private, but there is something about these last organizations that misses the spirit of the associational revolution, and thus most researchers discount them as not warranting inclusion as NPOs or NGOs.

The Salamon and Anheier definition of NPOs distinguishes NPOs as nonprofit and formal organizations, but this fails to account for the enormous number of ways people in Latin America and the rest of the developing world organize themselves *informally*. Moreover, at times people organize with the goal of generating and distributing profits. Think of a farmer's co-op, for instance. Finally, there is a lack of correspondence between what Salamon and Anheier call NPOs (their focus in studies of the associational revolution) and NGOs, the focus of those who study development in places like Latin America. On one hand, NGOs may be a more inclusive term, allowing informal organizations into the definition, while on the other hand NPOs might be more inclusive, because NPOs include unions, business/professional organizations, and religious organizations.

By now it should be clear that no definition of NGOs is likely to satisfy everyone. A telling example of this comes from my own experience: An article I had written with two colleagues, about NGOs in the state of Rondonia in the Brazilian Amazon, created confusion among Brazilian scholars from Rondonia (Brown, Brown, and Desposato, 2002). These scholars said things to me like, "the groups you are writing about in Rondonia are not NGOs. They are community-based organizations. NGOs are different. They do not work directly with people from communities, but they help community-based organizations raise funds and have greater contact with the international aid community." These Brazilian scholars were referring to organizations that were staffed only by professionals who would work to raise money from large international aid organizations like OXFAM (U.K.) and channel those funds to organizations that work with groups of people organized at the community level. Only a small number of the 250 groups in Rondonia that were a part of my study were such "NGOs," so to the Brazilian scholars, my study was not about NGOs at all. One does need to settle on a definition, though, so following the lead of a number of scholars on the issue, this chapter uses an NGO definition based on structural/organizational terms that includes organizations that are autonomous, private, not-for-profit, and designed to improve the quality of life for people who are economically or politically disadvantaged or otherwise vulnerable; thus we are leaving out NPOs that might have some type of business/professional focus or NPOs that serve the interests of people in the upper classes of society.

Such a definition is so general—it would include so many different groups—that some type of classification scheme is needed to clarify what type of NGO is being discussed. Researchers Bebbington and Farrington (1992) came up with just such a classification scheme that is quite useful. The scheme is based on the NGO's location, scale, ownership, orientation, approach, and operation. First of all, the location of an NGO is important, for it affects a whole range of other characteristics such as how the NGO carries out its operations, how it relates to the state, and where it gets its support. NGOs involved in Latin America may actually be located in the developed North; to accomplish goals in Latin America, they must interface somehow with NGOs working at the local level in Latin American communities. Another possibility is that the NGO is a northern NGO, staffed by people from developed countries, but it is stationed in Latin America. Finally, the NGO may be located in Latin America and staffed by Latin Americans. Location is then inextricably linked to the scale of NGO work. An NGO might operate at a national or international level with the goal of helping NGOs working locally to communicate with one another and build common goals. An example of this would be an organization located in a major city that works to make sure all the NGOs representing indigenous peoples at the local level across the country act in concert with one another on a set number of important issues. Such an NGO might be called an umbrella organization, under which scores of others are affiliated and organized.

Another useful characteristic to classify NGOs is their type of ownership. Are they "membership support" NGOs, in which the organization is staffed and elected by the clients it serves, or is it a "grassroots support" organization, a professionally staffed one, in which the clients of an organization have no effective control over the operations of the NGO? The next distinction is whether the group has any profit-driven motives to its work at all, or whether it is purely "value-driven." (Recall, an earlier definition above requires NGOs to be nonprofit!) A value-driven NGO will exhibit a wide spectrum of approaches to its work, from those that are top-down, in which NGO leaders/directors tell clients what is best for them to do in a given situation. The opposite end of the spectrum involves approaches that are fully participatory; everything from the goals of the organization to execution of programs and their evaluation is done entirely by the clients of the organization themselves, with the purpose of empowering them to change the circumstances of their very lives. Finally, researchers separate those organizations that are directed toward research and innovation from those that are directed toward carrying out direct actions and implementing new ways of doing things.

All in all, this practice of trying to classify NGOs is complicated and may seem more geared toward inventing "alphabet soups" of confusing new acronyms that in the end do little to get to the bottom of what NGOs really are (Vakil, 1997). If this is all so confusing and involves splitting hairs, then why go through the process of deciding what is or is not an NGO? One reason is simply to recognize the incredible diversity of NGOs around the world. Another is that only by coming up with some type of NGO classification scheme can researchers make within- and cross-country comparisons in studies on the associational revolution. Finally, if a scheme to standardize the classification of NGOs were developed, it would help NGOs themselves benefit from others' experiences. They would be more readily able to locate other organizations around the world that are similar. Increased communication among such organizations could lead to insights into improving the effectiveness of their programs.

NGOs AND THE POLITICS OF SCALE

NGOs form an extremely diverse set of human organizational forms. It is difficult to compare them across countries and within countries. One way to get past the confusing names and the problems with them is to classify NGOs in terms of the scale of their organization. What is meant by "scale"? This section argues that common uses of the word "scale" often don't help us understand the nature of NGOs, but that a literature in geography known as the "politics of scale" is useful.

We commonly use the word "scale" to signify the size or reach of an operation. Calling something large- or small-scale says something about, for example, how many people, how much capital, or how much technology is involved in a given human activity. In common usage, it appears that such language also contains information about the type of people involved in a given human activity. "Small-scale" implies the "little guy," the worker, the family farmer, the members of the family business, and often in the developing world, the peasant and the indigenous person—people often viewed as being harmed by globalization. "Large-scale" implies "big-timers," capitalists, big-businessmen, corporations, and rich people—people often viewed as being helped by globalization.

Geographer Mark Purcell and I have argued elsewhere that there are problems with such tendencies to associate certain scales of human organization with certain human activities and certain people or actors (Brown and Purcell, 2005; Purcell and Brown, 2005). Such thinking involves a lack of understanding of two important conclusions from a literature that has developed over the past few decades largely within political economic studies of the urban landscape. As a whole, the literature is given the name "the politics of scale," and its first main finding, simply stated, is that scale is socially constructed. What this means is that people produce scales of human organization as part of their struggle for social and political power in a given situation. An organization of peasants from a particular area might create a *local*-scale organization in order to make demands from the municipal government for better roads, for example. In this sense, the scale of the organization is more a part of a strategy to achieve a goal than anything else. Thus, the scale itself does not lead to a given human or environmental outcome such as better roads. Rather, it is the increased power of the people—working at a particular scale of organization with a particular agenda—that leads to an outcome, namely, better roads.

Another main finding of the politics of scale literature is that scales are highly dynamic. Recall that people utilize scale to gain power of some sort. So, as people constantly shift strategies to jockey for power, the differing scales of human organization are constantly being created, deployed, and dismantled in order to achieve that power. At times in history, the particular scale at which certain types of organizations operate may seem to be dominant. It may become so dominant that people tend to think it is fixed that way and always will remain that way. Perhaps it is when the scales of organizations become fixed like this that people come to believe that the scales themselves, as opposed to the actual organizations, have some type of inherent qualities or characteristics, and it is then that people begin to associate particular scales with particular actors. We know from history, though, that scales of human organization rarely if ever remain fixed forever. Political geographer John Agnew makes the point that though today state sovereignty is organized at the national scale, it has not always been, and will not remain, that way. Consider that each nation on earth organizes its own domestic and foreign policies, its defense, and its economy primarily at the scale of the national territory. This was certainly not the case before the creation of modern nation-states, however, and state sovereignty is likely to be organized at different scales in the future. Agnew points to the European Union, a current example of human organization in which state sovereignty at the national scale is being challenged and reorganized in favor of sovereignty at a scale one might call continental (Agnew, 1994).

The implication of such thinking is that there is nothing essentially good or bad about any scale of human organization. Scales of organization themselves do not have any preknown effect on the outcome of any human activity. For example, while we may tend to think that small-scale, family farmers take better care of their land from an environmental standpoint than, say, a large-scale corporate farm, it is not the scale of the organization of the farm that creates the good or bad effect of farming. Rather, the social or environmental outcomes of farming depend on the goals and practices of the people in charge of the farming operation. If the goal of a farmer is to make money regardless of the social and environmental costs of that farming, then the outcome is likely to be socially and environmentally harmful. Both small-scale and large-scale farmers may do this. In contrast, the goal of a farmer may be to improve social and environmental conditions of his farming operation, even if it cuts into his immediate profits. Again, both small- and large-scale farmers may do this.

Still, many of us tend to believe that small-scale, or "local"-organized human activities are preferable to large-scale or more "global"-organized activities. With respect to Latin Americans, part of that tendency comes from experiences with the spectacular failure of Latin American development programs in the 1970s–1980s that were supposed to make life better for the poor while improving the condition of the environment. There will be more on this later, but suffice it to say that those programs were largely organized as extremely large-scale projects, the vision and financing for which came from centralized, often authoritarian national governments and globally organized financial institutions like the World Bank. If such large-scale projects were so damaging, then conventional wisdom dictated that smaller-scale, decentralized development projects would correct those problems. Local people would be in more control over the development money and decisions that affect their lives.

Taken as a whole, this theory about scale is a useful guide for a discussion of NGOs in Latin America. The theory suggests looking for diversity in the ways NGOs organize, matching the scale of their organization to their myriad goals. One can also expect to see them using scale as a tool to challenge the power of other actors organized at similar or different scales. Finally, the theory directs us to be aware of romanticizing or giving essential qualities to NGOs in Latin America simply because they are organized often at smaller scales than international corporations and national governments. Rather than expecting to see particular outcomes from the actions of these organizations, the goal is to investigate links between the agendas of NGOs and the outcomes of pursuing those agendas.

THE SOCIAL AND ENVIRONMENTAL CONTEXT OF THE ASSOCIATIONAL REVOLUTION

The associational revolution arose within a context of past political, economic, cultural, and environmental events both in Latin American countries and internationally. In broad terms, the development of NGOs in Latin America can be told as a story of a slowly emerging separate sector in society that arguably was always present in society ever since pre-Columbian times. Then, as the Catholic Church and the modern state impacted those societies with their own forms of human organization, this sector of society would gradually differentiate itself into the more defined sector that it is today. All societies have some form of informal human organization that is designed to step in and help people in some way when other, often more formal, institutions fail. Before the state and the modern market were invented, people in Latin America and elsewhere had their own forms of societal and cultural institutions to rely on. Authors who have contributed to Salamon and Anheier's studies on the nonprofit sector in Latin America all mention pre-Columbian societal forms as an important contributor to what would eventually become known as part of the nonprofit sector and NGOs. For example, a principle known today as "Andean reciprocity" was the basis of an organizational system ensuring that hunger and misery among less advantaged groups was addressed through redistribution of excess production from more fortunate groups. This organization was based on kinship ties among different groups of people.

The next important point in this history is the introduction of colonial forms of human organization that would build on pre-Columbian forms. Most importantly, colonization brought the Church and its Christian ideals of charity and assistance to the poor. Colonial governments gave the Church broad powers for hundreds of years to establish sanctioned schools, hospitals, asylums, and other "charitable" organizations. The strong relationship between the colonial state and the Church would not last, however, and by the 1800s and the independence of Latin American countries from European power, governments wrested from the Church much of the power it had in society. It was during this period that the Church would begin more independently to continue its works by establishing "brotherhoods" and "sisterhoods," private charitable organizations among the elite, which would provide assistance to the needy outside the realm of state action.

Moving into the twentieth century, Latin American societies and economies began to modernize, and with these changes, new groups in civil society began to develop that organized people in much greater numbers than ever. In Latin America's growing cities and in the countryside, labor unions and peasant groups organized to demand better working and living conditions from more powerful groups. Such demands put the state in a difficult political position. It could meet those demands with the power it had to legislate changes to benefit the lower classes. But if it did this, it would alienate the powerful landed elite and emerging entrepreneurial, urban classes that helped keep in power those individuals who controlled government. In some cases, when demands were not met, revolution resulted. In others, military dictatorships took over the state in order to maintain order. In yet other cases, populist governments attempted to please both the elite and the poor by supporting the development of the civil society sector in a way that allowed government to control the demands such groups could make on the state and on the elite. From the Cold War through the early to mid-1980s, many Latin American countries, often with material and ideological support from the U.S. government, were ruled by military dictatorships that brutally repressed any type of non-state-sponsored organizations. Universities, unions, political parties, and other organizations were no longer avenues for people to attempt to work toward change.

During the time of the authoritarian regimes, the only non-state-sponsored organization that continued to develop its works among underprivileged classes was the Catholic Church. After having been aligned so often with the interests of the elite and state in Latin America, many in the Catholic Church spurred a new theological movement in the 1960s and 1970s called Liberation Theology. This had a profound impact on the subsequent development of NGOs in Latin America, because for the first time, the Church worked to organize people outside of the direct control of Rome and even of the diocese and local churches. Liberation Theology was a movement to use the teachings of Christ and the Bible to motivate the poor and oppressed of Latin America to rise up, organize, and address their need for basic human rights and a more secure livelihood. (The feature film *Romero*, starring Raul Julia, is a classic depiction of the life of Oscar Romero, an El Salvadoran priest who advocated Liberation Theology and was assassinated in 1980.) Though it was an overarching ideology, it was markedly decentralized in that what actions were dictated to improve peoples' lives did not come down from authoritative figures at some national level, but rather the ideology itself was designed to encourage each group (known as Christian Base Communities—Comunidades Eclesiasticas de Base, or CEBs) to address their problems in their own particular way. Liberation theology was also infused with a strong element of Marxist revolutionary thinking. Thus, Latin American intellectuals influenced by the Marxism of the time had much sympathy for these Church-related movements. Liberation Theology was a motivating ideology that allowed poor people to create local-scale organizations to gain a greater influence over the course of their own lives.

What was happening not just in Latin America but also around the world in the 1980s and 1990s set the stage for an explosion in the growth of NGOs in the most recent past. Internationally, since the 1970s, growth in the difference between rich and poor between and within nations and growing alarm over environmental degradation have precipitated the convening of numerous international government-level meetings to assess the state of the world and proposals for its improvement. Amid the problems of acid rain, global warming, holes in the ozone layer, and extinction crises wherever tropical forests were falling, it became very clear that the forces of "modern" development were raising questions of social and environmental justice in development. The massive social and environmental harm done by national-scale, planned megadevelopment projects both in Latin America and around the world actually helped force greater demands for ordinary citizens to be involved more directly in the way development was practiced. The very scale and intensity of development projects like dam building and agricultural colonization in rain forests elicited an unprecedented campaign by concerned citizens around the world to stop the resulting environmental destruction. These development projects were obvious and shocking evidence of violations of basic rights and interests of poor, rural peoples. One of the most well publicized and galvanizing development failures was that of the series of colonization projects that took place in the Brazilian Amazon during Brazil's military dictatorship in the 1970s and 1980s. Designed to bring the distant Amazon within the national economic sphere, development projects involving billions of dollars constructed roads through the jungle and settled peasant farmers from more densely populated regions. Tax incentives given to large companies resulted in conversion of enormous areas of rainforest land into cattle ranches. Illegal gold mining, logging, and occupation of indigenous lands resulted as well, leading to high deforestation rates and predictions that the Amazon forest would be destroyed by the year 2000. As part of the response by civil society to this destruction, rubber tappers of the Amazon began to organize unions to demand their forestlands be protected from development. Their leader, Chico Mendes, was assassinated by cattle ranchers who were threatened by Mendes's successful organizing efforts and the great amount of attention he was drawing from very sympathetic environmental and human rights organizers from Brazil and around the world. His death in 1988 inspired a feature film (again starring Raul Julia) documenting his struggle to preserve the rubber tappers' way of life.

In Latin America and around the world, the 1980s and 1990s brought the rise of democratic governments and with them the political space needed for the participation of ordinary citizens in carrying out processes like development. This democratization gave increased legitimacy to an organized civil society making demands on government as Chico Mendes had done in Brazil. The problem was that these demands were being made when the state had little revenue to meet those demands. Latin America was in the midst of a serious debt crisis, a situation resulting from the fact that the governments of the past, mostly authoritarian, had borrowed so much money to fund development programs like the Amazonian development projects that newly formed democracies were forced to pay out huge percentages of the country's gross domestic product merely to pay the interest on its loans. If countries were to spend money to improve the lives of citizens, they would have to borrow more money. Here, the interests of multilateral agencies like the World Bank, the International Monetary Fund (IMF), and governments converged. States needed money, and lending agencies like the World Bank needed a way to increase their legitimacy as an organization concerned about helping the poor directly in a socially and environmentally sound way. A new ideology in development helped provide the final circumstance in Latin America that would help propel NGOs to their level of prominence in society today: neoliberalism.

The rise of neoliberalism in development theory and policy has had tremendous implications for the formation and strengthening of NGOs. Amid the economic recession and debt crisis of the early 1980s, it was clear to policymakers that the state-directed import substitution industrialization (ISI) model of development had failed. The state was also seen as an inefficient institution that could not be relied on to raise the capital needed to improve society. As a result, the World Bank and the IMF forced indebted countries wanting to borrow more money to implement structural adjustment programs (SAPs). These programs embraced the power of a trimmed-down state, privatized industries and services, and overall freed markets to contribute toward export-oriented economic growth that would generate the income required to pay off debt. By the end of the 1980s, these programs had been adopted by most indebted Third World nations. With state expenditures slashed, even less money remained in state coffers for social, health, and environmental programs. (For a study showing that trade openness is not necessarily related to decreased spending on social programs, see Avelino et al., 2005) This is where NGOs come to the fore in their most recent form. Some form of human organization had to fill the gap left by the relative weakening of the state and entrance of the logic of global market capitalism to Latin America. NGOs would enter the stage as local, regional, national, and international forms of human organization given at least modest recognition by the state and the market as independent "players" that now had to be given some level of consideration in efforts to improve people's lives and livelihoods.

CASE STUDY:
THE ASSOCIATIONAL REVOLUTION, THE POLITICS OF SCALE, AND PEOPLE'S EFFORTS TO IMPROVE LIFE IN BOLIVIA

This section is a case study of water resource management in Bolivia. It is designed to show how the politics of scale literature can be used to examine the outcome of an associational revolution in a particular Latin American country. The purpose here is not simply to list the names and locations of a few organizations and list some of their characteristics and activities over the years with respect to water resource management. The point is to show that these organizations are what they are today because of how they developed within a larger political, economic, and ecological context. As they developed, their interests and tactics may have changed as they came to relate to other more powerful or less powerful interests. Moreover, although the groups mentioned in the case study could be classified as NGOs, the outcomes of their activities for both people and the environment may or may not be good.

Bolivia today retains a very high level of indigenous identity among its peoples. The vast majority of indigenous peoples are part of the Aymara and Quechua groups, whose livelihoods are centered in Bolivia's Andean highlands. Dozens of other indigenous groups are located in Bolivia's lowland areas in the east. Together, they form the majority of the country's population. Mestizos, however, who are more educated, more connected to global consumer culture, and more economically powerful, have always held most of Bolivia's political power over the years. As will be seen, however, this power has been challenged over the years, and will be challenged as individuals representing Bolivia's indigenous peoples gain significant levels of power.

Bolivia's economic development, as is the case in many Latin American countries, has been geared toward supplying international markets with a select few export products, namely tin and natural gas. Having an economy so reliant on a few export products has caused wide economic fluctuations as world prices for commodities change drastically over time. Exporting raw materials like this does not lead toward stable jobs or an even distribution of wealth that is necessary for the development of a strong internal economy. Tin exports, for example, used to make up approximately 50 percent of Bolivia's legal export income (I say "legal" because Bolivia is also a major exporter of coca/cocaine). When tin prices crashed in 1985, it created a crisis, since thousands of Bolivia's poor were employed by the mining industry. The event brought dramatic changes for the political economic organization of the country. Bolivia adopted an economic plan that forced the beginning of privatization of state-owned industries, including in the mining sector. A shrinking economy and cuts in social services by the state left Bolivia's poor, mostly indigenous peoples, without a state or market they could rely on to improve their circumstances. Up to 1985, the Central Obrera Boliviano (COB—the nation's central union organization) derived its power from mining's central importance in the country's economy and its huge membership. Not only miners were organized under the COB umbrella. Numerous other interest groups, from rural peasant unions to organizations of indigenous peoples, were part of the COB. Up until the tin crash, tin production was centrally, nationally organized and operated, and as so central to society, the labor union representing miners ended up representing numerous other groups in a nationally organized labor movement.

The national scale of production and union activity would change with the tin crash. The COB's organizing capability was severely limited once miners lost their economic power. Privatization of the mining industry and other sectors left workers with management structures that could operate without any promises or concerns about the collective well-being of workers nationally. Other groups in society began to feel that their interests would be better served if they were not organized nationally in the way the COB had been for so long. Some groups maintained a national-level organization but separated themselves from other sectors of society to fight for their particular concerns. Others began to decentralize their organizations, operating more regionally and locally than before. In short, Bolivia entered a period after 1985 in which the dominant scale of the economy and of NGOs began to be challenged by neoliberalism, leading NGOs to strategize new scales of organization that could help them achieve their goals.

The management of water as a resource is especially interesting to study given that the scale of its management has much to do with the meaning it has in people's lives. One geographer who has written much about water resource management in Bolivia, Thomas Perreault, illustrates a number of points from our discussion above in a case study of water management in rural areas (Perreault, 2005). By studying water use governance, Perreault is dealing with one of the very substances that supports us as natural organisms—one cannot survive without it—and who gets access to it and how that access is governed are all related to political economic circumstances in local, national, and international arenas. Scale politics is a major way in which Perreault interprets the struggle NGOs, the state, and private capitalist interests are having over water governance.

The political economic logic of leaders during the 1980s and 1990s was to remove the command-and-control jurisdiction the state had over resources in the country and to decentralize operations to the local, municipal level. The outcome for water management was extremely complicated, and it left water users—both urban poor and rural peasants and irrigators—in a position in which they had to organize to fight to retain their access to water resources on their own terms. The outcome in rural areas showed this complexity well. Under laws passed in 1994, individual municipalities were put in charge of establishing and maintaining irrigation systems, and they had authority over the use and monitoring of springs and streams. These laws were in conflict with others that had already established central state control over rights to water use. Under such conflicting laws, both local peasants and transnational corporations interested in investing in water systems could make claims on water. Moreover, no single law governed water use in Bolivia. Rather, each sector of the economy that relied on water (mining, agriculture, industry, households) had its own rules that put members of each of these sectors in competition with one another for this precious resource. Efforts to correct this confusing situation included laws in the late 1990s and early 2000s to reassert national-level control over water resource management. While rights to water for indigenous peoples and rural peasants are guaranteed in the law, the law still did not address the competing claims that other sectors of the economy have on water, and so indigenous peoples and peasant irrigators felt that the national-level superintendent of water, heavily influenced by and sympathetic to the goals of neoliberalism, would favor those sectors—mining and export agriculture—that generated export income for Bolivia to make payments on its large foreign debt. While centralizing authority over water like this does not match the typical neoliberal approach, it did end up facilitating the achievement of another important goal—the privatization of water provision—which occured in La Paz and El Alto in 1997. Private interests attempted to take over water resource management in Cochabamba and Potosí, but these efforts met with great protest, much of it organized by NGOs, and privatization efforts there eventually failed.

Rural peasant irrigator NGOs, meanwhile, began to organize in ways like never before to fight for their rights to water in the midst of this confusing politics of decentralization and then recentralization of water resource management. Amid all this politics of water, it was very difficult for them to implement and codify the most important organizing principle in their water management, something called *usos y costumbres* (customary uses). These uses are important to peasant irrigators. They differ greatly from place to place, since they are based on tradition, local knowledge, and local environmental conditions. As such, these practices help form a part of the identity of each particular group. When irrigator NGOs from across the country met in Bolivia in 2001, their challenge was to find a way to get national, legal recognition for *usos y costumbres*, practices that differ greatly from place to place. They made an important step toward this by engaging in a complicated politics of scale of their own. Locally organized NGOs were made aware of these national-level issues about water resource management by umbrella NGOs and Bolivian intellectuals. Those larger-scale organizations were in turn advised and funded by NGOs that operate at the international scale. In short, the irrigator NGOs organized nationally and internationally for the very first time in order to counter the Bolivian state's own centralization/internationalization privatization project. Rather than remain only locally organized, the irrigator NGOs now brought their numbers, their shared knowledge, and the help of national- and international-level NGOs to thwart the power of the state and internationally organized capital. The catchphrase for such changing of scale from local to higher levels has been "scaling up." The new organization that arose from this politics of scale was the National Association of Irrigators and Community Drinking Water Systems. The new organization pushes for national, legal recognition of local, traditional water management rights and practices. Moreover, for the first time, the irrigators and rural households have a chance to compete officially for access to water with more powerful economic sectors.

At this writing, we are only a few years since the formation of the new national-level irrigators' organization, and it remains to be seen how successful the group is at achieving its goal under the continued pressure of neoliberalism. Moreover, Evo Morales, an indigenous politician, has recently become Bolivia's president. His "Movement Toward Socialism" political group and others who are against neoliberalism are working quickly to reverse many neoliberal reforms by strenghthening the power of the national scale in important areas of investment. Most importantly, he announced the nationalization of Bolivia's natural gas and oil industry, and he appears extremely sympathetic to the water resource management issues in urban and rural areas that have plagued Bolivia in recent decades. In some respects, he has attempted to strengthen central government control over water provision and management, no better demonstrated than his creation in January 2006 of a central Ministry of Water. With this ministry, Morales is attempting to strengthen national sovereignty over water provision and management, which was threatened by the privatization attempts of the 1990s. Like the efforts of the irrigators mentioned above, Morales's efforts will have to balance creating this national scale of control with the desire to be attentive to the particular water needs one finds in local areas across Bolivia. While Morales wants everyone to see access to water as a basic human right as part of a national project, the various interests at play (city dwellers, industry, rural irrigators, for example) will no doubt marshall their own scales of organization to respond to Morales's efforts to control this essential resource for the future of Bolivia as a whole.

CONCLUSION

NGOs have attracted the attention of academics interested in understanding changes in society and how it is structured to provide people with the things they need to survive. While not always clear what is and what is not considered an NGO, they tend to be formal institutions that work outside the two dominant institutions that have organized people's lives in recent history, the state and the market. NGOs have their roots in pre-Columbian civilizations, before the modern state and market were ever in existence (though they certainly were not called that), and they have and will continue to evolve as NGOs both create and react to changes in political economic circumstances. NGOs are not always locally organized groups of people, nor are they always large, regional, national, or international groups. That's where scale comes in. People will operate at whatever scale necessary, even a combination of local and global scales, to accomplish their goals and projects. In the case of peasant irrigators in Bolivia, locally organized NGOs eventually "scaled up" their efforts to include national- and international-level organizations to ensure their access to water in the countryside. Latin America has a deep history of people organizing in one way or another to ensure social justice. Studying how NGOs respond to the challenges presented by the state and neoliberal capitalism reveals much about how ordinary citizens confront the complexities of everyday life in an age of globalization.

SUGGESTED WEBSITES

Johns Hopkins Institute for Policy Studies, Center for Civil Society Studies conducts numerous ongoing research projects on the nonprofit sector around the world. Their publications and reports can be browsed at: http://www.jhu.edu/~ccss/.

The World Bank in recent years has made nearly all of its reports and publications available to the public through its website, which contains a wealth of information on bank involvement with NGOs and civil society. You can browse for publications from their main page: http://www.worldbank.org/.

The North American Congress on Latin America publishes articles dealing with a wide variety of political, economic, and ecological issues in Latin America, including the water resource issues in Bolivia mentioned above. You can browse through articles and issues at their website: http://www.nacla.org.

SUGGESTED READINGS

Bebbington, A., and G. Thiele. *Non-Governmental Organizations and the State in Latin America: Rethinking Roles in Sustainable Agricultural Development.* London, New York: Routledge, 1993.

Carroll, T. F. *Intermediary NGOs: The Supporting Link in Grassroots Development.* West Hartford, Conn.: Kumarian Press, 1992.

Farrington, J., and A. Bebbington. *Reluctant Partners? Non-Governmental Organizations, the State and Sustainable Agricultural Development.* London, New York: Routledge, 1993.

BIBLIOGRAPHY

Agnew, J. "The Territorial Trap: The Geographical Assumptions of International Relations Theory." *Review of International Political Economy* 1, no. 1 (1994): 53–80.

Avelino, G., D. S. Brown, and W. Hunter. "The Effects of Capital Mobility, Trade
Openness, and Democracy on Social Spending in Latin America, 1980–1999."
American Journal of Political Science 49, no. 3 (2005): 625–641.

Bebbington, A., and J. Farrington. *The Scope for NGO-Government Interaction in Agricultural Technology Development: An International Overview.* London: Agricultural
Administration (Research and Extension) Network, Overseas Development Institute, 1992.

Brown, D. S., J. C. Brown, and S. W. Desposato. "Left Turn on Green? The Unin-
tended Consequences of International Funding for Sustainable Development in
Brazil." *Comparative Political Studies* 35, no. 7 (2002): 814–838.

Brown, J. C., and M. Purcell. "There's Nothing Inherent about Scale: Political Ecology, the Local Trap, and the Politics of Development in the Brazilian Amazon."
Geoforum 36, no. 5 (2005): 607–624.

Economist. "Sins of the Secular Missionaries." January 29, 2000.

Keck, M. E., and K. Sikkink. *Activists beyond Borders: Advocacy Networks in International
Politics.* Ithaca, N.Y.: Cornell University Press, 1998.

Perreault, T. "State Restructuring and the Scale Politics of Rural Water Governance in
Bolivia." *Environment and Planning A* 37, no. 2 (2005): 263–284.

Purcell, M., and J. C. Brown. "Against the Local Trap: Scale and the Study of Environment and Development." *Progress in Development Studies* 5, no. 4 (2005):
279–297.

Salamon, L. M. "The Rise of the Nonprofit Sector." *Foreign Affairs*, July/August 1994,
109–122.

Salamon, L. M., and H. K. Anheier. *The Emerging Sector Revisited.* Baltimore: Johns
Hopkins Center for Civil Society Studies, 1999.

Salamon, L. M., H. K. Anheier, R. List, S. Toepler, and S. Wojciech Sokolowski and
Associates. *Global Civil Society: Dimensions of the Nonprofit Sector.* Baltimore: Johns
Hopkins Center for Civil Society Studies, 1999.

Vakil, A. C. "Confronting the Classification Problem: Toward a Taxonomy of
NGOs." *World Development* 25, no. 12 (1997): 2057–2070.

World Bank. "The World Bank, NGOs and Civil Society." Washington, D.C.: World
Bank Group, 2000.

10

The Geographies of Latin American Social Movements

Fernando J. Bosco

As Latin America entered a new millennium, social movements continued or even increased their activism in the region. Latin America's civil society is dynamic and in a constant state of mobilization, with diverse groups ranging from human rights activists and poor people's movements to different ethnic, racial, and cultural minorities challenging the institutions of the nation-state and making claims for economic gains and cultural and political recognition. This chapter provides an overview of such contemporary Latin American social movements. The focus is on the *mobilization strategies* of activists, that is, on how social movements come and stay together, how social movements organize their activities and their strategies for recognition and visibility, and how social movements connect and network with each other to build coalitions across space-time. The focus is also on the *geographies* of social movements in Latin America. The chapter explicitly addresses the ways in which places (cities, neighborhoods, public spaces in cities) and events occurring at different geographic scales (local, regional, national, and transnational) play a crucial role in the mobilization of Latin American social movements. This perspective is important because it highlights the difference that thinking geographically makes in the understanding of social and political events that are often interpreted in nongeographic ways.

Human geographers have already argued that social movements do not operate on the head of a pin (Miller, 2000). Rather, their activities unfold in real places; often, the effectiveness of social movements' public actions depends on their visibility in specific places. For example, meeting points in public spaces in cities (such as parks and streets) provide an arena and stage for organization of activism (Mitchell, 2003). Moreover, activists often build transnational networks that transcend formal geographic boundaries to enhance their possibilities for success (Bosco, 2001). The Internet provides a medium for such transnational connections, but so do the friendships and emotional connections that people develop over time (Bosco, 2007). And, again, those friendships and emotional attachments develop in specific places at particular times (in a sit-in demonstration in a plaza, in a demonstration across a city, at a picket line, and so on) (Bosco, 2006).

Keeping these ideas in mind, the goal of this chapter is to make connections between established geographic thinking and theorizing on collective action and existing accounts of the activism of Latin American social movements. The discussion in this chapter is informed by making reference to actual practices of collective action in Latin America, such as the activities of human rights movements in Argentina, Chile, Guatemala, and beyond, movements of urban unemployed and rural landless people in Brazil, indigenous movements seeking economic and political recognition in Bolivia, Colombia, Guatemala, and Ecuador, and other groups seeking cultural gains in the largest urban areas in Latin America.

It is not possible to cover all of the social movements currently active in the region. Rather, through the examination of some specific cases, this chapter works as an analytical tool to help interpret other forms of collective action from a geographic perspective. The chapter also presents a unique view on the way social movements claim spaces in the city by offering a section called "Notes from the Field," which describes the geographic dimensions of women's human rights activism in Argentina. Finally, the discussion in this chapter complements the other discussions of activism presented in chapter 9 and chapter 11. Together, these three chapters provide an overview of the political geographies of civil society in Latin America.

DEFINING AND CONTEXTUALIZING
LATIN AMERICAN SOCIAL MOVEMENTS

A recent report on the current social, political, and economic state of Latin America explained that one of the major tensions facing the region is "that between the included and the excluded—those who can regularly participate in the formal institutions of society, politics and the economy, and those who are able to do so only intermittently, or not at all" (NACLA, 2005). The binary of inclusion/exclusion is at the crux of the formation of Latin American social movements. Indeed, this issue is at the core of what defines social movements as such, because social movements often involve people engaged in noninstitutionalized discourses and practices designed to challenge and change society as they define it (Garner, 1996).

It is easy to apply this definition to contemporary social movements in Latin America. For example, excluded and disempowered groups of indigenous peasants in many Andean countries, such as Bolivia, Ecuador, Colombia, and Brazil, have been at the forefront of social mobilization in South America. The participants in these movements are attempting to change society because they feel that current economic, social, and political structures in line with neoliberalism (see chapters 1 and 2) benefit only a few people at the expense of the majority.

In the case of Bolivian social movements, the struggles of recent years have been over access to important resources such as natural gas and oil and over the rights to economic benefits that would come out of their sale to foreign multinational corporations. Specifically, activists oppose foreign exploitation of natural resources and would prefer that more of the benefits generated by the sale of resources such as natural gas and oil would go toward improving the lives of ordinary Bolivians (see also chapters 9 and 11 on the issue of Bolivian "water wars" and environmental politics more generally). Because activists feel that they have no true representation in the formal institutions of the state, they attempt to bring about change by getting involved in noninstitutionalized practices, such as coordinated blocking of roads and massive mobilizations of peasants in the streets, among other strategies of resistance. Activists hope that these practices will force the government to pay attention to their plight and consider them active participants in economic decisions that shape the future distribution of benefits in the country. The relation between access to natural resources and grassroots mobilizations has become an important part of the landscape of activism in Latin America. This kind of struggle is now often identified as an issue of "resource nationalism."

The broad definition of social movements provided above can be applied and made relevant to concrete situations such as the struggle of Bolivian peasants. But the binary of inclusion/exclusion and the noninstitutionalized practices that social movements follow in an attempt to alter their members' livelihoods are not necessarily circumscribed to the economic realm, as might have been implied by the example of the struggle for access to resources mentioned above. On the contrary, many of the current struggles of social movements in Latin America can be defined as involving *cultural politics*. Cultural politics are processes enacted when sets of social actors shaped by, and embodying, different cultural meanings and practices come into conflict with each other. Meanings and practices often considered marginal or residual in relation to a dominant cultural order can become the sources of political processes. For example, social movements that talk about alternative conceptions of democracy, justice, nature, and citizenship enact a cultural politics because the meanings that they attach to those concepts seek to redefine social power in either explicit or implicit ways (Alvarez, Dagnino, and Escobar, 1998:7).

The case of a broad "Pan Mayan" movement that has operated in Guatemala since the mid-1980s is a good example of a social movement that has organized and mobilized in an attempt to make visible important cultural and ethnic identities. Led by well-educated Mayan people including lawyers, teachers, development workers, linguists, and social scientists, the explicit goal of the movement has been to undermine the authoritativeness of non-Mayan accounts that dominate portrayals of the Mayan culture (Warren, 1998). In an attempt to reverse this situation, the movement has concentrated its efforts on the promotion and revitalization of Mayan language, revitalization of chronicles of culture and history of Mayan resistance in school texts, and the promotion of Mayan forms of leadership. One of the most interesting dimensions of this cultural politics has been the use of indigenous religion to subvert dominant themes of Catholicism in contemporary Guatemala (Warren, 1998).

There are many other examples of Latin American social movements that fit the formal definition provided above, and whose struggles also revolve around both issues of distribution/economy and issues of inclusion/cultural politics. Rather than providing more examples, the remainder of this chapter will focus on explaining how the struggles of social movements in Latin America are geographic and how their effectiveness and/or failure often also depends on geographic dimensions, such as the way in which activists mobilize in places, build networks across space, and act collectively across many geographic scales simultaneously.

LATIN AMERICAN SOCIAL MOVEMENTS AND THE IMPORTANCE OF PLACE

The struggles and the identities of resistance are often borne locally through activists' sense and experience of place (Pile and Keith, 1997). Many Latin American social movements mobilize because of attachments to place or territory, in many cases because their existence is tied to their ability to claim land or a place that they can call their own.

One relevant, contemporary example that illustrates the connection between place and social movement mobilization is the Movement of Rural Landless Workers, or MST (Movimento dos Trabalhadores Rurais Sem Terra) in Brazil. The movement began in the southern Brazilian states of Rio Grande do Sul and Santa Catarina in 1984, but has now expanded to 22 of 26 Brazilian states (Wolford, 2004). Set in the context of poor rural and urban areas, the movement's main strategy has involved the occupation of "unproductive" lands. The explicit goal of the movement is to obtain rights to property, and to secure land for those who actually work it. Over the years, the movement has been involved in over 23,000 occupations and created about 1,000 settlements. On April 17, 1997, over 50,000 people loosely affiliated with the MST marched and demonstrated in Brasilia, giving visibility to the largest grassroots social movement in Brazil's history (Wolford, 2004). Over 20 years later, the movement keeps demanding of the government further rights to property for an increasingly landless population in Brazil. In May 2005, the movement conducted a mass mobilization to the Brazilian capital, where they met the president to persuade him to accelerate the conversion of "unproductive" and empty lands to lands that can be settled by peasants to improve their livelihoods.

Other Latin American social movements involved in cultural politics (as explained in the previous section) are also involved in a very active politics of place. Often, for social movements, "being" and "having a place to be" are difficult to separate. This is a dimension of activism that demonstrates the intrinsic place-based nature of many social movements' struggles. For example, Colombia's broad "Black Movement" (another movement that seeks ethnic recognition) has tied its struggle for inclusion to simultaneous claims for territory. People who live in the forested areas along Colombia's Pacific coast have long been demanding integration into Colombian society *and* recognition as an ethnic group (e.g., the right to be "black") in conjunction with demands for rights to a territory (e.g., right to space for being) (Grueso, Rosero, and Escobar, 1998). Recent research on the sociopolitical organizational structure of these communities has also shown that there is an "aquatic space" (as opposed to artificial political boundaries) that is the method of organization for black and indigenous populations living in the river basins and deltas throughout the region. This aquatic space is a set of spatialized social relationships among Afro-Colombians that not only facilitates political organization but is also the foundation for their organization and mobilization (Oslander, 2004).

Geographers also have argued that a social movement's sense and experience of place entails much more than location. Sense of place is about the complex interplay of processes in a context that may or may not be geographically circumscribed. Especially in the case of social movements that are spread across space, a sense of place can be symbolic. A symbolic sense of place for a social movement refers to its "home," a common meeting ground that is associated with a spatial imaginary (Ettlinger and Bosco, 2004). One of the best documented examples of the relation between a Latin American social movement and a symbolic sense of place is the case of the Madres de Plaza de Mayo in Argentina (Bosco, 2001; Bosco, 2004). The Madres de Plaza de Mayo began meeting in the Plaza de Mayo in downtown Buenos Aires (figure 10.1) in 1977 as a local group of a few women searching for their missing sons and daughters who had been kidnapped by the government. The Madres got together with (and actively recruited) more women like them, and by 1984, there were 21 groups of Madres de Plaza de Mayo across Argentina. And as women had done first in the Plaza de Mayo, many mothers of the disappeared started to conduct public demonstrations

Figure 10.1.   The Plaza de Mayo in downtown Buenos Aires, Argentina.

in the main plazas of their cities at the same day and time as the original group in Buenos Aires.

These original meetings of women in the plazas later became a collective ritual that united members and proved important for the survival of the overall movement of mothers of the disappeared in Argentina. Even today, three decades later, the Madres' weekly public meetings and marches still take place, every Thursday at 3:30 in the Plaza de Mayo and in public plazas across Argentina (figure 10.2). Over the years, the Madres' half-hour silent march around the obelisk in the center of the Plaza de Mayo in downtown Buenos Aires has become their signature public display of activism. Even though much has changed since the first time the Madres met in the Plaza de Mayo in 1977, the plaza remains a central symbolic gathering place for the Madres' movement. For the Madres de Plaza de Mayo, being in the plaza at a specific day and time knowing that other women like them are doing exactly the same in many other different places is a way to reinforce their feeling of membership in the social movement. Moreover, the plazas (irrespective of location, including plazas in other countries and continents!) have represented sites of resistance, recruitment, solidarity, and conflict resolution for the Madres (Bosco, 2004).

The case of the Madres de Plaza de Mayo in Argentina demonstrates how, for many Latin American social movements, the survival and continuity of activism is inextricably tied to places and to the creation of a symbolic sense of place (see next section, "Notes from the Field"). The practice of these collective rituals shows that, in the case of the Madres, activist bonds are not encouraged by proximity to one location but rather by a socially

Figure 10.2.   The Madres de Plaza de Mayo in the city of La Plata during one of their weekly marches.

constructed symbolic proximity based on the group's identification with a particular place (see "Notes from the Field"). The type of activism started by the Madres de Plaza de Mayo in Argentina in the 1970s continues through another movement of mothers of disappeared people that has been active in the border city of Ciudad Juarez, Mexico, since the late 1990s (see chapter 5). The mothers' movement in Ciudad Juarez is another excellent example of a social movement that has used the marking of symbolic places in the city as a strategy for movement visibility and survival.

NOTES FROM THE FIELD

The Madres de Plaza de Mayo and Their Sense of Place

It is a sunny afternoon at the end of September. I am in the Plaza de Mayo in downtown Buenos Aires waiting for the Madres, who, according to my information, should arrive in about a half hour. I look down to the ground and I see the emblems of the Madres de Plaza de Mayo painted on the ground: carefully drawn white headscarves form a perfect circle in the center of the plaza, reminding me of the circular silent marches that the Madres de Plaza de Mayo perform every Thursday here. Around the headscarves, I recognize other drawings on the ground. They are the white silhouettes of people that represent the disappeared.

I look around the plaza and I realize that the government in Argentina is very much concerned with the control of this space. I look toward the Casa Rosada (the seat of the executive power in Argentina) from the center of the plaza and I notice a heavy crowd-control fence that splits the Plaza de Mayo in two. I ask a man sitting on a bench if he knows why the fence is there. His answer is simple: "It is because they are afraid of the people." He is right. A few days ago, I had witnessed a large demonstration of workers and unions in the plaza. The fence had been placed to stop the crowd from getting too close to the Casa Rosada and to help police have more control of the situation. Suddenly, at about 2:45 PM, I see a group of city workers rushing down the plaza toward the fence. They quickly start to take it apart. I realize that the fence is partly over the empty circular space where the Madres walk every Thursday. If the fence were to stay, it would prevent the Madres from completing their many silent circles in the plaza. I wonder, then, whether the quick removal of the fence on this particular day and time has anything to do with the Madres' weekly walks. Since the Madres' walks have been taking place for over two decades and are publicly known, I suspect that the city, the police, and the government in general do not want to be seen as preventing the Madres from walking in the plaza. I am sitting on a bench next to the man to whom I have been talking for the last 15 minutes, and I ask him if he knows why there is such a rush in taking the fence down and moving it. He looks at me and replies: "The Madres are coming."

At 3 PM, I see a group of women emerging from one of the subway stations located under the Plaza de Mayo. From different directions in the plaza, I see other groups of women walking slowly along the paths toward the center. Two women stop to talk to the city workers who are removing the fence. They cordially smile at them and exchange a few words. I hear the men reassuring the women that the fence will be completely taken apart in a matter of minutes. I then realize that something has changed about the way the space of this plaza is controlled since the Madres became active. Whereas the police attempt to control other popular demonstrations in the Plaza de Mayo by dividing the space and making it difficult to navigate, the presence of a small group of older women prompts the opening of the plaza and the removal of any obstacles. The women get together in the center of the plaza and I see them smile, hug each other, kiss, and hold hands. They seem incredibly happy to be out here, some of them very emotional. They slowly start walking in small groups. Thirty years ago, the Madres de Plaza de Mayo left their homes, went out to the streets, and through constant resistance, claimed, reclaimed, and finally constructed the small circular space in the center of the Plaza de Mayo as their own. And they are here again today, three decades later. (Field notes by Fernando J. Bosco, Buenos Aires, September 2000.)

LATIN AMERICAN SOCIAL MOVEMENTS AND NETWORKS ACROSS GEOGRAPHIC SCALES

The symbolic sense of place that social movements build does not have to be *necessarily* associated with a material place. For example, a social movement attempting to mobilize members through the Internet might also utilize a symbolic sense of place, since particular locations in cyberspace (websites, for example) often act as homes for networks of activists in different locations. The use of the Internet by social movements relates to the mobilization of activists across space through the creation of networks. It also relates to social movements' sense of space and to their mobilization across geographic scales.

The strategic use of place and a sense of place are critical to most social movements in Latin America. However, equally important to a social movement is a sense of space and its spatial arenas of operation or potential operation. As we have indicated, although networks of resistance are rooted in places, they are not necessarily local. Social movements and activism in general are seen as "networks of networks" (Diani and McAdam, 2003) and as intricate webs of social relations constituted by shared practices between individual activists and formal and informal organizations, embedded in places and also operating across space in multiscalar political action. Scholars have already shown that whereas the politics of resistance are often organized around place-specific struggles, what also gets diffused and organized across space is the "common ground" shared by different groups—often the result of groups' entangled interests (Routledge, 2000:27). These entangled interests and common ground is what scholars typically refer to when they talk about social movement networks that group individuals and groups of activists in many places (across scales) simultaneously. Geographers pay attention to the effects of geographic scale in the mobilizing strategies of social movements. For example, it is now commonly argued that the effective mobilization of activists often requires "scaling up"—making connections outside of the local, creating transnational webs—or even developing "multiscalar" strategies of collective action (Cox, 1998; Castree, 2001) (see chapter 9 for an explanation of the politics of scale).

There are many examples of these strategies of networking across scales in Latin American social movements. During the process of Chilean democratization, the women's movement in Chile was enlarged and supported by activists who formed new networks of nongovernmental organizations (NGOs) and grassroots organizations. The networks were national in scope but transcended the Chilean confines since many of the NGOs obtained funding from other European NGOs in countries such as Sweden (Schild, 1998).

The case of the Madres de Plaza de Mayo is again relevant here. To enlarge their capacity of mobilization and effectiveness, over the years the Madres expanded their networks across scales to reach the international arena. This geographic strategy to enlarge their networks was based on the Madres' strategic use of emotional bonds and images and discourses of motherhood to reach and connect with distant others. Other human rights activists created support groups for the Madres de Plaza de Mayo both in Argentina and abroad, in Europe, North America, and even Australia. In most cases, it was other activists who approached the Madres with ideas about the creation of support groups. The support groups, which gave logistical support to the network of Madres and helped disseminate the Madres' goals and message, were created on the basis of feelings of love and admiration for the mothers.

Many of the activists in these support groups explain their devotion to the Madres de Plaza de Mayo in emotional ways, talking about their love for the Madres de Plaza de Mayo as if they were their own biological mothers—perhaps even drawing from a broader cultural template of love and devotion for mothers that, if not universal, is at least typical in Latin America. The groups abroad maintain and reaffirm the emotional connections with the Madres (which gave rise to the support groups in the first place) by organizing local events in which they discuss the Madres' activism. In these events, supporters often talk about the Madres in heroic ways, expressing their admiration for these women and mobilizing local support by framing emotions in ways in which they resonate with particular audiences. Occasionally, one or more Madres de Plaza de Mayo are able to visit the support groups abroad, and the personal visits cement their emotional connections even further and ensure the continuity of the groups' activities (Bosco, 2006).

Other Latin American social movements have also networked across scales to enlarge their mobilization potential by relying on the communication and organization capacity provided by new communications technology such as the Internet. For example, the case of the Zapatista movement in southern Mexico has been widely cited as an example of the successful use of the Internet to connect the plight of excluded indigenous peasants to the networks of knowledge and power of academics and activists in the United States and other countries of the industrialized world. The Internet allowed the Zapatistas to gather support for their claims from abroad, thus forcing the government in Mexico (at the national and local level) to begin to seriously consider the movement's demands.

But Latin American social movements have not just used the Internet to coordinate the mobilization of previously existing activists and organization across scales, as was the case with the Zapatistas. In some cases, the Internet has allowed social movements to come together in the first place. The connections between the geographic arrangements of activism in relation to new communications technology is well represented by a network of human rights activists called H.I.J.O.S. The network of H.I.J.O.S. was first born in Argentina, but it is now transnational in scope thanks in part to the Internet. H.I.JO.S. is a grassroots collective started by the children of people who were "disappeared" (i.e., illegally kidnapped, tortured, and murdered in a systematic plan of state-sponsored terrorism) during Argentina's "dirty war" of the late 1970s (in some cases, the members of H.I.J.O.S. are grandchildren to members of the Madres de Plaza de Mayo). The name of the network, H.I.J.O.S., meaning "children" in Spanish, is also an acronym that stands for Hijos por la Identidad y la Justicia y contra el Olvido y el Silencio (Children for Identity and Justice and against Forgetting and Silence). As a transnational network, H.I.J.O.S. has evolved to include the sons and daughters, both in Argentina and abroad, of people who were disappeared in Argentina and in some other Latin American countries, as well as children of survivors of imprisonment and of those who fled their countries into exile (Bosco, 2007).

In Argentina, H.I.J.O.S. followed the same trajectory as the Madres de Plaza de Mayo, forming local groups that gathered in specific places such as plazas and parks, and recruiting others who shared the same grievances. Over the years, H.I.J.O.S. organized over 18 local chapters throughout Argentina, and the network continues to grow even today. One unanticipated effect of the formation of H.I.J.O.S. in Argentina was that the network expanded even more with the incorporation of the sons and daughters of disappeared people living in exile in Europe and other countries in Latin America. The same grievances that brought together H.I.J.O.S. in Argentina also allowed distant activists to begin communicating with one another, giving rise to a broad transnational network of H.I.J.O.S., with more than 16 chapters across Latin America and Europe. But in the case of the transnational network of H.I.J.O.S., coming together first did not mean meeting in a physical place like the Plaza de Mayo, or in collective gatherings in universities or other places to commemorate the disappeared, but rather gathering using the Internet. The Internet became a site of gathering for the network of H.I.J.O.S. in exile, and what generated that gathering was the need to find an outlet for their shared past experiences and grievances. For example, in many websites hosted around the world, members of H.I.J.O.S. (or HIJ@S, as they name themselves in cyberspace) began posting narratives describing their experiences of what it felt like to be a son or daughter of a disappeared person—regardless of one's physical location. Soon, through the Internet and personal contacts, the physical network of H.I.J.O.S. in Argentina became linked to the virtual network of H.I.J.O.S. around the world.

Interestingly, those participating in the virtual network felt the need to experience their activism in a more direct and personal way. So H.I.J.O.S.

abroad (in cities in Spain, in Sweden, in Mexico, for example) decided to follow the example of the H.I.J.O.S. network in Argentina and came together in retreats and gatherings in their respective locations. This was the beginning of the regional gatherings of different local groups of H.I.J.O.S. in each country, a practice that also continues today. Such regional gatherings have proved to be crucial for furthering the political and activist dimensions of the transnational network of H.I.J.O.S. These practices also demonstrate the relation between the transnational dimensions of activism and the importance of place for social movements.

In addition, the sons and daughters of disappeared people in other countries, who had never had an outlet for their grievances, have also used the Internet to get to know each other and form new activist networks. Recently, a new group of H.I.J.O.S. was formed in Guatemala, not by Argentines in exile but rather by sons and daughters of some of the more than 200,000 disappeared in Guatemala during the 1980s. The group in Guatemala adopted the same name as the transnational network of H.I.J.O.S. formed first in Argentina, giving rise to a truly transnational network of sons and daughters of disappeared people that transcends formal political boundaries and national identities and affiliations. In sum, the case of the transnational network of H.I.J.O.S. demonstrates how the formation and consolidation of some Latin American social movements has become dependent on the existence of communication technologies that have allowed people separated by large geographic distances to come together and organize collectively around specific goals.

CONCLUSION

The study of social movements has enjoyed a renaissance of sorts in the past two decades. Today, social movement studies is one of the most dynamic subdisciplines within contemporary sociology, political science, cultural anthropology, and even cultural studies, in addition to geography. In recent years, geographers interested in the study of activism in Latin America have made significant contributions to more geographic understandings of the activities of social movements and grassroots networks of activists in the region. This chapter has emphasized how geographic dimensions such as place and scale play a role in the mobilization of Latin American social movements. This chapter also highlighted the main dimensions along which one can analyze social movements from a geographic perspective. These two avenues can be summarized as follows. First, to understand the formation and duration of social movements, it is necessary to think and analyze activism in relation to places, both material and symbolic. Second, to understand the effectiveness and or failure of mobilization of activists, it is important to pay attention to how social movement and grassroots networks begin to adopt more global perspectives in their actions. This focus informed the last section of the chapter, and includes the analysis of the mobilization of transnational activists who are resisting the discourses and practices of global capitalism and attempting to find alternatives they believe to be more just and equitable.

In sum, a geographic analysis of Latin American social movements is concerned with understanding the spatialities of mobilization—that is, how social movements come together and how activists organize and build organizations and coalitions in place and across space. The geographic strategies of social movements certainly do not guarantee their success, but it is very difficult to understand how and why social movements fail and/or succeed in their action without paying attention to the role of geographic dimensions, whether these are explicitly part of the mobilization activities of social movements or not.

SUGGESTED READINGS

Alvarez, S., E. Dagnino, and A. Escobar, eds. *Cultures of Politics, Politics of Cultures: Re-visioning Latin American Social Movements*. Boulder, Colo.: Westview Press, 1998.

Bouvard Guzman, M. *Revolutionizing Motherhood: The Mothers of the Plaza de Mayo*. Wilmington, Del.: SR Books, 1994.

Eckstein, S., and M. Garreton Merino. *Power and Popular Protest: Latin American Social Movements*. Berkeley: University of California Press, 2001.

Scarpaci, Joseph L. "Primary-Care Decentralization in the Southern Cone: Shanty-town Health Care as Urban Social Movement." *Annals of the Association of American Geographers* 81, no. 1 (1991): 103–126.

Scarpaci, Joseph L., and Lessie Jo Frazier. "State Terror: Ideology, Protest, and the Gendering of Landscapes." *Progress in Human Geography* 17, no. 1 (1993): 1–21.

Stephen, L. *Women and Social Movements in Latin America: Power from Below*. Austin: University of Texas Press, 1997.

Warren, K., and J. Jackson, eds. *Indigenous Movements, Self-Representation, and the State in Latin America*. Austin: University of Texas Press, 2003.

BIBLIOGRAPHY

Alvarez, S., E. Dagnino, and A. Escobar, eds. *Cultures of Politics, Politics of Cultures: Re-visioning Latin American Social Movements*. Boulder, Colo.: Westview Press, 1998.

Bosco, F. "Place, Space, Networks and the Sustainability of Collective Action: The Madres de Plaza de Mayo." *Global Networks* 1, no. 4 (2001): 307–329.

Bosco, F. "Human Rights Politics and Scaled Performances of Memory: Conflicts among the Madres de Plaza de Mayo in Argentina." *Social and Cultural Geography* 5, no. 3 (2004): 381–402.

Bosco, F. "The Madres de Plaza de Mayo and Three Decades of Human Rights Activism: Embeddedness, Emotions and Social Movements." *Annals of the Association of American Geographers* 96, no. 2 (2006): 342–365.

Bosco, F. "Emotions That Build Networks: Geographies of Two Human Rights Movements in Argentina and Beyond." *Tijdschrift voor Economische en Sociale Geografie* 98, no. 5 (2007): 545–563.

Castree, N. "Geographic Scale and Grass-Roots Internationalism: The Liverpool Dock Dispute, 1995–1998." *Economic Geography* 76 (2001): 272–292.

Cox, K. "Spaces of Dependence, Spaces of Engagement and the Politics of Scale; or, Looking for Local Politics." *Political Geography* 17 (1998): 1–23.

Diani, M., and D. McAdam. *Social Movements and Networks: Relational Approaches to Collective Action.* New York: Oxford University Press, 2003.

Ettlinger, N., and F. Bosco. "Thinking through Networks and Their Spatiality: A Critique of the US (Public) War on Terrorism and Its Geographic Discourse." *Antipode* 36, no. 2 (2004): 249–271.

Garner, R. *Contemporary Movements and Ideologies.* New York: McGraw-Hill, 1996.

Grueso, L., C. Rosero, and A. Escobar. "The Process of Black Community Organizing in the Southern Pacific Coast Region of Colombia." In *Cultures of Politics, Politics of Cultures: Re-visioning Latin American Social Movements*, edited by S. Alvarez, E. Dagnino, and A. Escobar, pp. 196–219. Boulder, Colo: Westview Press, 1998.

Miller, B. *Geography and Social Movements.* Minneapolis: University of Minnesota Press, 2000.

Mitchell, D. *The Right to the City: Social Justice and the Fight for Public Space.* New York: Guilford Press, 2003.

NACLA (North American Congress on Latin America). "Social Movements: Building from the Ground Up." *NACLA Report on the Americas* 38 (2005): 5.

Oslander, U. "Fleshing Out the Geographies of Social Movements: Colombia's Pacific Coast Black Communities and the 'Aquatic Space.'" *Political Geography* 23 (2004): 957–985.

Pile, S., and M. Keith. *Geographies of Resistance.* London: Routledge, 1997.

Routledge, P. "'Our Resistance Will Be as Transnational as Capital': Convergence Space and Strategy in Globalizing Resistance." *Geojournal* 52 (2000): 25–33.

Schild, V. "New Subjects of Rights? Women's Movements and the Construction of Citizenship in the "New Democracies." In *Cultures of Politics, Politics of Cultures: Re-visioning Latin American Social Movements*, edited by S. Alvarez, E. Dagnino, and A. Escobar, pp. 93–117. Boulder, Colo.: Westview Press, 1998.

Warren, K. B. "Indigenous Movements as a Challenge to the Unified Social Movement Paradigm for Guatemala." In *Cultures of Politics, Politics of Cultures: Re-visioning Latin American Social Movements*, edited by S. Alvarez, E. Dagnino, and A. Escobar, pp. 165–195. Boulder, Colo.: Westview Press, 1998.

Wolford, W. "This Land Is Ours Now: Spatial Imaginaries and the Struggle for Land in Brazil." *Annals of the Association of American Geographers* 94, no. 2 (2004): 409–424.

11

Urban Environmental Politics in Latin America

Sarah A. Moore

Oaxaca de Juarez, in the southern Mexican state of Oaxaca, is a lovely destination for tourists, language students, and visitors of all ages and nationalities. It is also home to over 300,000 people and the center of an urban area whose population is almost 700,000. In March 2001, Oaxaca's dual roles as tourist destination and municipal area were put into sharp contrast when hundreds of tons of garbage began to pile up on the cobblestone sidewalks, in the urban parks, and against the colonial buildings. The area's one municipal dump had caught fire. This prompted residents who lived near it to block the access road in order to keep city garbage trucks from discharging their loads. These residents were upset at the city's inability to prevent fires at the site and the city's lack of compliance with earlier accords determining how the dump should be managed. The municipal government of Oaxaca was forced to suspend garbage collection and citizens and tourists alike were made to live with their own waste (see figure 11.1). This event and others like it have forced the city of Oaxaca to negotiate with neighborhood organizations, and with the state and federal governments, to change the way that municipal solid waste (MSW) is managed in the area.

These struggles over the management of MSW in the city of Oaxaca highlight a number of important common themes in urban environmental politics in Latin America. In discussing this and other case studies from the region, I will highlight three of these: 1) the ways in which the challenges of urban environmental management often lead to shifts in the responsibilities of governmental and nongovernmental entities; 2) the ways in which local populations have been able to shape urban ecologies through popular movements and protests; and 3) how conflicts over urban environments,

Figure 11.1.   Market area during a garbage crisis in Oaxaca.

in turn, play an important role in shaping local political identities. Before turning to these three points, though, it is necessary to define the major terms used in this chapter.

DEFINING THE URBAN ENVIRONMENT

Any discussion of environmental problems in the context of Latin American cities must begin with definitions of the terms "urban" and "environment." Rather than thinking of the city in terms of area—that is as a static, circumscribed place separate from "rural" area—it is useful to think of the urban as the result of a set of practices that creates what are identified as "urban" landscapes. This more dynamic view focuses on the ways that both institutions and citizens make and remake urban areas continuously. Further, it is important to note that this making and remaking of the city is not separate from the making and remaking of rural areas. The two are tied by the exchange of resources, people, technologies, and environmental goods and bads, among other things. While most of this chapter will deal with the activities of people and institutions who call the city their home, it must be noted that the flows of cities, particularly those of waste and water, often have a negative impact on surrounding areas and people.

In both the global North and the global South many types of ecological thinking concentrate on the conservation or preservation of what we call "nature," often defined as pristine areas separate from human interference. Urban environmental movements, on the other hand, have sought to redefine the environment as, "where we live, work and play." Given this definition, there are many urban ecologies. Urban gardening, either for subsistence purposes or to create community spaces, is one example of the relationship between urban spaces and nature. Urban greenspace plans, aimed at providing parks and pleasant thoroughfares for residents, are also important parts of Latin American urban ecologies. Though these particular parts of the urban ecoscape are beyond the scope of this chapter, they are important factors in the constitution of urban environments.

This chapter concentrates on the flows of environmental resources and risks in Latin American cities. As Carlos Minc puts it, "ecology in the Third World begins with water, garbage, and sewage" (Roberts and Thanos, 2003:99). All three issues are tied to the distribution of vital resources (e.g., water) *through* the city or the elimination of wastes *from* the city. These processes of distribution and elimination are essential factors in the health of the populace, which has led observers to describe environmentalism in urban Latin America as "the environmentalization of public health issues" (Roberts and Thanos, 2003:99). The public, though, is not a homogeneous body, but rather a complex and varied group. Therefore, it is important to note that such factors as class, ethnicity, and gender influence access to and use of urban environmental resources as well as exposure to pollution. Some issues, like smog, can be termed relatively "democratic" because they affect people of diverse backgrounds in the same ways, though some people may have more choice in how to react to them. On the other hand, "water, sewer service, and garbage collection are relatively less democratic and therefore, less often solved by the big municipalities" (Roberts and Thanos, 2003:104).

According to recent research, there is no obvious link between the population size, the population growth rate, or the population density of a city and the level of urban environmental problems (Satterthwaite, 1998:70–71). Rather, the most reliable indicator of environmental problems in Latin American cities and other places in the global South is affluence. The production and accumulation of wealth in urban areas, along with a lack of comprehensive development planning, has had many environmentally damaging effects. While some cities are able to use their economic wealth to attack these externalities, many others cannot. Because municipal governments are often burdened with the responsibility of environmental management in urban areas, their inability to solve such problems has huge implications for urban governance and livelihoods.

DEFINITIONS

Ecology

The branch of biology that deals with the relations of living organisms to their surroundings, their habits and modes of life, and so forth.

Political Ecology

Political Ecology is a field of research that explores and explains environmental change and conflict through direct reference to interactions of power between people, institutions, and states.

Environmental Politics

Environmental Politics is a diverse term that could include conservation and preservationist movements, as well as contests over environmental justice. In short, any power struggle over the distribution of environmental goods and bads could be considered environmental politics.

Environmental Justice

Environmental Justice is both a social movement and an area of research. The social movement in the United States began in protest of the concentration of waste processing and dumping facilities in minority and lower-class communities. Many researchers in this field are concerned with documenting such inequitable spatial phenomena, while others investigate the political economic contexts in which such unequal relationships emerged.

RESPONSIBILITY FOR THE URBAN ENVIRONMENT

Many urban residents in Latin America feel that it is the responsibility of the municipal government to assure a clean and healthy living and working environment (Roberts and Thanos, 2003). This expectation is embedded in the historical relationship between urban centers and citizens' rights. Those people identified by the state as "citizens" have entered into a contract of sorts with the municipal government, which is bound to them by a set of rights and obligations. While it is the responsibility of citizens to participate in the production of the city through their everyday lives, it is the responsibility of the city to provide the services necessary for the social reproduction of urban citizens. Historically, the city's responsibility for the public health of citizens can be traced to earlier periods of modernization (Gonzalez-Stephan, 2003).

In the above example of garbage blockades in Oaxaca, the appropriation of public space through its colonization by garbage upsets the status quo, mainly by denying more powerful citizens the ability to export pollution. It works, in the short term at least, by relying on the fact that citizens hold the municipality responsible for distancing them from their own waste. As McGrannahan and Songsore state:

> Many environmental services such as piped water, sewerage connections, electricity, and door to door garbage collection not only export pollution (from the household to the city) but also shift both the intellectual and practical burdens of environmental management for the household to the government or utility. (In Satterthwaite, 1998:74)

This relationship between the city and the citizen rarely exists in its ideal form, but the obligations of the municipality to provide sanitation systems, potable water, and solid waste collection have been written into many city ordinances. It is also a part of constitutional law in many places, as well as the subject of newer environmental legislation at state and federal levels. However, the relative obligations of different levels of government as well as the availability of resources to meet those obligations are constantly shifting because of external and internal pressures.

Deregulation in many Latin American countries has left urban environmental problems exclusively in the hands of municipal entities. However, many environmental problems, such as air or water pollution, cross these political lines. This leads to the potential for "joint irresponsibility" (Roberts and Thanos, 2003:108) where no individual municipality is willing to attend to such collective environmental bads or to the provision of services to avoid these. In many cases, international agencies such as the World Bank (WB) are called on to fund projects dealing with these challenges. Since the early 1990s, when it acknowledged that "health costs resulting from urban water, air and solid waste pollution can reach up to 10% of urban income" (Roberts and Thanos, 2003:111), the WB has instituted a number of urban environmental projects in Latin America. Many of these projects, due to their technocratic approach, address only short-term needs rather than the deeper social problems at the root of environmental issues (Roberts and Thanos, 2003:111). Instead of concentrating on the political-economic, historical, and social context of particular urban environmental problems, World Bank loans have traditionally encouraged countries to focus on technological fixes, which may or may not be appropriate to the situation. For example, the WB-funded National Urban Solid Waste Management Project currently underway in Argentina allocates 83 percent of its 54-million-dollar budget to building landfills in the country. While this may improve environmental conditions in some areas temporarily, it will do little to address the problems of increased consumption, the spatial inequities of dump location, or lack of recycling.

External pressure from international organizations such as the World Bank challenges local authority and autonomy. At the same time, the involvement of these institutions in the development of Latin America has led to pressure to "neoliberalize" the economies (and ecologies) of Latin American countries (see chapters 1 and 2). This has also meant shifts in the responsibilities of local, state, and federal governments and the private sector. Privatization of natural resources and environmental management services has been pursued in some areas to increase efficiency and lower costs to the state. As we shall see in the next section, many of these new strategies for managing urban environments in Latin America have engendered significant public opposition.

POPULAR MOVEMENTS AND PROTESTS

Oaxaca's Dump

Struggles for environmental justice (see Definitions above) take many forms in the cities of Latin America. In Oaxaca (see figure 11.2), one of the most visible is that over management of municipal solid waste. The city has, in recent years, pursued programs that have increased the area and frequency of garbage collection. In this way, the municipal government has responded to its mandate from the citizens to keep the city clean. In order to fully make good on that responsibility, though, the city must expel the garbage outside of its borders. Oaxaca has dumped its garbage in the same 16-hectare spot located about 8 miles southeast of the city center for almost 20 years (see figure 11.3). However, the dump was only made official in 1992, when the city used new property laws to take control of the area. Since that time, all of the garbage from the city of Oaxaca and its surrounding suburbs has been disposed of in the open-air dump. High rates of rural to urban migration, as well as political discrimination and increasing property prices within the city, have led people to settle on the cheap land near the dump. There are also, in fact, communities of people who live on the dump (called *pepenadores*), making their living recycling what they find there.

Residents of communities around the dump have argued with city officials for many years over how the dump is managed. Along with some environmental groups, they have advocated the construction of a sanitary landfill on the site to prevent much of the air, land, and water pollution that exists. The city has responded with rhetoric about its plans to develop a sanitary landfill, but in the end these marginalized communities and groups had very little success in changing management on the ground.

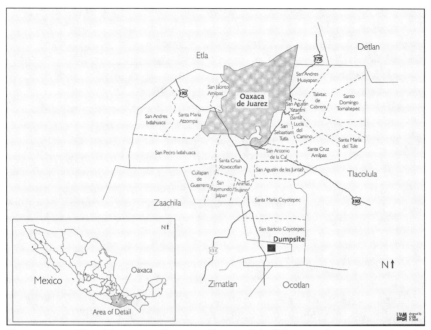

Figure 11.2. City of Oaxaca and surrounding municipalities. Map by C-GIS, University of Wisconsin, Madison

Figure 11.3. Oaxaca's dump.

Then, in 2000, these communities developed the more successful strategy of blocking the city's access to the dump. This means that the city cannot expel its waste. In addition to logistic difficulties, this disruption in the typical flow of garbage out of the city also puts into question the legitimacy of the municipal government itself. That is to say, if the city cannot get the garbage out of the way of its citizens, then it has failed one of the litmus tests of modern urban competency. This one community's struggle over the dumpsite, therefore, turns into a citywide debate over the management of the site and Oaxaca's environmental situation more broadly. Further, this strains the already difficult relationship between the state and municipal governments, while at the same time putting pressure on local industries and businesses to reduce waste. In this battle, public protest has changed not only the lives of the community members involved, but also the city.

NEOLIBERAL POLICIES AND OPPOSITION POLITICS

As mentioned above, the adaptation of neoliberal policies by the states of Latin America has meant the following in terms of environmental management. First, at the same time that municipalities are expected to pursue economic growth, they are given less federal and state support to mediate the effects of such growth on urban ecologies. Second, many important services are privatized, either in full or in part, in order to defray costs for urban governments. Additionally, at the same time that urban pollution is increasing and services are becoming affordable for fewer and fewer people, funding for public health services is often reduced. This section focuses on struggles over the privatization of vital resources, though it should be obvious that this has direct implications for the public health issues that are at the center of environmental politics in Latin America. The following cases of water privatization in Ecuador, Bolivia, and Brazil highlight how these practices are contested by local groups and with what effects.

Contest over Water

In his study of struggles over access to water resources in Guayaquil, Ecuador, Eric Swyngedouw describes the ways in which a private market for water distribution systems has led to manufactured scarcity, with the result that many people are denied access to potable water. He then describes four basic responses to the limitation of access through these (often corrupt) market distribution systems. They are passive acceptance, individual resistance, self-help (self-constructing and financing), and social protest/mobilization (2004:150).

While some people accept the limited access to water, others act individually by taking advantage of traditional clientelist networks to ensure their personal access to the resource. While such strategies may have positive results for any particular person, they have little effect on the overall system of distribution (Swyngedouw, 2004:151). Alternatively, some community groups organize and pool labor and resources to build their own infrastructure. While these communities are sometimes able to get funding from government aid programs or other groups, they are often limited in scope, scale, and time-period.

However, in contrast to these reactions, there are also times when resistance becomes more virulent and effective. In Guayaquil, women's activism has managed to stop the flow of water, at least for short periods (Swyngedouw, 2004:156). Despite the presence of this type of activity, though, Swyngedouw comes to a fairly pessimistic conclusion that denies the possibility of substantial change through these political actions. The next section, in contrast, highlights a situation in which social protest was more effective. As we see below, public activism and resistance often shape environmental politics and policies in Latin America.

Water in Bolivia

In January 2004, angry residents of El Alto, Bolivia, staged a protest against the high cost of water in that city. They forced the president to cancel the contract of Aguas del Illimani, a subsidiary of the $53 billion French Suez (Forero, 2005). This came on the heels of the broadly opposed attempt on the part of now-ousted President Gonzalo Sánchez de Lozada, to sell Bolivia's natural gas to multinational companies. This particular incident can be seen as part of a larger antiprivatization backlash that has spread across many of the countries of Latin America. Peru, for example, has experienced a downturn in foreign investment in its oil resources as indigenous peoples and environmental groups have opposed ownership by foreign companies (Forero, 2005).

In Bolivia, the first of these major public uprisings came in 2000. The Andean city of Cochabamba planned to give the U.S.-based firm Bechtel a major concession for the city's water services. Rather than accept this, many of the city's 600,000 residents took to the streets, forcing the city to back down from its original plan. The oil company, phone company, national airline, electric company, and national train system had all been privatized already, but without the anticipated improvement in services and with increased costs to consumers (Shultz, 2003). When Bechtel, just weeks after taking over water services, decided to increase fees 200 percent, the Coalition for the Defense of Water and Life was born. The group managed a three-day, citywide strike and pressured the government to sign an agreement to review water rates. The government did not, however, carry through on this promise. The coalition organized another march, but this time it was violently suppressed with military force. While this quelled some of the protests, it also led to outrage among the public, forcing a rollback in rates. In an effort to cancel the privatization permanently, the coalition organized more actions the following month. The government responded by declaring martial law. Public response to this declaration was further outrage and a large Internet e-mail campaign, which led Bechtel to flee the country (Shultz, 2003). The end result was a cancellation of the agreement between the government and Bechtel as well as a shift to broader public support for political candidates who voiced opposition to privatization (Shultz, 2003). The success of this protest helped provide fuel to defeat other privatization schemes in Bolivia (Perreault, 2005). More than this, the example of Cochabamba has become a rallying cry for further protest movements in Latin America more broadly.

Bolivia continues to be a country in which popular protests over environmental issues drive policy changes and political futures. After ousting two presidents in as many years, on December 18, 2005, the people of Bolivia elected Evo Morales Ayma, an indigenous activist, president. This preceded Bechtel's announcement that it would drop its lawsuit against the government of Bolivia, which was started after the Bolivian government canceled its contract with the corporate giant. Morales's administration has called for continued nationalization of the country's energy sector, particularly in natural gas holdings.

Unlike the case of Bolivia, activism in São Paulo, Brazil, did not eliminate the privatization of water, but it did impact the way in which privatization was pursued. While this may not be ideal, it does leave room for optimism among researchers like Margaret Keck, who explained,

> During the 1990s, Sao Paulo, followed by other states and the federal government, passed laws mandating a new regime of water resource management, in which users would pay for what had previously been a free good. The laws called for new institutions (watershed committees and agencies) to manage the complex relationships among producers, consumers and the public. They implicitly understood water issues to involve political problems, rather than strictly technical ones, and thus to require (not simply allow) participation and organizations of civil society. These new institutions are still embryonic, in that parts of the reform still await enabling legislation. . . . Nonetheless, we find some reasons for a bias toward hope in the persistence of the professionals and activists who have long waged the battle for livability. (Keck, 2002:164).

This long-running battle over livability alters relationships between local groups, municipalities, and state and national governments. It also changes the relationship between different groups of people within the city itself.

Often, it inspires political action and claims of citizenship from groups previously excluded from the political realm.

POLITICAL IDENTITIES AND URBAN ENVIRONMENTAL CONFLICTS

In the above sections, we have seen some of the ways that popular movements have changed urban environments in Latin America. Many of these struggles have also altered the structure of urban citizenship itself. That is to say that they all, in some way, represent the extension or return of rights to important environmental and public health services to groups who had been excluded from these. Here, we discuss how involvement in such environmental struggles becomes an important part of urban citizens' identities.

In the case of Guayaquil, the most effective (though still temporary) actions against water sellers were perpetuated by women. This is significant in that "the right to water is directly related to the right to the city and to the meaning and practice of being an urban citizen" (Swyngedouw, 2004:156). Thus, by participating in social movements to assure access to this vital resource, women are also insinuating themselves into the role of full and equal citizens. There are many other cases in which women have become public political actors through their association with urban environmental movements (Radcliffe and Westwood, 1993). In Oaxaca, for example, the neighborhood committee of Guillermo Gonzalez Guardado is comprised entirely of women who organize the protests and meet with government officials. They use their socially defined roles as mothers and wives to argue for clean environments for their children and families *and* to position themselves as having rights to the city services necessary to guarantee this. At the same time that they are fighting for improved local conditions, they are also arguing for full inclusion in the citizenry. While they do so as women, their argument has been generalized to include other marginal groups. It is often the boundary constructed by municipal services that defines the inside and outside of citizenship. That is to say, access to such services is an important part of gaining status and recognition as part of the urban community.

Similar citizenship demands can be seen in the case of struggles over water and gas privatization in Bolivia. Questions of who has the right to water emerged when ownership was to be handed over to foreign companies. An emphasis on water as a collective good meant that even recent migrants to the city were involved in struggles over services that they did not yet possess (Perreault, 2005). A sense of entitlement to urban services is one step toward full political participation and urban citizenship. In this way, water projects have the power to designate the inside and outside of urban citizenship, as Swyngedouw observes: "In the end [the problem of water control and access] raises the issue as to who has the right to the city and whose nature is, in the name of progress and modernization, so violently and oppressively appropriated by some at the exclusionary expense of others" (2004:176). In other words, urban environmental politics in Latin America are not about absolute scarcity of resources or inadequate technology, but rather the *distribution* of these resources to all groups through appropriate technologies.

CONCLUSION

The Ecotopia of the Americas

The city of Curitiba, located in southern Brazil, is heralded by many scholars as a model of environmental management. The city is broadly thought to provide its citizens with a high quality of life. There are many reasons for this. The transportation system is highly efficient and encourages the use of bicycles and public transportation. The water system works with the ecology of the city to prevent scarcity and to make clean water available. Further, garbage management has been innovative, encouraging high levels of recycling and low levels of informal disposal. As longtime mayor and urban designer Jaime Lerner describes it,

> In Curitiba, citizens sort trash into two bins: biodegradable and non-biode gradable. In the recycling plant . . . , the handicapped, recent immigrants, and the poor are reportedly given work separating materials to be reused and sold to local industries. . . . We transformed the garbage man into an environmental hero. (quoted in Roberts and Thanos, 2003:113)

This eco-friendly solid waste management has counted on two major programs. One is a combination of curbside recycling, which is provided by the city, with an educational component to describe "Garbage that isn't Garbage." The garbage purchase program, on the other hand, gives incentives to people who live outside of the areas that trucks can access (usually poor communities). People can bring their recyclables and trash to designated centers in exchange for eggs, milk, potatoes, bus tickets, and various other goods. The two programs together have helped Curitiba to achieve a recycling rate of almost 70 percent. This was done without high-tech solutions, but rather by integrating existing technology with the ecological system.

Given the success of such a program, it is possible to imagine that other Latin American cities, like Oaxaca, as well as cities in other regions of the world, might try to replicate these programs. Indeed, many have tried, but with varying success. To understand why such a system of environmental management might not work in Oaxaca and other cities, I will conclude by considering the *politics* of Curitiba's ecotopia.

As Traicoff points out, "Attributing the successes of Curitiba to the talents of the mayor and the perceptions of the populace towards their city begs the question as to how this culture was created and why it is absent in other Brazilian cities" (quoted in Roberts and Thanos, 2003:114). I would add that the answer to this question is extremely important for the viability of similar programs in other places. One factor in the success of Curitiba is its strong executive, a direct result of its military dictatorship. While this allows for the rapid passage and enforcement of legislation protecting the environment, it diminishes other freedoms. Moreover, rather than continuing public participation in planning, a general "boosterism" has taken hold, meaning that citizens are expected to extol the city's virtues. Even more importantly, a "belt of non-citizens" composed of poorer and more irregular municipalities surrounds Curitiba. So, while Curitiba is a positive model for environmental management in Latin America, it is "much less so for the consolidation of functional democracy" (Roberts and Thanos, 2003:116). If one judges the success of Curitiba's environmental initiatives purely on measures of ecological health, it is very easy to argue that it should be the model for Latin America to follow into the twenty-first century. On the other hand, if one evaluates Curitiba in terms of the status of the populace, one sees the same problems that still plague many of Latin America's cities. It is the uneven *distribution* of environmental goods and bads (and not the absolute level of these) throughout cities and their hinterlands that endangers the health of urban dwellers. Urban environmental politics aims to do more, therefore, than protect the health of cities. It also aims to empower marginalized groups to claim citizenship and join the political struggle over shaping urban places. In Oaxaca, it is not only the ecological health of the city that is contested through urban environmental politics, but also the value placed on the participation of women from the surrounding neighborhoods in determining municipal solid waste policy.

The complexity of this relationship—between urban ecologies and urban politics—illustrates the main point of this chapter. The environments of Latin American cities cannot be evaluated or understood separately from the daily lives of the people who live in them.

SUGGESTED READINGS

Roberts, J. T., and N. D. Thanos. *Trouble in Paradise: Globalization and Environmental Crises in Latin America*. New York: Routledge, 2003.

Swyngedouw, E. *Social Power and the Urbanization of Water: Flows of Power*. Oxford: Oxford University Press, 2004.

BIBLIOGRAPHY

"Ecology." *The Oxford English Dictionary Online*, http://dictionary.oed.com/cgi /entry/50071982?single=1&query_type=word&queryword=ecology&first=1&max _to_show=10 (accessed September 1, 2006).

Forero, J. "Latin America Fails to Deliver on Basic Needs." *New York Times*, February 22, 2005, A1.

Gonzalez Stephan, B. "On Citizenship: The Grammatology of the Body-Politic." In *Latin American Philosophy: Currents, Issues and Debates*, edited by E. Mendieta, pp. 188–206. Bloomington: Indiana University Press, 2003.

Keck, M. "Water, Water, Everywhere, Nor Any Drop to Drink: Land Use and Water Policy in São Paulo, Brazil." In *Livable Cities? Urban Struggles for Livelihood and Sustainability*, edited by P. Evans, pp. 162–194 . Berkeley: University of California Press, 2002.

Perreault, T. "State Restructuring and the Scale Politics of Rural Water Governance in Bolivia." *Environment and Planning A* 37, no. 2 (2005): 263–284.

Radcliffe, S., and S. Westwood. "Gender, Racism and the Politics of Identities in Latin America." In *Viva: Women and Popular Protest in Latin America*. London: Routledge, 1993.

Roberts, J. T., and N. D. Thanos. *Trouble in Paradise: Globalization and Environmental Crises in Latin America*. New York: Routledge, 2003.

Satterthwaite, D. "Environmental Problems in Cities in the South: Sharing My Confusions." In *Environmental Strategies for Sustainable Development in Urban Areas: Lessons from Africa and Latin America*, edited by E. Fernandes, pp. 62–83. Aldershot, U.K.; Brookfield, Vt.: Ashgate, 1998.

Shultz, J. "Bolivia: The Water War Widens." *NACLA* 36, no. 3 (2003): 34–38.

Swyngedouw, E. *Social Power and the Urbanization of Water: Flows of Power*. Oxford: Oxford University Press, 2004.

12

Transnational Communities, Identities, and Moving Populations

Susan P. Mains

As can be seen from the previous chapters, Latin America is a vast and diverse region, and Latin American populations represent a range of identities and cultural practices. Of course, these places and cultures cannot always be easily demarcated (see chapter 5), and have frequently influenced activities and ideas far beyond the traditional territories of the region. To understand the ways in which Latin America has stretched and transcended traditional nation-state boundaries, this chapter will examine transnational communities and identities and their importance for understanding this part of the world as simultaneously constitutive of local, national, regional, and international spaces, and the links between different spaces of Latin American diasporas.

The following discussion will be divided into two sections. The first section will provide an overview of what is meant by the concept of transnationalism and transnational communities. The goal of this discussion is to introduce concepts and literature related to the theoretical concept of transnationalism and—using specific brief case studies—how this can be conceptualized in the context of the region. The second section will examine concepts of migration and movements of Latin American citizens—where and why they move to different places—and how these represent examples of transnational relations. Case studies will be explored relating to the U.S.-Mexico border and Colombian cultural geographies. These case studies will explore the ways in which Latin Americans have forged transnational identities through a range of cultural practices and experiences. The conclusion will provide a brief overview of the key points raised in the chapter and suggest some possibilities for future research topics on Latin American communities.

UNDERSTANDING TRANSNATIONALISM

Within and beyond the discipline of geography, "transnationalism" has become a very popular term. It is also frequently utilized in mainstream media—in conjunction with the term "globalization"—to refer to changing political and economic events in specific locales (Swyngedouw, 1997). Indeed, globalization and transnationalism have been used interchangeably in some contexts, however, the nuances of their different meanings are worth bearing in mind. Globalization is generally taken to refer to the movements, processes, and relationships that intensify connections throughout the world, albeit in an uneven manner (Amin, 1997; Dicken, 2003). Although a fairly recent term, geographers have noted that globalization has a long and complex history (Blaut, 1993).

Transnationalism, although also international in scope, refers more specifically to relationships that cross traditional nation-state territorial boundaries, but which still also maintain some connection to (multiple) national identities (Anderson, 2002). In this sense, we could say that globalization involves transnational processes or that transnational practices are part of intensified globalization. The two, of course, are interlinked; however, to focus our exploration in the course of this chapter, we will concentrate on different understandings and practices of transnationalism, particularly in relation to movements of people.

If we turn to more closely examine the term "transnationalism" itself, we begin to see that it is a concept, relationship, and/or practice that reflects activities that are ongoing—are about the sustained or varying interconnections across (and often, in spite of) state boundaries—and are also all about *movement*. Transnationalism is an inherently geographic practice in that people, objects, and ideas that are part of transnational relationships have moved from one place to another (and then, perhaps, returned) (Mitchell, 1997). These kinds of relationships are particularly important in the context of Latin America given the diverse and substantial movements of people within and between the region and other locations. There are several types of transnational relationships in Latin America that provide a focus for understanding how these movements take place: these include social, cultural, political, and economic practices.

SOCIAL AND CULTURAL ASPECTS OF TRANSNATIONALISM

In terms of social and cultural practices transnationalism encompasses a myriad of activities and social attitudes. To explain this more fully it is helpful to look at some specific examples. Cultural identities and social relationships do not simply fit within regional or national boundaries—while they may define state divisions, political districts do not act as neat dividers for demarcating differences in ideas or histories—and in many ways cultural and social practices are among the most fluid in terms of an ability to move back and forth across official political lines. If we take, for example, movements of music and architecture, the U.S.-Mexico border region illustrates the dynamic and transnational nature of these cultural practices (see also chapter 5). In both northern Mexico and California, Mexican hip-hop, ranchero music, and U.S. rock have had a significant presence and influence in wider musical productions on both sides of the border (and far beyond the border region). Such music is often bilingual and makes references to experiences from a range of cultural contexts, while often drawing on additional musical traditions from further afield (Aparicio and Jaquez, 2002). At the same time, if we examine the built environment of cities such as Los Angeles or Tijuana, in both places we can see the influence of Spanish colonial plazas and gardens, indigenous adobe materials, modernist office buildings, and graffiti. In some cases (e.g., in relation to pueblo churches), particular architectural styles were manifested on the physical landscape prior to the current U.S.-Mexico border (formalized in its most recent form in 1848), and have been adapted in more recent constructions. In others (e.g., graffiti and transborder art events such as La Frontera/The Border Arts Project between San Diego and Tijuana), the notion of a "border" and how it is demarcated comes under ongoing intensive scrutiny and challenges by the many people who seek to move beyond the notion of belonging in one place or another (CEMA, 2002). These latter practices often celebrate transnationalism as a positive connection between populations in different countries that share common cultural identities, and illustrate how Latin American cultures are present in places that are often thought of as being "outside" the region in terms of mainstream political and geographic discourse (e.g., as can be noted in salsa dances found in San Diego, New York, London, Tokyo, and Madrid). Gloria Anzaldúa has written extensively about this process of being "inbetween" cultures and provides a critical perspective on how we think about transnational—or border—identities (see, for example, Anzaldúa, 1987). This approach encourages individuals to think beyond traditional physical, linguistic, gendered, and racial boundaries in order to understand the constantly changing connections between people and places that may at first glance appear distinct.

POLITICAL AND ECONOMIC ASPECTS OF TRANSNATIONALISM

Politically and economically, transnationalism is significant in that it challenges the primacy of the nation-state. Traditionally, in much geographic research, national governments have been viewed as the key level and institutional framework through which policy decision-making has been made. This is not to say that the nation-state is no longer important—indeed, many would argue that in some ways it is even more so, as a monitor and filter of local and international programs—but rather to suggest that its relationship to other processes functioning on a range of scales has altered over time and in different locales. There are many different examples of transnational political and economic movements and organizations, which range from neighborhood associations, to regional corporate organizations, to international human rights institutions. In the context of Latin America, the International Monetary Fund (IMF) and the World Bank are two highly influential financial institutions that have held a significant influence over the development paths and fiscal policy changes for most governments (Escobar, 1994).

Although financially focused, we can consider these institutions examples of transnational politics in that they cut across national boundaries in their significance, and because they shape the political decision-making in a way that has led to neoliberal policies increasingly dominating the region during the last fifteen years. This is not to say, however, that such "top-down" institutions (i.e., organizations led from above, through, for example, decisions made by executives or national leaders) function unchallenged, and in fact if we turn to the example of a "bottom-up" organization (i.e., networks arranged through a system of decentralized power, or through a range of locally based organizations), such as the Americas World Social Forum, we have a framework of locally based organizations that are transnational in their outlook, and through their connections to a range of grassroots organizations throughout the region and the world have created a global activist space (see chapters 9 and 10). One of the central foci of this latter group has been to challenge the assumption that middle- and low-income countries should repay their (often extremely high interest) debts to institutions like the World Bank or the Inter-American Development Bank, and to argue that instead these countries should focus their energies on social and educational programs while independently "auditing" international financial practices themselves (WSF, 2005). This challenge to the authority of international financial and political institutions and policymakers has illustrated the ways in which political and economic decision-making are intertwined, and despite historical depictions to the contrary, has shown fiscal decision-making to be part of highly subjective practices.

In the context of Latin America, two trade groupings (among others, such as the Andean Community and the proposed Free Trade of the Americas) that function as important examples of economic transnational communities are MERCOSUR (Mercado Comun del Sur/Southern Common Market) and NAFTA (North America Free Trade Agreement). MERCOSUR was initiated in 1991, formalizing commerce and customs linkages between Argentina, Brazil, Paraguay, and Uruguay. The stated goals of MERCOSUR have been to improve economic integration between member states through an opening up of trade markets and through policies geared toward furthering economic development. Additional countries have also been working with the original MERCOSUR members in order to expand the markets covered. These more recent states negotiating membership include Chile, Bolivia, Colombia, Peru, and Ecuador (which all have associate member status), Mexico (which currently has observer status), and Venezuela (which became a full member in July 2006).

Focusing on the northern connections between the Americas, NAFTA was formally launched in 1994 with a signing of the free trade agreement between Canada, the United States, and Mexico. Similar to MERCOSUR, the goal of this framework was to facilitate trade between member countries and to limit tariffs on goods and services exchanged within the region. Discussion has also been underway regarding the possible expansion of the NAFTA area. Despite this ongoing presence of trade organizations and agreements such as NAFTA and MERCOSUR, they are not without their critics. Transnational social movements and trade unions have pointed to the undermining of local economies, job losses, and the financial difficulties faced by small-scale business owners in the wake of "liberalized" large businesses, the latter of which are functioning at economies of scale with which small businesses can rarely compete. The freedom of multinational companies to move to where labor supplies and taxes are cheapest, and where environmental monitoring is less stringent, has motivated many local organizations to create links with other organizations nationally and internationally to illustrate the growing concerns of underrepresented groups. What these trade agreement processes can be seen as illustrating are the ways in which different forms of transnationalism may be seen as benefiting some groups while disadvantaging others. In addition, transnational policymaking frequently functions in a way that limits the possibilities for local input, and as a result those local groups can become organized into a national and transnational movement of resistance.

While trade organizations provide a form of transnationalism that is largely run at the international level and with a largely top-down focus, remittances provide an example of a means by which transnational communities are economically and socially supported through a series of informal, locally based, internationally circuited, and locally and nationally accumulated series of contributions. Remittances can be defined as transfers of money, or in-kind support, between households, where the sender is usually residing in a different country from the remittance receiver (often, migrants who move or work abroad send remittances to other family members or friends who remain in the home country). The volume of remittances into Latin America is substantial, and provides a significant percentage of foreign exchange earnings for many countries (Orozco, 2002). The Inter-American Development Bank (IDB), which states that remittances in 2004 were greater than U.S.$45 billion, notes the extent of this economic support (IDB, 2005a). Migrants often view these contributions as an important means by which they can contribute to the social and economic well-being of their families, as well as charities and organizations, from afar, while also helping to maintain transnational connections in a practical way.

TRANSNATIONAL COMMUNITIES AND IDENTITIES

Just as the concept of transnationalism encompasses a range of interrelated components and relationships, the concept of transnational communities is equally diverse. Benedict Anderson (1983) explored the idea of a nation being an "imagined community" where, even though very few citizens had come into direct contact with each other, there was a sense of connection and shared ideals through forums such as newspapers, elected representatives, music, and literature. Transnational communities also share an understanding of connection between far-flung people, including individuals, families, and organizations. Of course, not everyone will agree with what the central identification should be—just as there are often conflicts over how to define what the key characteristics of a specific nation should be—but there is some kind of investment made in claiming a transnational and diasporic identity (where an ethnic group moves from one locale and disperses to different places), that resonates with others (Portes, 1997). At the same time, transnational communities often include members who belong to multiple national, local, and regional communities. If we take, for example, the (imaginary, but not unlikely) case study of a Colombian migrant, Frederico, who moves from Bogotá to Toronto, Canada, we can start to see some of these overlapping identities and communities. Frederico moves to Toronto to take up a teaching position in an anthropology department in a large state university. Once in Canada he becomes friends with other colleagues and neighbors who are from different parts of Latin America, including Colombia. At the same time he establishes a circle of colleagues and friends who work in anthropology in different universities in Toronto and other cities in Canada and the United States, and who come from a range of ethnic and national backgrounds. While in Toronto, Frederico attends film screenings held by a Colombian popular culture group, and becomes involved in an international migrants' outreach network. In addition, he assists his family residing in Colombia by sending monthly remittances, has regular get-togethers with an aunt and uncle who were already living in nearby Scarborough, and assists his daughter with a visa application in order to attend graduate school in Toronto. When possible he visits Bogotá in July and while there spends time with family and friends, while also conducting some field research.

From the brief example above we can already begin to see just some of the many varied communities to which someone like Frederico could belong: a middle-class educated international academic community; a Canadian middle class; a Colombian diaspora interested in popular culture; a working-class family in Bogotá and extended middle-class diasporic family networks; an international flow of migrants who negotiate documentation procedures (at certain moments marginalized due to ethnicity and/or citizenship status); English- and Spanish-speaking Toronto- and internationally based friends; and trans-American international finance communities, among others. Of course the regularity and intensity of the ties to these different communities may vary quite considerably and change over time, but they also illustrate the dynamic and situated nature of identity and place relationships.

Identity, therefore, is something that shifts relative to varying geographic and historical contexts. An individual or cultural group does not simply carry one unifying identity, but usually works through an ongoing process of negotiation about which characteristics (or places) are of significance, and which are to be prioritized over others. In this sense, transnational identities are provocative in that one of their defining features is the notion that there can be a simultaneous bond with more than one nationality and that national identities can travel with, and adapt to, an individual's changing physical and social locations. The following section will be a more in-depth discussion of specific migrant movements, the creation of transnational spaces, and the contexts to, and from which, Latin Americans have moved.

LATIN AMERICAN TRANSNATIONALISM AND MOBILITY

An Introduction to Concepts in Migration

Transnationalism and mobility are very much intertwined concepts; it is partially through the ability to move (at some point) that transnational communities come into being.[1] Migration, in particular, is a central characteristic of transnational Latin American communities and this section provides a discussion of some popular representations of migration, selected case studies of how Latin American populations move, and how these are manifested in specific landscapes.[2]

Migrants and migration exist on a variety of scales both in terms of where and how people move, and in terms of the meanings ascribed to mobility: from the movements of individual migrants' bodies, to official national ports of entry, to large-scale immigration policy. In order to understand how population movements function at a range of interrelated scales it is helpful to examine more closely some definitions of migration. At a general level, migrants can be defined as people who move from their region/country of origin with the intention of living in another region and/or country. In addition, "return" migration develops another dimension to the *ongoing* processes of migration. In the context of Latin America and the Caribbean, for example, for decades we can see movements of people back and forth between origin and destination country. For many migrants from this region the maintenance of ties with home communities, while physically distant, is an important component of sustaining and securing a respected social identity, maintaining a certain degree of mobility, and the possibility of returning home if need be. Return migration exemplifies the diversity of international movements. King (2000:10–11) comments that return migration can encompass several different types of movement: occasional returns (for short/periodic stays); seasonal returns (related to variations in the availability of cyclical work, e.g., agricultural employment); temporary returns (where people move back to the country of origin for a significant time but with the intention to emigrate; and permanent returnees (those who return to their countries of origin and settle). This typology can also be combined with various practices in terms of migrants' intentions to stay or return to a specific location and the material act of carrying the journey out (for example, as King explains, many students migrate to study with the intention of returning home at the completion of their degrees, but they then find further research or employment, and decide to stay abroad). It is also important to note that many migrants do not necessarily have specific intentions about length of stay or the nature of future migrations, and so the decision-making process is often unclear, lengthy, and linked to other personal factors. The economic ability to return is a particularly important factor in the likelihood of migrants actually returning, as many migrants may simply be unable to *afford* an international move (Ghosh, 2000).

In combination with different forms of movement and return come varied concerns and definitions around the topic of choice. Past research on Latin American migration has tended to distinguish between voluntary movements (e.g., migration for work) and forced migration (e.g., seeking asylum due to civil conflict). In practice many migrants who have been categorized as "voluntary" have faced less obvious limitations that have pressured them into moving (e.g., other family members already overseas, high crime rates, a lack of job diversity, restrictive social attitudes). Choice and mobility are therefore interwoven, and sometimes complicated by factors beyond economics, but by social factors, such as new personal ties made in destination countries (Chambers, 1994). It can be argued, therefore, that choice is also a spatial construct, in that decisions about movements are situated in relation to the physical, economic, and social conditions that migrants negotiate. These decisions are *located* in the context of particular social and physical settings in which understandings and images of day-to-day life help to shape decision making (e.g., while a 25-year-old Guatemalan woman may be able to stay in Guatemala City employed as a domestic worker, a devaluation of the local currency, increased living costs, a recently hospitalized relative's medical bills, and a reduction in working hours may make a move to Mexico City more desirable due to its proximity to her home country, language similarities, and a perception of greater employment opportunities).

Increases in the scale and diversity of migration to and from—and within—Latin America are linked into increases in the internationalization of capital and demand/supply of labor, the increased displacement of people (e.g., as a result of civil conflict and/or environmental devastation), and growing cultural ties across (and between) a variety of locations (e.g., between relatives and friends who have moved overseas and developed new employment and social networks in their destination countries). Contrary to many popular state discourses that promote globalization and transnationalism as leading to increased mobility that will benefit all, in the context of Latin America these increased flows of people and products frequently create a state of flux or "turbulence" (Papastergiadis, 2000), where competing interests and spaces in countries of origin and destination produce "fundamental problems of livelihood, equity, suffering, justice, and governance" (Appadurai, 2001:6). These disjunctures are both local and global. As Appadurai (2001:6) notes, for example, disjunctures come in various forms:

> Media flows across national boundaries that produce images of wellbeing that cannot be satisfied by national standards of living and consumer capabilities; flows of discourses of human rights that generate demands from workforces that are repressed by state violence which is itself backed by global arms flows; ideas about gender and modernity that circulate to create large female workforces at the same time that cross-national ideologies of "culture," "authenticity," and national honor put increasing pressure on various communities to morally discipline just these working women who are vital to emerging markets and manufacturing sites.

In examining the human geographies of Latin American migrations, such contradictions and contested expectations about mobility and cultural identity can also be noted in relation to shifting concepts of transnationalism.

During the last fifty years, there has been a tendency of higher income countries, such as the United States, United Kingdom, France, and Spain, to view international immigration from middle- and lower-income Latin American and Caribbean countries with increasing concern in relation to the ease of choice or mobility of migrants. This concern has been manifested in the introduction of increasingly stringent visa and residency regulations in destination countries. Yet, it is important to note that migrants do not simply flow from low- to high-income countries—nor only from South to North—but also between low- and middle-income countries, and this is increasingly the case when wealthy countries introduce new immigration restrictions. In Latin America, for example, we can find "significant communities of Bolivian migrants in Argentina, Nicaraguans in Costa Rica, Guatemalans in Mexico, Peruvians in Chile, and Haitians in the Dominican Republic" (MIF-IDB, 2002).

For many Latin American countries facing economic challenges, emigration has been a significant issue resulting in large numbers of younger (and more recently, older) people moving from their home nations to seek other opportunities while leaving behind a reduction in the working-age population (particularly in rural areas). At the same time this migrant population provides significant revenue in the form of remittances to their countries of origin. At an individual level these remittances form an important component of economic and social transnational relations, providing assistance with children's educational costs, rent, and health costs, while at a national level the income can rival industries such as tourism for the provision of highly desired foreign exchange, and exceeds Official Development Assistance (ODA) (IDB, 2005b).

For many Latin American migrants the negotiation of the bureaucratic processes involved in movement can be daunting and expensive. Who makes decisions about work permits or immigration policy, and where these decisions take place seems far removed from migrants who often feel that they can have very little input to the decisions being made about their legal status in their country of destination. While the idea of being able to move back and forth and contribute to a range of communities sounds positive, the lived experience for migrants frequently involves the confrontation of several political and legal obstacles (such as a minimum amount of savings, a return-flight ticket, proof of work history, a current driver's license, or sponsorship by an employer). Migrants may also face racial and gender discrimination that excludes them from certain kinds of work or living in particular neighborhoods. Wealthier individuals often have a greater range of mobility (and due to their economic resources and social networks, access to a smoother bureaucratic process), while economically poorer individuals are viewed with suspicion.

By developing an understanding of the important role that migrants play—within, from, and to Latin America—in contributing toward the exchange of ideas, talent, income and transnational/international relations, we can perhaps take a step toward developing more inclusive systems of population policies and political representation.

TRANSNATIONALISM, INTERNATIONAL MIGRATION, AND THE U.S.-MEXICO BORDER

Given the many official changes in the U.S.-Mexico border during the last 300 years, it is easy to see why there are so many cultural, political, and economic links (and tensions) in this region, and why it is viewed as a point at which Latin America and the United States coalesce and collide. Indeed, a common phrase for many Latino and Mexican communities responding to anti-immigrant sentiments in the United States—"We didn't cross the border, the border crossed us"—highlights this (not always mutually agreed) transnationalism, and the frequently arbitrary nature of international boundaries.

Movements of people have crisscrossed the Americas—North and South— for centuries. The United States, for example, as with most countries, has a long history of immigration from various parts of the world. Despite (or in spite of) this shared history and geography, policymakers and immigration-control advocates have frequently attempted to delineate boundaries between the United States and Latin America (Mains, 2000). Such efforts to delimit the social and physical territories of the United States, for example, as reflected in anti-immigrant sentiments, visa restrictions, a reduction of migrants' access to social services, and intensified policing of the U.S.-Mexico border, are intriguing and problematic, especially given the extent to which migrants have contributed to the culture, economy, and political structures of the nation:

> The pace of recent US economic growth would have been impossible without immigration. Since 1990, immigrants have contributed to job growth in three main ways: they fill an increasing share of jobs overall, they take jobs in labor-scarce regions, and they fill the types of jobs native workers often shun. The foreign-born make up only 11.3 percent of the US population and 14 percent of the labor force. (Orrenius, 2003)

There have been several temporary work programs (such as the late Bracero program), where Mexican workers have been hired to undertake seasonal work (e.g., as H2A agricultural workers). In addition, many people who cross from the Tijuana area to San Diego do so for short-term visits, often for shopping, entertainment, or to visit relatives who live in Southern California. In an analysis of data focusing on Latino, and particularly Mexican, support of the U.S. economy, the Institute of Mexicans Abroad notes the substantial volume of this financial presence:

> The purchasing power of Hispanics in the United States in 2005 was estimated at 736 billion dollars. . . . The US population of Mexican origin (including migrants and Mexican Americans) contributes close to US $635 billion dollars to the US economy, which represents 5% of the US GDP. (IME 2006, 3)

While much of the mainstream media in the United States has tended to focus on migrants who cross the border without papers, many migrants do file for, and obtain work visas, permanent residency (a "green card"), or U.S. citizenship (Mains, 2002). In addition, a significant number of San Diego–based residents cross the border to Mexico daily in order to work in factories in the maquiladora zone (foreign-owned factories concentrated in northern Mexico), and for leisure and family visits. Migration at the border, therefore, is not unidirectional, but is part of the production of diverse transnational movements and identities. Indeed, this westernmost section of the U.S.-Mexico border is one of the busiest international boundaries in the world.

In terms of long-term immigration to the United States, Mexico has been one of the main sending countries, and the U.S.-Mexico border has been depicted as the sole gateway for this movement. However, significant numbers of migrants come from areas throughout the world, including other Latin American countries, Europe, Asia, and Africa, and arrive through a variety of official (and unofficial) ports of entry. Some migrants arrive legally and after a period of time they may—for a variety of reasons—overstay their visas and become undocumented. What we see, then, in terms of some U.S. perceptions of Mexican migrants, is an assumption that most people who come from Latin America, or are of Latin American descent, come from Mexico across the southern border without appropriate papers: an entire region becomes generalized to one place. However, at closer examination, it becomes clear that there is a vast range of origin countries represented, and many Latinos are first-, second-, or third-generation migrants, have been born in the United States, and consider themselves to be "American" (in both a national and continental sense).

At this point you may (or should!) be asking—given the difficulty of migration and the increased controls on Latin American migrants, why move? This is an important question with no simple answers, but the following section will briefly outline some of the possible push and pull factors in relation to Latin American migration to the United States.

Push Factors

There are many different push factors that have led to migrants' leaving Latin America (often with the intention of eventually returning), and many of them are interlinked. One of the striking things about the relationship between Mexico and its northern neighbor, for example, is the disparity in income levels between the two countries, and this has been an important aspect of the migratory process from Latin America in general. Although all countries' economies have fluctuated during the last century, the United States has dominated the region during the last 50 years (economically and politically). In 2004 the purchasing power per person (in U.S. dollars) was $39,710 in the United States; $9,590 in Mexico; $13,920 in Argentina; $8,230 in Brazil; $7,150 in the Dominican Republic; and $7,950 on average for the entire region of Latin America and the Caribbean (Population Reference Bureau, 2006a). Many Latin Americans, therefore, have been pushed to leave their native countries due to an unstable economy, limited job opportunities, limited opportunities for women (in terms of work diversity), and occasionally fear of persecution if they have been critical of government/political policies.

Pull Factors

Factors that have drawn migrants to the United States are also diverse. Relatives and friends living in specific areas of the United States often act as a "pull" factor in the sense that they provide a social network and a sense of community in a new place (this is one factor that helps to partially explain why we tend to see concentrations of migrant groups in certain cities, for example, Colombians in New York, Cubans and Haitians in Miami, Mexicans and Guatemalans in Los Angeles). Because the U.S. economy is stronger than those further south, many migrants look north believing that they will have better job opportunities than they do in Latin America—some do—but many migrants have found themselves in poorly paid work, with little protection in terms of benefits or unionization, as Smith (1999:48) notes below:

> Poor economic conditions and lack of any prospect of a decent livelihood induce people to look for work—the push. Flourishing economies in which there are not enough people to do necessary jobs provide possibilities for employment—the pull.
>
> Though wealthier countries need migrant labor, they do not usually treat migrant laborers well. Low pay, no social rights (or no information about their rights, which amounts to the same thing), employers who steal the workers' passports, illegal and dangerous and expensive transport to countries where jobs might be available, discrimination in the housing market, semi-criminal landlords renting out places in sub-standard dormitories and hostels—the list of abuses against migrant workers is long.

The possibility of improved accessibility to health care and educational facilities, has also provided an important draw, although if a migrant does not have adequate immigration or employment papers it can be extremely difficult to access such services.

Migrant advocacy groups, such as the American Friends Service Committee, Mexican American Legal Defense Fund, and the American Immigration Law Foundation, have stated that migration from Latin America to the

United States is inevitable, given the history of, and disparity in wealth between, the two areas (Mason, 2006). These groups also state that increased mortality rates for undocumented migrants attempting to travel north during the last decade is a matter of considerable urgency that should be addressed by both sending and receiving countries, and as such they have attempted to draw attention to this loss of life by holding demonstrations and candlelight vigils at the border. The border fence itself, therefore, becomes a transnational activist space that organizations use to physically and symbolically mobilize public sentiment and political policy (which is also true of immigration-control groups, e.g., the Minuteman Project, a voluntary vigilante group patrolling the U.S. side of the border). Increasingly prohibitive immigration policies and the intensified use of surveillance technologies and border patrols in recent years have resulted in undocumented migrants' need to travel through more remote terrain. The move to less visible areas has resulted in growing death rates, increased exposure to robberies, assaults, heat exposure, and vast increases in smugglers' fees: "Data gathered from surveys of Mexican migrants indicate smugglers' prices rose from about $500 [US] in 1993 to $1,000 in 1998. Today, migrants reportedly pay about $1,500 to $2,000 for a typical crossing" (Orrenius, 2003).

In a period when the increased mobility of goods, services, and people has received growing government attention in relation to globalization and intensified trade connections throughout the Americas, physical deterrents to mobility have become increasingly visible at the U.S.-Mexico border. This contrast between concepts of mobility and transnationalism can be seen just a few miles east of the heavily monitored San Ysidro port of entry in Southern California, where, at the Otay Mesa border crossing, a considerable amount of business traffic moves between the two countries. This crossing links into many transnational economic flows and has a "Dedicated Commuter Lane," which runs a system called SENTRI, where—after an FBI background check—business commuters are issued a "PortPASS" identity card that they can swipe through a machine at the border checkpoint where they then are free to cross (Mains, 1999). This system has rapidly sped up the process for regular business cross-border commuters. Here we can see that depending on occupation, class, and ethnicity the experience of the border can be very different, and its permeability can vary considerably depending on social group—that is, it is easier to become a mobile transnational citizen if you have greater economic means and look as though you "fit" with the most powerful ethnic or racial group.

The U.S.-Mexico border and its interconnectedness with people and places throughout the Americas illustrate transnationalism in several ways and at a variety of scales. Economically, politically, and artistically the borderlands have become an international focal point for immigration and foreign policy and the exchange of ideas between the United States and

Central and South America. Regionally, this has been significant in terms of NAFTA and the movement of people and trading ties (including undocumented movements of people and goods) to and from Central and South America, the United States, and Canada. At the local scale a Latin American presence can be felt through the ethnic, national, linguistic, architectural, and religious diversity of the population in Northern Mexico and the United States; in U.S.-owned maquiladora factories and fast-food chains in Ciudad Juarez; in taco stands and reconstructed historical Mexican old town streets in Los Angeles; in public parks, marches, and art projects celebrating Latino identities in Arizona, Texas, and Southern California (e.g., in Barrio Logan in San Diego); in surveillance cameras trained on the border fence at Imperial Beach; and at spring break rock concerts and migrant shelters (e.g., Casa Del Migrante) in Tijuana. Transnationalism, therefore, works through complementary (and sometimes competing) social practices that connect places by giving meaning to different identities. To examine another context in which transnationalism functions in Latin America, we will now turn to a South American setting—Colombia.

MOBILITY AND TRANSNATIONAL SPACES IN COLOMBIA

Mass media representations of Colombia outside of the country are dominated by images of drug trafficking and armed conflict. While both of these practices are a significant part of this cultural landscape, such depictions fail to communicate the rich and diverse social character and geography nurtured by the country. As is common with much popular media, such as primetime television newscasts, a narrow range of places and themes is often used as shorthand in a context in which journalists are restricted by time limitations and format constraints. The stories that we view, therefore, often fail to explain the reasons behind the events that are depicted or their connections to other places and practices. In the following discussion we will attempt to tease out some of the hidden stories of selected cultural and political landscapes in Colombia in an effort to explore and understand their transnational dimensions.

Past Population and Cultural Movements

Before turning to examples of transnationalism in the migratory movements of Colombians today, the diversity of the domestic population itself is a testimony to the transnational nature of the country's history. Similar to other South American countries, a large majority of the current population reflects a coalescing of indigenous Amerindian groups, African slaves, and European immigrants. This diversity illustrates past transnational geographies (prior to the creation of today's nation-state boundaries), such as extensive regional indigenous empires (e.g., cultures linked to the Chibchas and Incas, at San Augustín and Tumaco), the slave trade (e.g., slaves who were forced to travel from West Africa to the Caribbean coast), and European colonialism (e.g., Spaniards who sought to conquer the area as they set out in search of the mythical gold of the fabled El Dorado in the country's interior).

Although rapidly reduced in number through repression, disease, and dispossession of lands at the hands of European settlers from the sixteenth century onward, some examples of the pre-Columbian indigenous presence can still be found in the built environment. One exemplary landscape illustrating these highly skilled and accomplished cultures is found in the southwestern department of Huila at the ceremonial burial sites of San Augustín (which includes a range of detailed stone statues, shown in figure 12.1). Artifacts and art dating from this period illustrate connections and influences between different indigenous groups (whether this be in the Andean areas or along coastal plains of the region, including the Caribbean).

European influences can be seen in the dominant language, Spanish, and the religious practices and architecture of Colombia's many cathedrals and central plazas (particularly in relation to Roman Catholicism, see

Figure 12.1.   Transnational landscapes of the past: sculptures in San Augustín, Colombia.

Figure 12.2.   Religion and the built environment: Spanish influences seen in the Primary Cathedral of Bogotá and the adjacent plaza.

figure 12.2). For example, the Cerro de Monserrate—a mountain overlooking the capital city of Bogotá—is marked by the church at its peak (figure 12.3), which is a symbol of transnationalism encompassing strong Spanish design and religious influences, national cultural traditions found in food and craft stalls concentrated around the church, local pilgrimages to the Statue of the Fallen Christ, and contemporary international ties through visiting tourists.

Strong links between Africa and Latin America can be found in the musical mélange of cumbia sounds on the Caribbean coast, and through the cassava (or yucca) found in Colombia (e.g., to make *pasteles de yuca*, or cassava patties, shown in figure 12.4). These connections are also seen in the current extensive production of the root in Africa (and Asia) following its introduction from South America. The most populous ethnic category—mestizo—a mixture of the main ethnic groups, also reflects the interconnected and international ties that have brought people together through both conflict and collaboration.

Popular Culture and Contemporary Transnationalism

A new arrival to Bogotá may be struck by the city's impressive physical setting within a mountain range of the Andean system that cuts across the

Figure 12.3. A site of pilgrimage: the Iglesia de la Tercera Orden overlooks the city of Bogotá.

Figure 12.4. Transnational cuisine: cassava patties are a popular snack.

northern part of the South American continent. Indeed, Bogotá attracts a vast and diverse population from many rural areas within the country and across its borders from neighboring countries such as Ecuador and Venezuela. Although immigration to the country is far less than its emigration, this flow of people has nonetheless added to its ethnic and cultural mix.

Looking at the built environment of Bogotá itself, again we see various aspects of a transnational landscape. There is a range of architecture from different time periods embodying local and international influences, and more recently, the development of small gated communities with European village design influences (figure 12.5). Cars manufactured in the United States, Brazil, Japan, and Europe travel along the congested streets. If we turn to focus on media industries, we can also see the linkages that this commercial activity has made between the built and social landscape— locally, nationally, and internationally. The offices of one of the main national daily newspapers, *El Tiempo*, and television news and entertainment broadcasters, Citytv, share a building in the downtown section of the city (figure 12.6). Both the newspaper and television station are owned by Casa Editorial El Tiempo, with the television name and brand being licensed from the Canadian station of the same name. Local residents can view news shows being filmed live on the building's balconies or record commentary

Figure 12.5.   Gated residences: European and Latin American urban spaces combine.

Figure 12.6. Media connections: *El Tiempo* **and Citytv provide and produce important connections to local, national, regional, and international places and cultures.**

in a video booth (*City Cápsula*) placed outside the building, while also being able to view broadcasts of national news coverage and dubbed or subtitled programs from the Canadian *Citytv* broadcasts.

Interestingly, a comedy series, *Ugly Betty*—picked up by the U.S. ABC channel and the Canadian Citytv station and began airing in September 2006—is a reworking of the immensely popular Colombian *telenovela* (or soap opera), *Yo soy Betty, la fea* (I am Betty, the ugly one), which was syndicated to a broad range of countries. The series focused on the "unattractive," but intelligent Betty, who emerges from the proverbial ugly duckling to become the successful swan managing a fashion company (Hodgson, 2000). Betty's character was viewed as transcending regional and national boundaries through her promotion of the "ordinary" worker. In general, Colombian *telenovelas* have been a significant source of revenue for the national media industry, with several shows being broadcast in other Latin American countries and on Miami-based Spanish-language television broadcasters, and *Yo soy Betty* has expanded this presence even further.

These vibrant representations, landscapes, and activities illustrate a view of Colombian life that highlights a diversity of transnational spaces, which survive despite many limitations and mainstream media depictions to the contrary. It is important to recognize this ongoing dynamism while also trying to understand the more negative aspects of transnationalism—for example, displacement and political conflict—in a broader historical and geographic context. While acting as a catalyst for a diversity of artistic and economic developments, Colombia also continues to struggle with prevailing poverty, civil conflict, and crime—all three of which have been interconnected to some degree. *Telenovelas* may offer a brief escape from the harsher realities of daily living, but a closer look at the larger-scale movements of Colombians is necessary to understand this more difficult side to transnationalism.

Placing the Displaced: Colombian Migratory Spaces

Migration has become a central component of Colombian identities. This movement of people is due to several economic, political, and social instabilities. Economic factors have been marked by limited domestic and foreign markets for investment, goods, and services; austerity measures being used to rein in government spending on social and welfare programs; high unemployment and underemployment; and a substantial informal economy (including widespread corruption and the drug trade in cocaine). Economic difficulties were exacerbated following a recession in 1999, however, the economy appears to have been stabilizing and gradually growing in recent years. Despite this relative improvement there are still major concerns about the pervasiveness of poverty and the unequal distribution of wealth: the GNI PPP (gross national income purchasing power parity) per capita in 2004 was US$7,420, and the percentage of the population living on less than US$2 per day was 18 percent (Population Reference Bureau, 2006b).

Politically and socially, Colombia has struggled with an internal armed conflict that has lasted over 40 years, resulting in substantial rates of extrajudicial killings, internally displaced citizens, and ongoing emigration: "In the last decade, large-scale emigration has marked Colombian society, with roughly one of every 10 Colombians living abroad" (Bérubé, 2005). The conflict is complicated, involving a range of groups— left-wing guerrillas (the Revolutionary Armed Forces [FARC] and the National Liberation Army [ELN]), the Colombian government's official forces, and extreme-right-wing paramilitary organizations (under the umbrella of the United Self-Defense Forces of Colombia [AUC]). The conflict has also changed its focus over the years: from an armed movement to establish a communist government, to several conflicting groups attempting to secure earnings from the drug trade and the land from which it originates: "The armed confrontation has evolved from an ideology-based conflict to one driven by territorial control and economic interests. Today, irregular armed groups are involved in drug trafficking, kidnapping, and terrorist activities" (Bérubé, 2005). Although peace negotiations during recent years have haltingly made attempts to address these issues of violence and displacement, substantial areas of land and significant sections of the population continue to exist in a precarious and vulnerable state (for an overview of the conflict see the *Guardian Unlimited* [2006] interactive guide). Although the government agency Social Action estimates that the number of those displaced by the conflict is around 1.9 million, nongovernmental organizations (NGOs), such as the Consultancy on Human Rights and Displacement (COHES) and the Episcopalian Conference of Catholic Churches, state that the figure is greater than 3.8 million (of a total Colombian population of approximately 46 million) (Associated Press, 2006).

In Colombia, internally displaced persons (IDPs) are often forced to flee from rural communities, where a great deal of conflict violence and human rights abuses have been taking place (such as massacres at the hands of paramilitary groups), in order to reside instead in poor marginal communities in urban areas. IDPs are those who have been forced to leave their homes due to dangerous circumstances, such as armed conflict, human rights violations, or natural or human-made disasters, but have not crossed an international state border. In the Colombian case, the internally displaced population is overrepresented by indigenous and Afro-Colombian people, and has increased recently during the period 1999–2002, and then again from 2004 to the present day (Bérubé, 2005).

While we may look at the situation of IDPs as one that appears to be largely local and national in character, at closer inspection we can also see that this "internal diaspora" is bound up in transnational relations (Villaveces-Izquierdo, 1999). IDPs may become asylum seekers and refugees in other countries due to an ongoing fear for their safety and continued persecution if they continue to reside within the country. Colombians living as refugees in the Americas, although difficult to track, are estimated at 290,000 for 2004 (Bérubé, 2005). For the period from 1996 to 2003 Colombians made up the largest percentage of asylum seekers from the region of Latin America and the Caribbean, at 24 percent of total applications (or 89,100 claims). The majority stayed within the region (39,200—mostly received by Ecuador and Costa Rica), followed by the United States and Canada (32,200), and Europe (16,700) (UNHCR, 2004). According to the Population Data Unit of the United Nations High Commissioner for Refugees (UNHCR) (2004) this movement of Colombians appears to be one that will continue for some time:

> Recently, the number of Colombian asylum-seekers has sharply increased, from just over 2,000 in the late 1990s to more than 20,000 per year since 2001. While the number of Colombians seeking asylum in the region continues to rise, Europe and North America have received fewer applications recently.

For those who are filing for asylum there is at least some hope of improved security, but the process can be lengthy and often under extremely tense circumstances, which can make accessing adequate housing and income difficult in the destination country:

> Juan Carlos and Nancy, aged 26 and 24, recently arrived from Colombia and claimed asylum. They have an eight-year-old daughter. They were temporarily placed in a reception center. . . . There was a man living in the neighboring room with an alcohol problem. He lurched at their child in the corridor and when Juan Carlos went to protect her, the neighbor started shouting abuse at him. . . . A heated row ensued. The police arrived. . . . The neighbor did all the talking (benefiting from the language advantage) and Juan Carlos was arrested. . . . From what he understood, the police threatened to deport him and his wife and take away the child. With support from the Medical Foundation, they convinced the council to move them to other temporary accommodation. (CARILA, n.d.:18, in Torres/ICAR 2003:37).

There is a need, therefore, for countries to work together to develop transnationally collaborative and culturally sensitive policies addressing refugees and settlement programs, which—apart from repatriation (the mandatory return of individuals to their country of origin)—so far have tended to receive limited attention.

Transnational relations have also been forged by national and international NGOs, such as the Red Cross and Amnesty International, who have played an important role in documenting human rights violations and putting pressure on national and international institutions to address issues of institutional corruption and displaced populations. A large part of the reason why people have been unable to maintain a livelihood and have fled their land has been due to competing forces attempting to control the drug trade—and while a substantial proportion of cocaine may originate in Colombia, its largest market is in the United States (although the market is also growing in other destinations). Without an international market and a transnational network of producers and consumers, therefore, this illicit substance would have a far reduced presence. The United States has also been intertwined with the current government's Plan Colombia efforts to curb drug trafficking by providing financial and military assistance (with limited effect). However, as national and international agencies have noted, in many impoverished communities with almost nonexistent social welfare, unless there is an alternative crop or source of income as lucrative as cocaine there is little incentive to divest from this economy. Focusing on cocaine production itself is viewed as failing to address the wider problems of international demand, neoliberal policies advocating limited social spending, and global and national socioeconomic inequalities. In addition, crop eradication campaigns, such as aerial herbicide spraying, have been opposed by rural communities in Colombia, Ecuador, and Bolivia, which have pointed out the procedure's indiscriminate nature and deleterious effect on other nearby crops and public health, resulting, for example, in Ecuadorian residents' demands for a cessation of the programs (Lucas, 2000).

Of course, not all Colombian migration is forced—although again we are faced with the muddied area of how much "choice" migrants truly have—a significant proportion of the population has been "pushed" toward leaving due to unstable economic situations, poor labor conditions, and generally high levels of violence, while being "pulled" toward destinations that offer greater employment diversity, more stable currencies for wages and savings, the potential for further education, and previously migrated family members. It is estimated that over 4 million Colombians live abroad, although the number of migrants officially registered with consulates is far lower—770,000 in 2003 (Bérubé, 2005). Regionally, estimates for the Colombian migrant population in 2003 are as follows: the United States and Canada, 2,035,621; Central America, 70,499; the Caribbean and Antilles, 39,676; South America, 1,583,571; Europe, 475,243; and Africa, Asia, and Oceania combined, 38,598; with key destinations being the United States (2,023,200), Venezuela (1,338,000), Spain (240,390), Ecuador (192,891), and the United Kingdom (90,000) (Bérubé, 2005). As immigration controls have been reinforced in some countries (e.g., the United States following 9/11), migrants have shifted toward other destinations (e.g., select European countries). Additionally, these tightened immigration policies have resulted in increases in undocumented migration and an increasing vulnerability of this population to human smuggling and trafficking of women and children (estimated to include 50,000 overseas Colombians).

Colombians living abroad maintain transnational economic and social ties through their substantial contributions of remittances, adding up to U.S.$3,857 million in 2004 (the third-largest amount for Latin American migrants after Mexico [U.S.$16,613 million] and Brazil [U.S.$5,624 million]) (IDB, 2005b). The Colombian government has been seeking to regularize these flows and facilitate the process of money-sending through discussions addressing reduced transfer fees. Politically, Colombians have the possibility of being official transnational citizens due to their ability to maintain dual nationality, although the political activism of the Colombian diaspora has been limited. This reticence to become politically involved in a transnational context could be reflective of the politically volatile situation that migrants have been required to negotiate in Colombia and have attempted to leave behind through moving. In studies of Latin American diaspora communities in the United States it has been noted that Colombians have tended to be more disparate than other nationals (e.g., Cubans in Miami or Dominicans in New York), with key transnational relations being sustained through contacts with close family, friends, and through ongoing provision of financial support from earnings saved abroad, rather than an involvement in more formal organizations and government institutions (Guarnizo, Portes, and Haller, 2003; Collier and Gamarra, 2003). These distinctive transnational practices and relations also suggest, therefore, the need to understand the different experiences and contexts of Latin Americans, rather than conceptualizing one single overgeneralized "transnational" community.

Exercise: Transnational Street Scene

To help us understand how we might use the context of Colombia to interpret transnationalism in a practical way, let us undertake a brief landscape-reading exercise. The street scene shown in figure 12.7 depicts one of the main thoroughfares in the small southwestern Colombian town of San Augustín on a weekday morning. At first glance this may not appear to be a particularly transnational landscape, but if we start to look more closely we can begin to see aspects that we initially missed. (Before reading on, try to note a few of the characteristics of the image that could be used as examples of transnationalism, and why.)

Figure 12.7. Reading a transnational landscape: In what ways does this San Augustín street scene depict local and global connections?

We can begin with the dominant elements of the photograph: the Pitalito bus that is stopped on the street, the two schoolboys walking away from our view, and the woman holding a basket on the left. The bus appears to be an old-fashioned rural vehicle containing bench seats and significant signs of wear and tear. If we look at the bus front, however, we can also see that the vehicle has been made by a U.S. manufacturer, Chevrolet (and if we had the chance to look in more detail at other vehicles on the road we would also notice other U.S.- and Japanese-produced vehicles). This alone illustrates the presence of transnational commodities, such as those used for transportation. Looking at the clothes the boys are wearing we might be able to deduce that these are local school uniforms, but at the same time these (and the clothing and shoes the woman is wearing to the left) are possibly made in mass-produced textile factories in Colombia or Asia (particularly the People's Republic of China). If we make a link between attending school and the curriculum that students study, we can also reflect on the content, which is taught in Spanish (historically, linked to European colonialism, but also the dominant language in most Latin American countries—with the exception of Brazil), and which has also helped influence Colombian migrants' decisions to move to more economically stable locales where Spanish is widely spoken, such as Madrid, Miami, and New York. The woman carries a traditional woven *canasto*, or basket, often used to transport goods such as vegetables to and from markets. Some of this produce, grown throughout southwestern Colombia, helps to contribute to the large agricultural sector of the country's economy, a significant proportion of which is exported. In addition, items made using traditional skills, such as weaving, while used by the local population for everyday tasks, are also viewed as desirable goods purchased by visiting tourists from the global North. Less obviously, we may also notice the web of telephone and electrical wires that frame the street. While these latter features represent the presence of local and national infrastructural practices (e.g., telephone and electricity companies, such as the national carrier, Telecom), they also symbolize connections to a range of local, regional, and international communities through a vast range of e-mail and web pages, and a growing number of Internet cafés (including such a café just a block away from the scene pictured).

While the landscape interpretation above is a very brief reading—many of you will be able to recognize other potentially transnational characteristics in the image—we can already note some of the diverse ways in which Latin American settings, such as this, embody growing and dynamic relationships with many places and populations. Hopefully, you will find undertaking similar exercises a useful starting point for unearthing some of the obvious and not-so-obvious transnational geographies of Latin America.

CONCLUSION

While much transnational activity is a form of extraterritoriality conducted national politics, most of it is quotidian. (Smith, Cordero-Guzmán, and Crosfoguel, 2001:11)

Transnationalism is a concept that encompasses a broad diversity of practices and ideas. In addition, Latin America embodies a vast range of cultural and physical landscapes. To rephrase the quotation above, while we may tend to think of transnationalism as being linked to the national political activities that take place beyond nation-state territorial boundaries, the majority of these practices are those occurring daily and often at the local scale. As the case studies discussed illustrate, different types of transnational relations—economic, social, and political—can be seen in landscapes as diverse as rural villages in southwestern Colombia, the beaches of Brazil, the meeting rooms of the European Union, kitchens of restaurants in New York, and plazas in Mexico City.

By focusing on the links between mobility and transnationalism we can see that in many ways locations such as New York, Madrid, Bogotá, and San Diego are all Latin American even though this list extends beyond the traditional physical boundaries of Latin America—socially and economically all these locations are intricately interwoven with the region. In this sense the idea of a "Latin American" identity is represented by a *transnational* imagined community, which is as much about cultural ties and a sense of regional identity as it is about ties to land.

Given this broad field of study, there are endless possibilities for further areas of exploration, but some potential avenues include: the role of media organizations in transnational depictions of Latin America; diaspora communities and political organizing; the representation and challenging of place images through Latin American literature and film; the role of sports and regional sporting events as a process of (trans)nationalism; and the production of alternative transnationalisms through social activism. These are just a few suggestions, but they point to the potentially rich and significant explorations that can work toward placing Latin America and Latin Americans.

NOTES

1. Part of this discussion is adapted from a presentation given at the UNU WIDER Conference on Migration, Poverty and Asylum—"Mobility and Exclusion"—in Helsinki, 2001, and a UWI GG10A Distance Education B.Ed. lecture series, 2003.

2. Before exploring specific migration case studies it is important to be familiar with key concepts in relation to different kinds of population movements. The following discussion will elaborate on selected terms through specific examples.

SUGGESTED WEBSITES

American Friends Service Committee, http://www.afsc.org/immigrants-rights /default.htm

El Tiempo, http://www.eltiempo.com

Mexican American Legal Defense and Educational Fund (MALDEF), http://www .maldef.org

Migration Information Source, http://www.migrationinformation.org

Minuteman Project, http://www.minutemanproject.com

Perry-Castañeda Library Map Collection: Colombian Maps, http://www.lib.utexas .edu/maps/colombia.html

Population Reference Bureau, http://www.prb.org/datafind/datafinder7.htm

Telenovelas in Latin America, http://www.zonalatina.com/Zldata70.htm

The Refugee Council, http://www.refugeecouncil.org.uk

World Social Forum, http://www2.forumsocialmundial.org.br/index.php?cd _language=2

BIBLIOGRAPHY

Amin, Samir. *Capitalism in the Age of Globalization: The Management of Contemporary Society*. London: Zed Books, 1997.

Anderson, Benedict. *Imagined Communities: Reflections on the Origins and Spread of Nationalism*. New York: Verso, 1983.

Anderson, Kay. "Transnationalism." In *Handbook of Cultural Geography*, edited by K. Anderson, P. Domosh, N. Thrift, and S. Pile. London: Sage, 2002.

Anzaldúa, Gloria. *La Frontera/Borderlands*. San Francisco: Aunt Lute Books, 1987.

Aparicio, Frances R., and Candida F. Jaquez, eds. *Musical Migrations: Transnationalism and Cultural Hybridity in Latin/o America*, vol. 1. London: Palgrave Macmillan, 2002.

Appadurai, Arjun., ed. *Globalization*. London: Duke University Press, 2001.

Associated Press. "Cifra de deplazados en Colombia es mayor que lo que admite el Gobierno, afirma ONG." *El Tiempo*, September 12, 2006, http://www.eltiempo .com/conflicto/noticias/ARTICULO-WEB-NOTA_INTERIOR-3240465.html (accessed September 12, 2006).

Bérubé, Myriam. "Migration Information Source—Colombia: In the Crossfire." *Migration Policy Institute*, 2005, http://www.migrationinformation.org/Profiles/print .cfm?ID=344 (accessed June 9, 2006).

Blaut, James. *The Colonizer's Model of the World*. New York: Guilford Press, 1993.

CEMA. "Border Arts Cultural Heritage Project." *California Ethnic and Multicultural Archives*, 2002, http://cemaweb.library.ucsb.edu/bach.html (accessed October 24, 2005).

Chambers, I. *Migrancy, Culture, Identity*. New York: Routledge, 1994.

Collier, Michael W., and Eduardo A. Gamarra. "The Colombian Diaspora in South Florida." Presentation at the Annual Meeting of the Latin American Studies Association, Dallas, Texas, 2003.

Dicken, Peter. *Global Shift: Reshaping the Global Economic Map in the 21st Century*. 4th edition. London: Sage, 2003.

Escobar, Arturo. *Encountering Development: The Making and Unmaking of the Third World*. Princeton, N.J.: Princeton University Press, 1994.

Ghosh, B. "Introduction." In *Return Migration: Journey of Hope or Despair?* edited by B. Ghosh, pp. 1–5. Geneva: IOM/UN, 2000.

Guardian Unlimited. "Colombia Conflict Explained (Interactive Guide)." *Guardian Unlimited*, 2006, http://www.guardian.co.uk/flash/0,635714,00.html (accessed September 10, 2006).

Guarnizo, Luis Eduardo, Alejandro Portes, and William Haller. "Assimilation and Transnationalism: Determinants of Transnational Political Action among Contemporary Migrants." *American Journal of Sociology* 108, no. 6 (2003): 1211–1248.

Hodgson, Martin. "Ugly Betty Woos Colombian Viewers Night after Night." *Guardian Unlimited*. September 18, 2000, http://www.guardian.co.uk/international /story/0,,369567,00.html (accessed September 3, 2006).

IDB. "Remittances to Latin American and Caribbean Countries Topped $45 Billion in 2004." *Inter-American Development Bank Press Release*, 2005a, http://www.iadb .org/NEWS/Display/PRView.cfm?PR_Num=41_05&Language=English (accessed October 28, 2005).

IDB. "Remittance Flows to Latin America and the Caribbean (LAC), 2004." *Inter-American Development Bank*, 2005b, http://www.iadb.org/mif/remittances /markets/index.cfm?language=En&parid=1 (accessed October 28, 2005).

IME. "US-Mexico Labor Market—Mexican Workers: A Key Element for Prosperity in the United States." *Instituto de Los Mexicanos en El Exterior*, 2006, http://www .ime.gob.mx/investigaciones/aportaciones/labor_market.pdf (accessed September 7, 2006).

King, R. "Generalizations from the History of Return Migration." In *Return Migration: Journey of Hope or Despair?* edited by B. Ghosh, pp. 7–55. Geneva: IOM/UN, 2000.

Lucas, Kintto. "Plan Colombia's Herbicide Spraying Causing Health and Environmental Problems." *InterPress Service*, 2000, http://www.commondreams.org /headlines/101700-01.htm (accessed September 8, 2006).

Mains, Susan P. "Statutes of Liberty: Migration and Urbanism in the Borderlands." *Yearbook of the Association of Pacific Coast Geographers* 61 (1999): 42–66.

Mains, Susan P. "An Anatomy of Race and Immigration Politics in California." *Journal of Social and Cultural Geography* 1, no. 2 (2000): 143–154.

Mains, Susan P. "Representing National Identity, Borders, and Migration: Making News in Southern California." *Hagar: International Social Science Review* 2 (2002): 271–298.

Mason, Eisha. "Exploitation without Borders." *The Black Commentator* 183 (May 11, 2006), http://www.blackcommentator.com/183/183_exploitation_without _borders_mason.html (accessed September 7, 2006).

MIF-IDB. "Remittances to Latin America and the Caribbean." *Inter-American Development Bank*, 2002, http://www.iadb.org/mif/v2/files/Pager2002.doc (accessed October 28, 2005).

Mitchell, Kathryn. "Transnational Discourse: Bringing Geography Back." *Antipode* 29, no. 2 (1997): 101–114.

Orozco, Manuel. "Globalization and Migration: The Impact of Family Remittances in Latin America." *Latin American Politics and Society* 44, no. 2 (2002): 41–66.

Orrenius, Pia M. "US Immigration and Economic Growth: Putting Policy on Hold." *Southwest Economy* 6 (November/December 2003), http://www.dallasfed.org /research/sw/2003/swe0306a.html (accessed September 7, 2006).

Papastergiadis, N. *The Turbulence of Migration.* Oxford: Polity Press, 2000.

Population Reference Bureau. *Population Reference Bureau Data Finder.* US: Population Reference Bureau, 2006a, http://www.prb.org/datafind/datafinder7.htm (accessed September 7, 2006).

Population Reference Bureau. *World Population Data Sheet.* US: Population Reference Bureau, 2006b, http://www.prb.org/pdf06/06WorldDataSheet.pdf (accessed May 15, 2007).

Portes, Alejandro. "Globalization from Below: The Ride of Transnational Communities." *Transnational Communities Progamme: Working Paper Series.* WPTC-81-01, 1997, http://www.transcomm.ox.ac.uk/working%20papers/portes.pdf (accessed October 24, 2005).

Smith, Dan. *The State of the World Atlas.* 6th edition. London: Penguin, 1999.

Smith, Robert C., Hector Cordero-Guzmán, and Ramón Crosfoguel. "Introduction: Migration, Transnationalization, and Ethnic and Racial Dynamics in a Changing New York." In *Migration, Transnationalization, and Race in a Changing New York,* edited by Robert C. Smith, Hector Cordero-Guzmán, and Ramón Crosfoguel, pp. 1–32. Philadelphia: Temple University Press, 2001.

Swyngedouw, Eric. "Neither Global nor Local: 'Glocalization' and the Politics of Scale." In *Spaces of Globalization: Reasserting the Power of the Local,* edited by K. Cox, pp. 137–166. New York: Guilford, 1997.

Torres, Anastasia Bermúdez/ICAR. "Navigation Guide to Refugee Populations: Colombians." *ICAR,* 2003, http://www.icar.org.uk/?lid=2021 (accessed September 7, 2006).

UNHCR. "Refugees and Asylum-Seekers in Latin America and the Caribbean: Levels and Trends, 1980–2003." *UNHCR,* 2004, http://www.unhcr.org/cgi-bin/texis /vtx/statistics/opendoc.pdf?tbl=STATISTICS&id=4198c2594 (accessed September 7, 2006).

Villaveces-Izquierdo, Santiago. "Internal Diaspora and State Imagination: Colombia's Failure to Envision a Nation." *International Union for the Scientific Study of Population (IUSSP) Working Paper,* 1999, http://www.iussp.org/members /restricted/publications/Cairo99/cairo-27.pdf (accessed September 7, 2006).

WSF. "What the World Social Forum Is." *World Social Forum,* 2005, http://www .forumsocialmundial.org.br/main.php?id_menu=19&cd_language=2 (accessed October 24, 2005).

13

Beyond the Nation-State

Scaling Claims to Latino/a Citizenship in the United States

Joel Jennings

The message from Los Angeles to the National Mall in Washington—as well as St. Louis and other cities in between—was broader: America's new immigrants intend to flex political muscle that matches their burgeoning numbers.

—*St. Louis Post Dispatch*, August 15, 2006

Spring 2006 had the makings of a watershed in Latino/a politics. The season was marked by a sudden emergence of a previously "invisible" Latino/a population across the United States. With cries of "Si, se puede," hundreds of thousands of Latino/a protesters and supporters took to the streets to demand recognition and the right to work legally in the United States. Seemingly overnight the question of Latino/a citizenship became a hotly debated topic across the spectrum of mass media in the United States. Protests, organized by unions, churches, and social activists, coincided with the decision of the 109th Congress to address issues of immigration reform. The possibility of change, after nearly 15 years without a major piece of federal immigration legislation, raised the hopes of immigrants and activists across the country.

During the past 20 years, the Latino/a population has overtaken the African American population as the largest minority in the United States. The population expanded by 58 percent between 1990 and 2000, from 22 million to more than 35 million, according to the United States census. A large majority of Latinos/as live in cities—78 percent living in the 100 largest cities in the United States (Brookings Institution, 2002). These figures highlight, furthermore, that Latino/a immigration is not a regional issue isolated in the Southwest and large cities like Chicago and New York. Rather, in the past decade Latino/a immigration has become a *national* process with a vast range of social impacts.

Immigration has become such a national issue that observers of the immigrants' rights protests and the subsequent media storm that accompanied the rallies would have been hard pressed to identify *any* Latino/a issues that were *not* tied to national questions of formal citizenship at the federal scale. Debate in Congress, in the media, and even among immigrant rights activists were polarized around two alternative sets of legislation. On the one hand, lawmakers were urged to consider punitive measures that were intended to punish undocumented immigrants and thus purportedly reduce the incentive for undocumented immigrants to enter the United States. At the other pole, activists supporting immigrant rights lobbied strongly for laws that would offer many undocumented immigrants an opportunity to eventually obtain full citizenship.

Ultimately, the failure of Congress to enact a legislative reform has ensured that citizenship remains the largest social issue facing the Latino/a community in the United States. The focus on establishing formal citizenship, however, has pushed other less visible struggles for Latino/a recognition into the shadows of the debate. This chapter will argue that struggles for Latino/a citizenship currently being advanced at *subnational* scales in the United States have significant implications for future claims of citizenship, even though, and indeed because, they are being negotiated at a scale other than that of the nation-state.

This chapter begins with an overview of the demographic and political contexts of Latino/a immigration in the United States. Next, it examines these national contexts in terms of a brief account of the current demographic, political, and social characteristics of the Latino population in St. Louis. The chapter moves on to analyze claims of belonging being made on behalf of recent migrants by Latino/a leaders in St. Louis. The argument is that despite media portrayals to the contrary, undocumented Latinos/as are not merely making claims to formal citizenship or even claiming the right to work. Rather, they are making claims to belonging and recognition based on less formal desires that may or may not be directly tied to attaining formal citizenship. The chapter concludes by suggesting that examining Latino/a claims to citizenship can be usefully analyzed through the theoretical lens of geographic scale.

Finally, the goal in this chapter is neither to provide a comprehensive account of Latino/a citizenship struggles in the United States nor a definitive ethnographic account of the Latino community in St. Louis. Rather, the goal is to identify a number of themes in the regional dynamics of St. Louis that may resonate with Latino/a struggles throughout the United States.

NEW DESTINATIONS:
NATIONAL TRENDS IN LATINO/A IMMIGRATION

Within the past decade, the Latino/a population surpassed African Americans as the largest minority group in the United States. This tremendously diverse population, originating from the United States and 22 states/countries throughout Latin America, collectively possesses very few characteristics that actually provide a unifying point of reference to the term "Latino/a." Broad characteristics such as Spanish language and origins in Latin America describe major segments of the Latino/a population, but may exclude others. Large numbers of indigenous people throughout Latin America, for example, do not speak Spanish, or Spanish is not their primary language. Similarly, Chicanos/as often simultaneously self-identify as both Latinos/as and as citizens of the United States, including many who come from families that have been U.S. citizens for many generations.

The development of this heterogeneous Latino population reflects the long and complex relationship between the United States and the rest of Latin America. While it is impossible in this chapter to examine the specific relationships between the United States and each of the Latin American countries, several broad trends have contributed to immigration patterns during the past half-century. Poor economic conditions, social instability, currency devaluations, and civil war have all, at various times, inspired waves of immigration from Latin America. Central American immigrants, particularly those fleeing conflict in Guatemala, for example, formed large communities in New York, New Jersey, and California. Mexican immigration in particular, caused in part by economic fallout from the NAFTA trade agreement coupled with the peso crisis, has risen significantly since the early 1990s.

The sheer demographic increase in immigration from Latin America, furthermore, has changed the traditional destinations for immigrants, particularly those from Mexico. While Los Angeles, New York, and Chicago have long been destination cities, recent studies suggest that Latino/a immigration patterns have become far more diverse in recent years.

A recent report by the Brookings Institution (2002) identifies four types of metropolitan areas in this most recent trend of Latino/a immigration: established Latino/a metros, new Latino/a destinations, fast-growing Latino/a hubs, and small Latino/a places. The report argues that while Latino/a immigration is increasing nationwide, there are significant differences in *ways* that urban populations are expanding. Established Latino/a metros (e.g., Los Angeles or Chicago), for example, grew faster than the national average, but slower than new Latino/a destinations like Atlanta or Orlando. Fast-growing Latino/a hubs, like San Diego, furthermore, traditionally have larger populations, and are growing faster than established Latino/a metros.

Finally, small Latino/a places, including St. Louis, had much smaller populations and growth rates—though, as I will demonstrate later in this chapter, even these smaller growth rates can have significant social impacts.

This increasing diversification of immigrant destinations, furthermore, serves as the vital context for my arguments about multiscalar citizenship. While the established Latino/a metros mentioned above have historically had substantial Latino/a immigrant populations, small Latino/a places like St. Louis and many cities throughout the South do not have a history of substantial Latino/a populations (see figure 13.1). Thus, while the U.S. government debates federal legislation to address immigration, state legislators and now even municipal governments across the United States are beginning to discuss laws that would intervene in what has traditionally been a federal-scale issue.

The rest of this chapter will examine the struggles to expand citizenship for Latino/a immigrants in St. Louis, Missouri. It is important to note, however, that St. Louis is not unique in terms of any of the social dynamics discussed. The growing demographic power and the increasingly dispersed geographic reality of Latinos/as in the United States ensures that citizenship for Latino/a immigrants will remain an important social debate in the coming years.

LATINO CITIZENSHIP: LEGAL STATUS, CLAIMS, AND POWER

While thousands marched in protests and attended rallies designed to demonstrate the political and social power of Latinos/as in the United States, they were met by counterrallies and heavily armed members of informal militia groups along the U.S.-Mexico border (see chapter 5). Underlying the spectacle of these performances, however, is a serious debate that has been contested in societies throughout Western history. Establishment of the parameters of citizenship, defined as the rights and responsibilities that accompany membership in a polity or state, has been a contested concept in many democratic societies. Citizenship, as it has been defined since T. H. Marshall's seminal work on citizenship and class in Great Britain, is thus not solely dependent on a legal relationship with the state, but rather based on participation within a given state (Marshall, 1950).

The idea that citizenship is bounded strictly by the nation-state has also been challenged by recent studies of transnational and postnational citizenship. Citizenship theorists such as Yasemin Soysal (1994), Aiwah Ong (1999), and others have argued that the nation-state has become increasingly less relevant to practices of citizenship. Soysal (1994), focusing on changing relationships between immigrants and states in Europe, has argued that nationally bounded citizenship is less relevant because states are recognizing immigrants and granting rights to noncitizen groups. Ong (1999), in contrast, focuses on

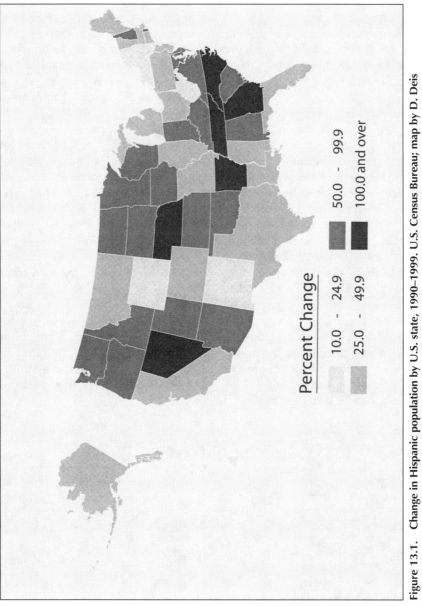

Percent Change

10.0 - 24.9	50.0 - 99.9
25.0 - 49.9	100.0 and over

Figure 13.1. Change in Hispanic population by U.S. state, 1990–1999. U.S. Census Bureau; map by D. Deis

the ways that Chinese immigrants demonstrate agency by using transnational citizenship as a means to enable flexible accumulation and maintain competitive advantages in the global economy. National citizenship then, according to this line of thought around citizenship, is being decentered and replaced by forms of citizenship that are no longer spatially constrained by the boundaries of the nation-state. Rather, they are based on the nation-state's recognition of citizenship developing at *other* scales (Soysal, 1994).

Scales of citizenship have also been an increasing focus of geographers during the past decade. Joe Painter (2003), for example, has suggested that regional citizenship *within* member-states of the European Union has become the focus of some attention as EU officials seek greater economic and social parity between regions. Ehrkamp and Leitner (2003), furthermore, have argued convincingly that citizenship is both relational and multiscalar. Their study of Turkish migrants in Germany suggests the negotiated construction of citizenship at multiple scales, but does not fully develop the relationship *between* scales.

If Latino/a citizenship in the United States is being decentered away from the scale of the nation-state, what scales should we examine in search of Latino/a citizenship practices? While Latino/a practices of transnational citizenship have been examined in a voluminous body of work, less research has been done investigating the role of scale in the development of subnational citizenship practices. This idea will be developed more fully in the final section of the chapter. First, however, it is important to establish the geographic context of St. Louis, the region where this chapter explores the multiscalar development of Latino/a citizenship.

DEFINITIONS

Latino/a

Latinos/as are individuals whose origin or ancestry can be traced to one of the twenty-two countries in Latin America.

Citizenship

Citizenship is generally thought of as membership in a state entailing rights and responsibilities for both parties.

Multiscalar

Originating, engaging, or occurring at multiple geographic levels (e.g., local, state, federal).

LATINOS/AS IN ST. LOUIS: REGIONAL DYNAMICS AND NATIONAL TRENDS

St. Louis, designed as a model modern city, failed spectacularly when it was unable to make the transition to postmodernity. The metropolitan area, with a population of nearly 3 million people, is anchored by the highly urbanized city of St. Louis and surrounded by eight suburban and exurban counties. Located in the heart of the Midwest and the largest metropolitan area in the majority rural state of Missouri, St. Louis was established and has grown at the conflux of the Mississippi and Missouri rivers.

The growth of the Latino/a population in the St. Louis area, as in many other cities in the Midwest and South, is a relatively new phenomenon that has predominantly developed since the early 1990s. After steady expansion throughout much of the twentieth century, the recent increase of Latinos/as in St. Louis has largely been driven by immigration from Mexico, followed by much smaller Central American, South American, and Puerto Rican populations (Puerto Ricans are U.S. citizens, but they are better thought of as migrants in this context). Mexican immigrants compose an estimated 70 percent of the Latino/a population in the St. Louis region, with Puerto Ricans adding another 15 percent and the rest coming from other countries through South and Central America. The various socioeconomic trends that have contributed to the growth of the St. Louis Latino/a population will be discussed in a moment, but first it is important to hypothesize about some traits that St. Louis has in common with other cities that have rapidly growing Latino/a populations.

St. Louis shares a number of common traits with other regions throughout the Midwest and South that are likewise experiencing similar demographic growth. These trends include economies with unmet demands for entry-level labor, lower housing costs than large megalopolises (e.g., Los Angeles), and less competition for jobs from other recently arrived immigrants. Academic studies in cities as diverse as Raleigh-Durham in North Carolina, Nashville, Tennessee, and Lincoln, Nebraska, have all reported significant growth of the Latino/a communities during the past decade.

While a growing Latino/a population has been vital in meeting the continuous demand for labor by the U.S. economy, this growth also raises challenges for cities that have not traditionally had significant Latino/a immigration. Providing culturally sensitive health care, educating hospital staff and police forces, and preparing school districts to address the needs of bilingual children and their often monolingual (non-English) parents are just a few of the adjustments that cities are seeking to address. The rest of this section focuses on the struggles for belonging and recognition of Latinos/as in St. Louis.

THE ST. LOUIS METROPOLITAN AREA

St. Louis has historically had a diverse economy composed of manufacturing, shipping and transportation, the defense industry, and breweries. Contemporary industry leaders in the region include beer-brewing giant Anheuser-Busch, defense-industry leader Boeing Corporation (formerly headquarters for McDonnell Douglas), and more technologically oriented companies like healthcare company Express Scripts.

The diversity of the St. Louis economy, however, is not matched by a similar ethnic diversity throughout the region. St. Louis City, the urban core of the region, has experienced "white flight" on a scale seen in few other cities during the past century. Since 1950, the City of St. Louis has lost more than 1 million residents to the counties and surrounding areas as city dwellers sought to escape the decaying neighborhoods, failing schools, and racial tensions of a city in decline.

Neighborhoods across St. Louis, furthermore, tend to be highly segregated both by ethnicity and country of origin. Delmar Avenue, a well-known avenue that loosely bisects the city, is widely recognized in St. Louis as the ethnic divide between African Americans in North St. Louis and white, middle-class communities of primarily European descent in South City. Families of German and Polish descent are prevalent throughout the southern parts of the city, while "The Hill" neighborhood is dominated by Italian-Americans. Bosnian, Vietnamese, and African communities are also present in smaller numbers throughout the central corridor of South City.

The Latino/a population in St. Louis, even relative to the more recently established Vietnamese and Bosnian communities, is very new. Middle-class flight, both African American and white, from the city to the suburbs, furthermore, has created opportunities for ethnic minorities to redevelop some neighborhoods within the city. Latinos/as, taking advantage of such opportunities, have created a small strip of ethnic shops on Cherokee Street. Though the Cherokee Street neighborhood is generally identified as being ethnically Latino/a, it is not an ethnic enclave in any traditional sense of the term. Unlike in other major cities, Latinos/as are scattered throughout the St. Louis region, and in no area do they comprise more than 4 percent of the total population.[1]

In contrast to St. Louis City, however, the rest of the suburban and exurban counties that comprise the St. Louis metropolitan area have experienced relatively consistent growth, both in terms of population and development. The availability of land for construction, strong public schools, and population growth has generated a westward expansion across St. Louis County and created significant exurban growth. This westward expansion, in turn, has created significant demand for laborers; particularly construction workers, roofers, and lawn-care workers. Service-industry and general entry-level workers are also in demand across the region.

Low housing costs, high availability of jobs, and lower levels of competition from other immigrants and ethnic groups have also made St. Louis a desirable destination for Latinos/as living within the United States. St. Louis, like many of the nontraditional immigrant destinations with growing populations, offers opportunities for work and an improved standard of living at a lower cost. Lower costs of living, in turn, allow immigrants to send money back to family members in their countries of origin—thus making cities like St. Louis even more desirable places to live.

A CLOSER LOOK:
EXAMINING CLAIMS TO LATINO/A CITIZENSHIP

Before evaluating Latino/a claims of citizenship, we must first identify what claims are being made—and on whose behalf they are being advanced. This research began by using several methods during 14 months of research, including participant observation, a quantitative survey, and more than 50 interviews with Latino/as from St. Louis. The majority of these interviews were conducted with community leaders, nearly all of whom are Latinos/as themselves. The study participants came from a range of backgrounds, including priests, social workers, political activists, and clinicians. A number of recent migrants, both documented and undocumented, from around the St. Louis area, were also interviewed.

These interview sessions used semistructured interviews to explore a number of themes including citizenship practices, transnationalism, and the ways that various citizenship practices were developing at different scales. A quantitative survey also was conducted with more than 570 members of the Latino/a community that examined, among other things, specific citizenship practices. This research with Latinos/as around the region included participant observation, including work in a community health clinic, an after-school tutoring program for the children of recent migrants, and participation in community meetings.

Several themes of Latino/a citizenship emerged from these various and complex methods of data collection. Though informants provided many examples of social processes from which undocumented Latinos/as are excluded or denied full access, three relatively consistent themes emerged from the interviews. The first theme, the need for undocumented immigrants to obtain valid driver's licenses, is a struggle that has historically been negotiated at the scale of the U.S. state (e.g., Missouri). The second theme, in-state college tuition for college students, is also a negotiation between Latinos/as and the U.S. state governments. The final theme, protecting workers' rights, is contested at many scales. This chapter, however, will focus on the local scale efforts to defend workers' rights.

Driver's Licenses as Citizenship?

The political struggle to provide undocumented immigrants access to driver's licenses is a theme that appeared numerous times throughout interviews with both Latino/a leaders and recent immigrants.[2] During an interview, a prominent Latina activist, Anna, was asked to identify the impacts of undocumented Latinos/as being unable to access driver's licenses. Her response highlighted the importance of differences between the policies of two adjoining states.

> ANNA: Well, the impact is that we have drivers out there without driver's licenses. They get [license] plates—cause in Illinois you can get plates without a driver's license. And then they drive here without license and insurance. Uh, what is the impact that sometimes when they have accidents sometimes they get scared and run away. So they get in more trouble.

Anna's answer highlights two roles that scale plays in the political struggle to pass state legislation granting undocumented immigrants access to driver's licenses. First, differences between Missouri and Illinois policies regarding license plates and driver's licenses create an opportunity for Latinos/as to *legally* obtain license plates, but leave them still unable to get valid driver's licenses. Excluding undocumented Latinos/as from obtaining driver's licenses, coupled with a very poorly developed public transportation system, exacerbates the types of scenarios that Anna describes. Second, the importance of geographic scale becomes apparent from the following comments by both an undocumented immigrant and an immigrant rights activist from St. Louis.

> JOSE: So, Manos Unidos is doing its job like that, like working more like in legal . . . she already made a couple trips to Jefferson [City] to try to pass a law so that we can have driver's licenses here in St. Louis. (F.P., undocumented, Mexican)
>
> MICHAEL: Uh huh. But I think you know, people for example, are making treks down to Jefferson City to talk to our representatives and to talk to the governor, if you could believe this, and the governor is standing in his office with all these undocumented people to talk about driver's licenses. (Michael, clergy, St. Louis native)

While Washington, D.C., is geographically remote and politically complex, even for experienced political activists, state governments are more accessible. Thus, as Michael's comment seems to suggest, local Latino/a activist groups can more easily organize their limited resources to access and lobby members of the state legislature and executive branch than federal legislators in Washington, D.C.

More important for the arguments around scale, however, is the fact that state governments have traditionally controlled the issuance of formal identification. Because there is no federal identification card for civilians in the United States, each state's legislature has set the standards for the issuance of driver's licenses. As a result, a number of state legislatures have opted to grant driver's licenses to undocumented immigrants, while others have required only minimal documentation that can be easily obtained by immigrants. While the majority of states have opted not to issue driver's licenses to undocumented immigrants, political groups lobbying on behalf of immigrants have succeeded in advancing driver's license legislation. Such political efforts vary from state to state, reflecting the importance of subnational scale efforts to advance the cause of citizenship for undocumented Latinos/as.

While these arguments may seem tenuous or only tangentially relevant to larger questions of Latino/a citizenship in the United States, it is important to point to the Good ID Law passed by the 109th Congress as suggesting the true relevance of such efforts. In the fall of 2005 conservatives in Congress felt that the long tradition of state power to provide identification for state residents was threatening the federal government's ability to govern. While the Good ID Law does not restrict states' abilities to issue independent driver's licenses, it did set a particularly high *federal* standard of proof for anyone wishing to obtain a driver's license or state identification.[3] This dramatic example of legislative power "jumping scale" (Cox, 1998) suggests how seriously a majority of the members of Congress took state-scale legislative efforts to advance Latino/a citizenship.

College Tuition and Latino/a Citizenship

JOEL: Ok. So, I was asking you about the Governor's Commission and what the role is there? What they are trying to do?

MARTINA: One of the big things we are working on is Missouri State tuition. To allow any Hispanic who graduated from, or essentially any immigrant-refugee student who graduated from high school in Missouri—and they can only have this for five years—and allow them to any public university. And would make them eligible for any kind of State [of Missouri] aid. (Martina, social worker, Latina)

The Missouri In-State Tuition Act is a second, and in some ways more complex, effort to expand citizenship opportunities for undocumented Latinos/as. Public universities are funded and governed at the U.S.-state scale. The University of Missouri, St. Louis, for example, is funded by the Missouri legislature through a budgeted appropriation bill. As a public university, admissions standards and tuition costs are also controlled and mandated by the state legislature.[4]

Currently, the children of undocumented immigrants who live in the state of Missouri are ineligible to attend public universities in Missouri unless they pay much higher "international student" tuition rates. The difference between in-state tuition rates and international student rates is greater than $6,000 dollars per year, putting university education well beyond the resources of many undocumented high school students. Thus, though many undocumented Latino/a high school graduates have lived in the United States for nearly their entire lives, upon completing public high school, many find themselves unable to continue with formal education.

Many of the same St. Louis–based activists and immigrants' rights organizations who have been fighting for immigrant access to driver's licenses are also lobbying Missouri legislators to pass an immigrant tuition bill. The Missouri Tuition Act would provide Latino/a graduates of public high school the opportunity to attend any public university in Missouri at the cost of in-state tuition.

The Missouri In-State Tuition Act, however, is more complex than lobbying efforts around driver's licenses because immigration activists have jumped (*down*) scale in their efforts to advance the cause of Latino/a citizenship[5] (see also chapter 9). The Missouri In-State Tuition Act is a state-scale legislative effort that mirrors the Dream Act, a similar bill that has been submitted at the federal scale. The nearly overwhelming amount of political capital required to pass federal legislation benefiting undocumented immigrants, however, has led immigrants' rights groups to adopt a bifurcated strategy. Employing the multiscalar approach of lobbying simultaneously at the state and federal scales allows Latino/a leaders to use geographic scale to manipulate *time*—essentially creating the possibility of doubling efforts to strengthen citizenship opportunities for undocumented Latinos/as.

Efforts to increase Latino/a immigrants' access to public universities in the United States highlights the ways that geographic scale is constantly negotiated for political benefit. Though Latino/activists were relatively successful in their early attempts to utilize geographic scale as a political tool, recent efforts by anti-immigrant activists to pass punitive laws at the municipal scale in St. Louis reaffirm the ways that geographic scale is a social construction that is constantly being renegotiated for political advantage.

Worker's Rights: Scaling the Federal to Local?

ANNA: These people [informal employers] come and promise they will pay them—and [undocumented immigrants] work and then at the end of the work—you know—the two weeks they tell them "We are not going to pay you—we don't have no money for you"—you know. And we are working on that. And now we have a partnership with Hourly Wage [Branch of Federal Department of Labor] and they truly go after these people. (Anna, activist, Latina)

Workers' rights are the final themes developed in this chapter. Unlike driver's licenses and lower costs of tuition for immigrant children, protecting workers' rights in St. Louis is concentrated much more at the local and personal scales. The discussion of workers' rights was intentionally left to the end because it is a process that is much more difficult to identify with a single geographic scale. As the vignette above would suggest, fighting for proper treatment of undocumented workers is a *multiscalar* process.

Combating abusive labor practices in St. Louis is multiscalar in the sense that *local* activists have enlisted the assistance of federal agencies such as the U.S. Department of Labor to assist with local efforts. While the federal government, through the "Hourly Wage" program, is making efforts to defend the rights of undocumented immigrant workers, such efforts are generally instigated by local activists, like Anna, who are local community organizers and have established the trust of undocumented residents in St. Louis. Without the assistance of local Latino/a leaders to engage the U.S. Department of Labor and to act as a conduit of information between Latino/a immigrants and government officials, the federal government would be far less effective at addressing labor injustices in the St. Louis region.

Despite some federal efforts to protect immigrant workers from fraud and abuse, most interventions are strictly local efforts by St. Louis activists.

JOSE: This woman, she was not, she was told that she was going to get fired if she kept talking in Spanish and they did not let her say a word in front of customers in Spanish or nothing. She couldn't communicate to her coworkers in Spanish at all . . . so she went to L.K. and L.K. went there. And they told, he promote this woman, and she was, the manager was about to fire her because she kept speaking Spanish and not English, and um . . . the manager did [de]mote her and the manager lowered her wage because she was not following what she was told. So, Lucacia went over there and F.R.V. too and the guy of course he retracts himself and he got the, he returned the old wages to this woman. (Jose, undocumented, Mexican)

Efforts to extend citizenship for undocumented Latino/a immigrants, in the case of labor rights, again highlight the ways that Latino/a activists and immigrants are able to negotiate changes between geographic scales to advance their claims to greater protections. By getting assistance from activists in St. Louis, undocumented immigrants are sometimes able to make claims for protection to the federal government.

As it was suggested above, fighting to protect workers' rights is a multi-scalar process that often involves both activists and officials at the local and federal scales. The very multiscalar nature of this process, however, suggests the important role that geographic scale plays in the development of citizenship. As the accounts above suggest, Latino/a citizenship is developing in the United States in part because immigrants and immigrant rights activists are able to create political windows of opportunity by contesting citizenship issues at various (and previously uncontested) scales.

CONCLUSION

This chapter has argued that subnational efforts to provide increased access to citizenship for undocumented Latinos/as in the United States are important for two reasons. First, amid the ongoing furor around the national citizenship debate, other efforts to increase the ability of undocumented Latinos/as to participate more fully in society are lost. Second, examining the ways that Latino/a leaders and recent immigrants in cities like St. Louis are fighting for greater citizenship in the United States reminds us that the role of geographic scale *is* important as a politically negotiated social process.

Federal-scale debates about the limits of formal citizenship in the United States tend to obscure Latino/a efforts to participate more fully in society at other geographic scales. State, regional, and local efforts to obtain recognition and greater access to citizenship are also vitally important to the development of Latino/a citizenship in the United States. Lobbying efforts to advance bills that would allow undocumented immigrants to obtain driver's licenses, attend state universities at the same fee rate as U.S. citizens, and be protected by U.S. labor laws all advance the ability of undocumented Latino/a immigrants to claim greater participation in U.S. society.

While the case study in this chapter addresses the development of Latino/a citizenship in St. Louis, similar processes are being documented around the United States. As the Latino/a population grows, struggles for citizenship and participation may develop in unexpected areas. Understanding these conflicts as negotiations for greater access to participation and belonging may help legislators, immigrants, and citizens alike to more fully assess the issue at hand.

Finally, exploring the ways that Latino/a activists have utilized geographic scale as part of a political strategy to advance citizenship and participation suggests interesting possibilities in ongoing debates about the proper role of scale in human geography. Geographic scale *is* a politically relevant and indeed central strategy employed by Latino/a activists and protesters to increase access to the informal process of citizenship, even as the formal process seems endlessly blocked by the legislative process at the federal scale.

NOTES

1. Based on Census 2000 data.

2. This is not a surprise given the small number and close relations between Latino/a leaders in the region, particularly in the political sphere. The fact that Latino/a leaders have chosen to focus on a given issue does not negate the importance of the issue.

3. The Good ID law requires that anyone seeking to obtain a driver's license must provide *four* valid sources of identification.

4. Provided the legislature remains within the bounds of the Missouri Constitution. University decisions to raise tuition at the University of Missouri in 1995, for example, were ruled unconstitutional and overturned by Missouri courts.

5. While a number of geographers (see, for example, Cox, 1998) have examined the ways that activist groups have jumped from local to regional or federal scales, the opposite process has been less examined.

SUGGESTED READINGS

Davis, M. *Magical Urbanism: Latinos Reinvent the US City*. London: Verso, 2000.
Suárez-Orozco, M., and M. Páez. *Latinos: Remaking America*. Berkeley: University of California Press, 2002.

BIBLIOGRAPHY

Cox, K. R. "Spaces of Dependence, Spaces of Engagement and the Politics of Scale; or, Looking for Local Politics." *Political Geography* 17, no. 1 (1998): 1–23.

Ehrkamp, P., and H. Leitner. "Turkish Immigrants and the (Re) Construction of Citizenship in Germany." *Political Geography* 24, no. 2 (2003): 127–146.

Marshall, T. H. *Citizenship and Social Class, and Other Essays*. Cambridge: Cambridge University Press, 1950.

Ong, A. *Flexible Citizenship: The Cultural Logics of Transnationality*. Durham, N.C.; London: Duke University Press, 1999.

Painter, J. "European Citizenship and Regions." *Queen's Papers on Europeanization*. Belfast: Queen's University, 2003.

Soysal, Y. N. G. *Limits of Citizenship: Migrants and Postnational Membership in Europe*. Chicago, London: University of Chicago Press, 1994.

Singer, A., and R. Suro. *Latino Growth in Metropolitan America: Changing Patterns, New Locations*. Brookings Institution: Washington, D.C., 2002.

14

Cinematic Spaces of Latin America

James Craine and Mirek Lipinski

The discipline of geography has long utilized visual representations of the world—how humans "see" their environment and how that image is then successfully constructed and reproduced for consumption by viewers is a continuously evolving project that engages some of the most interesting and vital research developed within the field of geography. Geographers have always been interested in investigating the "ways of seeing" that structure and represent geographical practices and ideas and, more recently, geographers have become more and more concerned with the ways in which landscape is shaped by, and carries within it, multiple articulations of cultural memory and identity.

To fully grasp our chapter it is important to realize that films operate as spatial forms—they represent space, place, and landscape within a series of frames and these spatial contexts have also shaped the practices of cinema and the meanings contained within films. This chapter is interested in how film, particularly Latin American cinema, can shape our perceptions of place by constructing "imaginative geographies" (see Driver, 1999; Gregory, 1994) that play central roles in constituting and sustaining both individual and collective notions of Latin American landscape and identities. In addition, film plays a central role in making social imagery concrete as part of the "real"—film has a material effect for those individuals and social groupings that construct and view them. Therefore, any analysis of the role of film in making "imaginative geographies" involves blurring the distinction between the real and the imagined. Geographers too often only consider space as the size of the geographical places and their associated processes. In other words, space is a macroenvironment that exists in space-time, having complex processes and meaning. But space can also be form or structure, or pure space, or even space as geometry. Blaut (1999:511) believes that "our ideas of pure space are distilled from our space-time experience, by the use of our powers of imagination, or by abstraction." Therefore, we engage Latin American cinema as a specific material object worth studying as a distinct geographical record within a broader set of practices and discourses that contain relationships that play a critical role in the construction of particular Latin American cultures.

It is important to understand that Latin American cinema (and any cinema for that matter) is a cultural production: it therefore visually *reproduces* the spatial interpretations of those who construct the film. Thus, the reproduction of culture is integral to the material structure of society and must take into account structures of dominance and oppression, as our two examples illustrate. According to Mitchell (2000:54), "reproduction can be defined as the everyday perpetuation of the social institutions and relations that make possible the material conditions of life. The important point is that social reproduction is never guaranteed, but is also a moment of potential struggle and transformation." Culture industries such as cinema circulate meaning, and through Latin American cinema we can explore how values are produced, circulated, and consumed and how spaces are the components of cultural production and consumption—or, as Mitchell states, we can discover how "aesthetic representations are turned into physical representations" (2000:77).

There exist within geographical research methodologies that can be used to derive the cultural relationships and productions encoded within the spaces of film. Visual geographic methodology pays critical attention to the content and construction of the images themselves, as well as to the contexts of their conception, production, dissemination, consumption, and preservation. One can argue that film and its technologies and practices have become so ubiquitous that they are, for all intents and purposes, invisible—in our chapter we want to make these images, technologies, and practices both visible and comprehensible. Films are produced and consumed in historically specific and carefully constructed ways and many factors combine to frame the ways in which meaning is generated. Thus, film cannot be engaged in isolation from, but rather must be linked in multiple and complex ways to, other forms of material evidence. We are concerned with film not merely as a visual reflection of the "real" world or as the intention of its maker but as discrete moments in the production and circulation of cultural meaning. Film is not only a technology of image making but, more importantly, it is a technology of information transfer and thus functions as an act of communication and it is, we believe, a chain of practices and processes by which geographical information is gathered, geographical facts are ordered, and our imaginative geographies are constructed.

Geography is shaped not only by the politics, philosophy, and economics of society, but also by its technology. The relationship isn't always clear: sometimes technological development leads to a change in geography; sometimes geographical requirements call for a new technology; often the development of the technology itself is the result of a combination of ideological and economic factors. Usually the relationships are broad: one could argue there would be no geography without the map, but the recent rapid increases in the technologies of geography have, so far, had little discernable effect on the how we *interpret* the visualization of geographic data. As a setting for a wide-ranging discourse on geographies, territorialities, and visual fields, cinema is a powerful marker of meaning and intention. Cinematic geographies *happen*—in a nonrepresentational sense, they *do*: they denote, depict, symbolize, and exemplify aspects of multiple actual worlds—and to completely understand geography, we must not submit to the orthodoxies of aesthetic appreciation as found in pure film criticism but we must find and make intelligible the geographies coded within these landscapes through the delineation and interrogation of the unique geographic qualities of cinema—cinematic geographies must be valid and valued on their own terms apart from a discourse imported from film studies. Through the specific works discussed in this chapter, we hope to explore how Latin American cinematic geographies arise from the conditions of their use and thus must be considered in terms of geographical value as well as their social and visual qualities.

In the discussion of Latin American cinema, the use of visual representations as a pedagogic tool can take many different forms and can offer great insight into the power relations between individuals and social institutions. Raymond Williams (1981:6) notes that "every human society has its own shape, its own purpose, its own meanings. Every human society expresses these, in institutions, and in arts and learning." Geographical shapes, meanings, and arts do many things. They are used as mimetic devices to represent real world places and people; they provide sites that permit the exploration of social issues ranging from gender and sexuality to spaces of resistance and contestation; and, perhaps foremost, geographical images create *landscapes*, the traditional domain of geographers, that allow the investigation of dominant ideologies and alternate forms of social contestation.

Since the publication of Sauer's *The Morphology of Landscape* in 1925, cultural geographers have recognized landscape as a central concept and subject, and have focused particularly on how landscapes reflect and symbolize the activities and cultural ideas of a place. Representational landscapes can be viewed as metaphors that are interpreted and analyzed in order to show the role of landscape in social and cultural creation and to help geographers understand space within a social and cultural context. That is, visual landscapes, the representational images of a landscape, can be interpreted to show the sociocultural and political processes that shape landscapes.

Gillian Rose (2001:14–15) clearly articulates the nature of the power relationships within social projects that account for how places, people, and events are made and constructed:

1. Visual representations have their own effects and can be used by many people for many different reasons.
2. Ways of *seeing* are geographically, historically, culturally, and socially specific; how we look at an image is not natural or innocent and is always constructed through various practices, technologies, and knowledges.
3. Visual representations both depend on and produce social inclusions and exclusions (what is seen and what is hidden).

However, regardless of the methodology or discourse, it is important to grasp how geography is embodied in a visual representation, be it a single static photograph or an animated series of photographs projected at a set rate (which is indeed what "cinema" is). One could argue (successfully, we believe), that the nineteenth century was the formative period when applications of photographic technology and habits of photographic seeing were shaped by, and in turn shaped, geographical concerns. During that time period, as ideas about vision and knowledge codified photographic practice, photographs influenced ways of "doing" geography, and shaped issues of geographic concern. One could further argue that photography as an image-making technology and photographs as visual images—independent of their status as art or science—helped people to know the world and articulate their relationship in it. Lowenthal (1976:3) observes, "The lineaments of the world we live in are both seen and shaped in accordance, or by contrast, with images we hold of other worlds—better worlds, past worlds, future worlds. We constantly compare the reality with the fancy. Indeed, without one we could neither visualize nor conceptualize the other." Sontag (1977:4) claims that photographic images "now provide most of the knowledge people have about the look of the past and the reach of the present," while Fyfe and Law (1988:2) state that "depiction, picturing and seeing are ubiquitous features of the process by which most human beings come to know the world as it really *is* for them." Thus, if the geographical imagination can be conceived broadly to include those practices and processes by which we situate ourselves in space and time, then film participates in three fundamental ways: in the empirical practices of gathering factual information in visual forms; in the cognitive processes of ordering that information to produce knowledge of places, peoples, and events; and in the imaginative processes of visualizing the world beyond our immediate experience.

While cinema might be engaged from the perspective of agency and causality, its narrative detail, its circulation, consumption, and impact, we are interested, in this case, in focusing on the way in which geographers might use film to allow us to more fully understand the spaces, identities, and power contained within the performance of a particular film or genre of films: the cinema of Latin America. Using cinema to think geographically can illuminate issues far beyond the narrative content of the images themselves. The constructions and performances found in the films discussed below are central elements in the ongoing and increasingly visual encounters between diverse cultures. The spatiality of social interaction within the realistic appearance of film is inscribed by sociopolitical relations of which cinema is simultaneously a medium and a product (Soja, 1989:6–7). While this constitutes the cultural formations that make the films possible, the films below cannot simply be reduced to signifiers of social forces and relations premised solely on models of *film theory*, nor to models of spectacle within a politically based culture war (cf. the recent controversies related to both Mel Gibson's *The Passion of the Christ* and Michael Moore's *Fahrenheit 9/11*).

The interpretation of geographical representations, in this case Latin American cinema, provides insight into how society and space in Latin America are ordered and how the construction and the representation of that space are manipulated by powerful groups through cultural codes that promote dominant ideologies. Uncovering the shared systems of meaning provides hints to the social, economic, and political circumstances of the societies that produce the visual image being analyzed. In the examples that follow, we look at how geography can provide knowledge of Latin America through a particular focus on two very different icons of Latin American cinema.

It is useful to ask, even rhetorically, whose visions and knowledges are being used to map the cinematic geographies discussed in this chapter. This is a crucial, if not all-defining, question that must be addressed to critically understand the cinematic landscape. Cinematic places and spaces are not neutral. Just how socialized power structures are involved in the transformation of these geographies reflects the response to a contested space. Latin American films are viable and unique spatialities that function as social constructions and geographic cultural reproductions in which we can discuss these contested geographies. And, like Latin America itself, its cinema is exceedingly regional, embodying the individuality of all the cultural geographies while at the same time serving as a visual representation for the currents that lie just beneath those tense borders between religion, government, and freedom of expression. The new century has seen a great upsurge in the international awareness of Latin American cinema, with films like Mexico's *Y Tu Mama Tambien, Amores Perros, Pan's Labyrinth,* and *The Devil's Backbone*; Brazil's *City of God*; the Colombian-based *Our Lady of the Assassins*; Argentina's *Nine Queens*; and the multinational *Motorcycle*

Diaries all capturing the interest of international audiences (please see our more all-encompassing list of Latin American favorites at the end of the chapter). There has also been renewed interest in looking into the darker memories of Latin America's history of military dictatorships, a vision often at odds with the region's integration into the globalized world of consumption-based economies. Copertari (2005:279), although speaking particularly of Argentina, says,

> If anything can be said to characterize the heterogeneous corpus of films and aesthetic projects that constitute the so-called "New Argentinian cinema" it is that they all stage narratives of disintegration (communitarian, political, social, cultural, familial and personal). These narratives articulate a social experience of *loss*. And it is well known that this social experience of loss is related to a very concrete process: the virtual vanishing of the state as a product of the neo-liberal policies that transformed Argentina during the 1990s.

The same sentiment is also expressed by Gundermann (2005:260), again in relation to the new Argentinian cinema:

> It is nothing new to say that the 1990s, the decade during which the New Argentine Cinema constituted itself, is the historical moment when transnational capitalism marched into Argentina on a large scale, producing the deregulation of the labour process, the breakdown of the welfare state, deindustrialization and massive unemployment. The 1990s brought into its own the plan that was originally designed and implemented by the military dictatorship in the 1970s and '80s.

These remarks are certainly applicable to much of Latin America and are illustrative of the social and economic conditions that form the geographies of Latin American cinema. We can therefore *see* Latin American cinema as unique cultural representations and cultural productions generated in particular historical spaces and embodying the dialectics of the region's respective nations. As Jaguaribe (2004:327) states in relation to the *favelas* of Brazil: "Contemporary literary and cinematographic productions are attempting to come to terms with new portraits of Brazil that focus on marginalized characters, favelas, drug cultures and the imaginaries of consumption." Indeed, Nouzeilles (2005:263) asks, "What kind of political responses are possible in societies in which spectacular images of pain and violence have become part of a mass-driven circus? And, moreover, how can the future be imagined in a culture transfixed by fetishized versions of the past and numbed by the unlimited promises of consumption?" We provide two distinct and very different answers to these questions through the works discussed below.

In this engagement of the geographies of Latin American cinema, this chapter moves away from place-based textual analysis and looks at the films as cultural productions, as a visual representation that both contains *and* transgresses the geographies of the region. The chapter focuses on two particular figures and delves into their films to explore the spatial relationship between the filmmaker and audience, a relationship that reveals a geographic depiction of a very different world, one without borders, that transgresses the subdivided cultures occupying the geographical spaces and places of Latin America.

BRAZIL:
COFFIN JOE AND TRANSGRESSIVE SOCIAL RESISTANCE

Brazil, one of the largest and most predominantly Catholic nations in the world, has long had a curious relationship with dictatorships and state-controlled media. In 1964, Brazilian military rule and censorship began in earnest as the newly installed junta outlawed political parties and did away with a constitution that had been in effect for less than two decades. The junta enacted the so-called Fifth Institutional Act that gave the government full latitude to ban any news or entertainment that might erode public morality and, as a result, Brazilian theaters were flooded with an influx of government-sanctioned R-rated films called *pornochanchadas*. Brazilian underground filmmakers countered this creative oppression with their own unapologetically provocative low-budget films. Collectively known as Mouth of Garbage Cinema, after the slums of São Paulo where many were produced, movies such as *Killed the Family and Went to the Cinema*, *Orgy; or, The Man Who Gave Birth*, and *How Tasty Was My Little Frenchman* were populated with cannibalistic doctors, cigar-chomping skulls, transvestite detectives, self-castrating men, and sadistic undertakers. Garbage cinema filmmakers thumbed their noses at officials with images influenced by surrealism and included everything from accidental electrocutions to murderous catfights set to Carmen Miranda tunes in their subversive and unsanctioned works. Fundamentally Catholic, but also peculiarly Brazilian in their *Carnival*-inspired tableaux of the netherworld, these films function as a major example of the cinema being used as a soapbox for self-analysis and self-expression.

Perhaps the best known of these cinematic renegades is Jose Mojica Marins, known as *Ze do Caixao* (or *Coffin Joe*) to his fans. One film in particular was intended to show Marins's particular displeasure with the state of Brazil: his *Hallucinations of a Deranged Mind* was a mixed-media compilation of every shot officially censored from his career prior to the restoration of democracy, including excruciatingly depicted body piercing, satanic-looking wax candles, hefty but scantily clad belly dancers, and a lingering sequence of Coffin Joe himself majestically descending a living human staircase. Mojica sought to uphold the motto of São Paulo's underground: a garbage-picker's cinema should be dirty, with only beauty pilfered from the squalor allowed. As Mojica has said, "I breathe and drink the essence of the primitive cinema." It is useful to put Coffin Joe in his proper context—a manifestation of fear who exists to help his audience understand and over- come the human frailties that sometimes define the difference between the geographies of survival and the geographies of victimization.

Jose Mojica Marins was born, appropriately, on Friday the 13th in March 1936, in São Paulo, the most populated and global city in the Southern Hemisphere. Bred in the city's working-class neighborhood, with its heated mix of Catholic ideology and macumba superstitions, Mojica grew up with a determined passion for cinema. His father managed a small movie theater, and as the family lived in back of it until Mojica reached eighteen, the young Jose found himself spending considerable time watching the films that played on the screen, everything from everyday Brazilian fare to American westerns, serials—and, especially, American horror films. A medical documentary about venereal disease also had a considerable im- pact on Mojica and undoubtedly led him to mimic its realistic shocks in the future films he would one day be directing. Gifts of an 8mm and then a 16mm film camera gave Mojica the opportunity to shoot short films in his teens that he then exhibited in the countryside for provincial audiences, sometimes under adverse conditions. Mojica made his feature-film direct- ing debut in 1959 with *The Adventurer's Fate*, a western (in widescreen) that contained strong violence and even nudity, and which would anticipate the use of these then-shocking elements in his later films.

In 1963 Mojica had a nightmare that changed the course of his life and international horror film history. In his dream, a man in black dragged him along the ground to a graveyard and to a grave that was revealed to be Moji- ca's own. The terrified dreamer read the accurate date of his birth, but could not bring himself to read further and discover the date of his death. The dreamer then looked more carefully at the man in black—and saw himself as his own tormentor. Mojica woke up screaming and pleading not to be taken away to his grave. Afterward, and having calmed down, Mojica imme- diately dropped his plans to produce a juvenile delinquency film, replacing that project with what would be Brazil's first true horror film, *At Midnight I Will Take Your Soul*, starring Mojica himself as the man in black who had appeared in his dream and who now had a name—Ze do Caixao.

Ze do Caixao, the black clad, black top-hatted character, with the equally black beard and the nauseatingly long fingernails, would quickly become ingrained in Brazil's national consciousness, much as Mojica's nightmare had become burned into his memory and his very soul. The color black represented evil and death, of course, the two great fears of mankind and the most common signifier of the horror genre, while the beard and long fingernails represented the character's admiration for the natural course of things—and, symbolically, unfettered artistic expression, which can be both fascinating and repulsive at the same time.

Mojica filled *At Midnight I Will Take Your Soul* with shocking images and blasphemies: a real tarantula on a woman's body, maggots on a face, Ze do Caixao's murder of his wife and rape of his best friend's wife, the eating of forbidden meat on Holy Friday, the negation of the Catholic faith and its symbols. Remarkably, considering the pervasive Catholic climate of Brazil, *At Midnight I Will Take Your Soul* was a huge hit in Brazil and most assuredly illustrated the strong need for rebellion against the status quo of the Brazilian military dictatorship and the religious restrictions that together formed the Brazilian cultural landscape of Mojica's São Paulo.

The film's 1967 follow-up, *This Night I Will Possess Your Soul*, benefited from a bigger budget and further cemented Mojica's reputation through both its subversive nature and its ability to shock audiences. Filming included eighty tarantulas and sixty snakes, the torment of six women (prospective brides for Ze do Caixao), and surrealistic color scenes of Mojica's vision of Hell that, one could argue, dramatically outdid Dante and his Inferno. Mojica once again had a huge hit on his hands, in monetary and

Figure 14.1. Jose Mojica as Ze do Caixao (better known to English-speaking audiences as Coffin Joe).

Figure 14.2.   From *At Midnight I Will Take Your Soul.*

critical terms, but the country's censorship board, bolstered by Brazil's military coup in 1964, began to seriously affect Mojica's work. *This Night I Will Possess Your Soul* suffered twenty minutes of cuts and, as a final insult, Mojica's original ending was redubbed. The censors removed Ze do Caixao's blasphemous lines: " God doesn't exist! I'll be back and I will kill all of you!" replacing those lines with "God! Yes, God is truth! I believe in your powers, master! Save me!" Mojica's anthology film *The Strange World of Ze do Caixao* (1968) had thirty minutes of cuts and alterations that completely changed all the endings of the film's stories. It fared better, however, than *Awakening of the Beast* (1970), which was banned completely by the Brazilian censors (a similar fate befell Stanley Kubrick's *A Clockwork Orange* in the United Kingdom—that film was not shown in English theaters until nearly thirty years after its initial release in the United States).

Having suffered such complete artistic humiliation by the Brazilian government, Mojica turned the tables on his tormentors. In 1982 he offered himself up as a servant and savior of his people: he entered politics, running for the Brazilian House of Representatives as a write-in candidate on his own unique platform: "In defense of gravediggers, garbage collectors and filmmakers." In an ironic twist worthy of his legend, Mojica would have won but for the popularity of his fictional character: instead of writing down his real name, voters wrote down the name of Ze do Caixao, and these votes for a nonexistent person were declared invalid, causing Mojica to lose the election.

Two years later and in need of financing for a new Ze Do Caixao film, Mojica entered the ultimate gritty realm of cinema: pornography. To secure the funds to produce the next Ze do Caixao tale, Mojica agreed to make a pornographic film while, in his mind at least, still staying true to the radical tenets of garbage-style cinema. With those principles at work, Mojica chose the ugliest women possible and included a sex scene between a dog and a woman, all in the hopes of so disgusting the viewer that cinemagoers would forever turn away from pornography. Ironies fill Mojica's life, however, and this case was no exception: the film, *24 Hours of Explicit Sex*, became a huge hit in Brazil and, instead of halting the production of pornographic films, Mojica's movie brought about a cinematic deluge of even more revolting pornographic films, most involving a much wider variety of animals. To further satirize the hypocrisy of Brazilian culture, Mojica followed *24 Hours* with another pornographic film, *48 Hours of Hallucinatory Sex*, which of course made even more money for his backers.

But it was for his horror films that Jose Mojica Marins was known. Raw and uncompromising as the slums of São Paulo the films metaphorically represented, gritty and superstitious as its people, these films, even in their censored versions, spared no one. The poorer classes, the bourgeoisie, the intelligentsia were all mocked and, at times, savagely debased. Given these things, it may be surprising that Mojica would become such a popular icon in the country. His Ze do Caixao character found permanent residence in Brazilian culture through cinema, television shows, radio programs, comic books, and horror exhibitions in theaters and under tents. Ze do Caixao became the country's boogeyman, used by parents to scare their children into behaving and becoming obedient Brazilians.

It was, however, the slums of São Paulo that held the secret to Mojica's power, their desperation creating the boisterousness of his nothing-to-lose pronouncements and taunting provocations, their stark realism gaining respect and admiration among those who had lost touch with their earthier, primal natures. The true feelings of the population needed to be expressed in a religious country under military rule from 1964 to 1985 and in a city of so many cultures where the discrepancy between the poor and the wealthy had been dramatically increasing year by year, the Ze do Caixao films functioned as representations of this cultural unrest (a theme found in the more recent *City of God* in which the main character, perhaps in tribute to Mojica, is named Little Ze).

Mojica's revolution was promoted by his sarcastic attitude against the forces and discipline of repression, and his ridicule of the classes and the very nature of man. In instances where his cinematic mirror commented unpleasantly on the viewer, the viewer's ego would safely negate the too personal message, even as it accepted that message as being justifiable and true for his closest neighbor. Or, if that failed, the viewer would be disturbed, possibly frightened, but certainly seduced by this black-attired madman who crafted with sadistic abandon predicaments that seared into the soul and self-identity, and who laughed with glee at the terror and destabilization that followed. However, in yet another ironic twist, the end of military rule saw the impetus and influence of Mojica's career considerably lessen. Redemocratization and a liberalization of Church ideology rendered his position in Brazil somewhat inconsequential. Mojica's long-promised third film of the Ze do Caixao trilogy has still not been completed and he hasn't finished a feature film in nearly two decades, though he continues to make the occasional acting appearance in films made by his friends and admirers. To many of his former viewers his famed black top hat may just be another old hat and, rumor has it, he is even pruning his transgressive nails.[1]

MEXICO: SANTO AND COLLECTIVE IDENTIFICATION

Our second figure comes from the distinctly Mexican universe of *Lucha Libre*, the sport of Mexican wrestling, where the rings are populated by a pantheon of masked, mythical warriors, including the most famous of them all—*Santo, el Enmascarado de Plata*. The man who was Santo—Rodolfo Guzman Huerta[2]—began wrestling in 1934, adopting various wrestling names before settling on Santo in 1942. His saintly moniker may have been a mischievously ironic choice because Guzman wrestled initially as a *rudo* (a brutish fighter who employs underhanded tricks in winning over his opponent). Only later, concurrent with the development of his screen persona, did he abandon his *rudo* ways to secure a reputation as an honorable and upstanding fighter. By then, a weekly comic book series, illustrated with photos, had filtered the character to homes middle-class and poor throughout Mexico. Even during Guzman's series of fifty-four Santo films, which began in 1958 and ended in 1981, he continued to wrestle in Mexico, submerging himself and his legend further in the soil from which he came. His stardom was not distant or pretentious; he never lost his touch with the people.

The geographies of victimization, so apparent in Mexican history, were overcome with triumph by this silver-masked figure who fought so successfully in the ring and on the screen. Several of his cinematic battles are against European-sourced demons and legends—Dracula, the Mummy, Frankenstein (the doctor, the monster, and the daughter). These screen match-ups take on a contemporary mythological significance in forming a hero and an audience receptive to creating one. The occasional use of indigenous legends and fables, like La Llorona (The Crying Woman) and Montezuma's treasure, validated homegrown traditions and strengthened the connection with Mexico's rich and frequently turbulent past.

Figure 14.3. Mexican *lucha libre* legend Santo.

Figure 14.4.   Santo in action.

The Santo films, though fantastical in many stories, would secure their
connection to reality by typically showing the silver-masked wrestler in at
least one wrestling match per film, frequently more and sometimes part-
nered with other wrestling icons such as Blue Demon. For non-Mexican
audiences these wrestling matches (some of which go on for over five
minutes) tend to be intrusive and annoying plot-stoppers, but for Mexicans

they validated the reality of Santo and his place among the people. They were the connecting link to his real wrestling matches occurring throughout Mexico and his history in the ring. The length of these matches (best out of three) and the hard work mandated to gain a victory further cemented the feeling among the populace that Santo was a worker like themselves—not afraid of sweat, intense in his labors, constant in his struggles. The wrestling ring became a symbolic platform for the labors of a people and Santo became their representative.

Though many scenes in Santo's cinematic oeuvre were shot in studios, location shooting took the silver-masked wrestler not only to Mexican locales, but to places like Cuba (right before Castro took control), Panama, Puerto Rico, even Spain, and confirmed the geographic hold and proud expanse of the Hispanic populace. Santo even managed to invade, peacefully, a desired territory held by Mexico over a hundred years earlier, when he shot scenes in Texas for *Misterio en las Bermudas* (*Mystery in Bermuda*, 1977).

Perhaps not surprisingly, influenced by their own Old World heritage and the prejudices of considering a European culture superior, a few filmmakers sought to give the character a proud European pedigree in films like *El hacha diabolica* (*The Diabolical Hatchet*, 1964) and *El Baron Brakola* (*Baron Brakola*, 1965). Undoubtedly these "origin-stories" made a connection to the Mexicans with solid links to European stock, but Guzman's silver mask could never hide the Indio features that were still visible—the nose, lips, and eyes. Furthermore, Guzman's brown torso was forever on display in the costume he wore (at least in the color films), and his short stature (probably 5'9" or less) rooted him even more to a non-European heritage. Before becoming a wrestler, the man without his silver mask could have been a farmer, a day worker, a peasant; at his core, he was clearly a simple man of the earth, and any viewings of these Santo films by foreigners, including the Anglos north of the border, must be lessened in impact without an awareness of this cultural distinction. This is why there is always some amusement on the part of many foreigners when looking at Santo and his adventures, a mocking condescension that these *lucha libre* adventure films are "bad" yet made bearable by the amusement one can find in their cultural strangeness. For Mexicans, though these films were considered entertainments, they were no joke. On January 26, 1984, there was no more pretense. Santo removed his mask on the variety talk show *Contrapunto*. Rodolfo Guzman Huerta stood before the live audience and the television viewers of Mexico, smiling and showing his distinctly Indio-featured Mexican face, now lined with age and his many wrestling battles.

Unlike the films of Brazil's Jose Mojica Marins, the Santo films were never transgressive; at most they were irritants to the intelligentsia, who could find nothing of value in either Santo's cinematic offerings, typically shown in cheaper theaters, or the *lucha libre* environment they were sourced from.

Though these films operated within the conventions of pulp sensationalism and comic-book plotting, they provided a spiritual nexus and a source of ennobling pride for a people, establishing through cinematic rites the legend and myth of Santo, Mexico's most famous fictional hero, who seemed, and in many ways was, a real man.

From this region geographers term "Latin America," we have presented two radically different examples of geographic representations. The Coffin Joe films of Brazil's Jose Mojica Marins consist of surreal and often terrifying landscapes that embody the zeitgeist of *his* geography, while the Santo films from Mexico embrace the social struggles of the Mexican people at a variety of levels. Santo's mask is the symbol of geographical change—it represents the possibility of political and economic transformation with Santo as that mechanism of revolution. For Brazilians, Ze do Caixao is everything they fear and cannot change—the nightmarish landscapes of Mojica's films become a visual representation of what the Brazilians themselves cannot and dare not speak of. Santo functions at a much more simple scale of resistance—he *is* the struggle between good and evil. Santo functions as a "social" wrestler capable of defeating the relentless corruption of the politicians and landowners. Both visions, however, employ the use of spectacle to engage the cultural spatialities of their respective place.

CONCLUSION

In terms of the geography of Latin America and the various cultures that inhabit those spaces, our glimpse into the geographies of Latin American filmspace show that the landscape representations within film *do* work. Raymond Williams was clear in his arguments that a critical analysis of the content of popular media is necessary to understand contemporary culture (Williams, 1981) because these representations map the material landscape by engaging audiences in the construction of new geographies that display the social and material world. As Mitchell (2000:102) indicates, the landscape is "a product of the work of people . . . it works on the people that make it" and, to go further back, Carl Sauer himself (1925:343) sought to understand the landscape as "fashioned from a natural landscape by a culture group." The regional landscapes of these two examples of Latin American cinema are, as Mitchell (2000:294) makes clear, "the product of human labor . . . thus encapsulating the dreams, desires, and all the injustices of the people and the social systems that make it . . . it acts as a social agent in the further development of a place." It is clear that the Latin American landscape is the work of structuring social relations between people and is thus ideological—meanings are naturalized in the landscape, and Coffin Joe and Santo become visual representations and cultural productions of these landscapes. The cultures of Brazil and Mexico are sets of social relations that contain structures of power, structures of dominance and subordination that are continuously struggled over. The landscapes of the films are manifestations of the cultures that make them—they are, therefore, a particularly ideological way of seeing the land and people's relationship to that land.

NOTES

1. Almost without warning, however, Jose Mojica Marins became a cult icon in the United States when the company Something Weird Video released videos and DVDs of his films in the 1990s, reinventing Mojica's character as "Coffin Joe" to replace the impossible to pronounce (for Americans anyway), Ze do Caixao. But Mojica hasn't been able to take significant advantage of this attention from one of the wealthiest countries on earth, apparently still rooted to the gritty, albeit cosmopolitan, city that bred him and made his work so impacting and necessary.

2. As with Jose Mojica Marins, "Huerta" is indeed Rodolfo Guzman Huerta's last name: however, in Spanish style, the family name is the middle one. So we use "Guzman" when referring to the wrestler. Also, we have dropped the "El" in "El Santo," as not being necessary.

BIBLIOGRAPHY

Blaut, J. M. "Maps and Spaces." *The Professional Geographer* 51, no. 4 (1999): 510–515.

Copertari, G. "Nine Queens: A Dark Day of Simulation and Justice." *Journal of Latin American Cultural Studies* 14, no. 3 (2005): 279–293.

Driver, F. "Imaginative Geographies." In *Introducing Human Geographies*, edited by P. Cloke, P. Crang, and M. Goodwin. London: Arnold, 1999.

Fyfe, G., and J. Law. "Introduction: On the Invisibility of the Visual." In *Picturing Power: Visual Depiction and Social Relations*, edited by G. Fyfe and J. Law. London: Routledge, 1988.

Gregory, D. *Geographical Imaginations*. Oxford: Blackwell Publishers, 1994.

Gundermann, C. "The Stark Gaze of the New Argentine Cinema: Restoring Strangeness to the Object in the Perverse Age of Commodity Fetishism." *Journal of Latin American Cultural Studies* 14, no. 3 (2005): 241–261.

Jaguaribe, B. "Favelas and the Aesthetics of Realism: Representations in Film and Literature." *Journal of Latin American Cultural Studies* 13, no. 3 (2004): 327–342.

Lowenthal, D. "Introduction." In *Geographies of the Mind: Essays in Historical Geography in Honor of John Kirtland Wright*, edited by D. Lowenthal and M. Bowden. New York: Oxford University Press, 1976.

Mitchell, D. *Cultural Geography: A Critical Introduction*. Oxford: Blackwell Publishers, 2000.

Nouzeilles, G. "Postmemory Cinema and the Future of the Past in Albertina Carri's 'Los Rubios'." *Journal of Latin American Cultural Studies* 14, no. 3 (2005): 263–278.

Rose, G. *Visual Methodologies*. Thousand Oaks, Calif.: Sage Publications, 2001.

Sauer, Carl. "The Morphology of Landscape." In *Land and Life: Selections from the Writings of Carl Ortwin Sauer*, edited by J. Leighly. Berkeley: University of California Press, 1925.

Soja, E. *Postmodern Geographies: The Reassertion of Space in Critical Social Theory*. London: Verso, 1989.

Sontag, S. *On Photography*. New York: Dell, 1977.

Williams, Raymond. *Culture*. London: Fontana Press, 1981.

SOME RECOMMENDATIONS—IN NO PARTICULAR ORDER AND CERTAINLY NOT MEANT TO REPRESENT A CRITICAL "BEST OF" LIST

El Topo (1970), D: Alejandro Jodorowsky
The Holy Mountain (1973), D: Alejandro Jodorowsky
Santa Sangre (1989), D: Alejandro Jodorowsky
Los Olvidados (1950), D: Luis Buñuel
El (1953), D: Luis Buñuel
El Bruto (1953), D: Luis Buñuel
El Vampiro (1957), D: Fernando Mendez
Misterios de Ultratumba (1958), D: Fernando Mendez
El Santo contras las Mujeres Vampiro (English title: *Samson vs. the Vampire Women*) (1962), D: Alfonso Corona Blake
At Midnight I Will Take Your Soul (1964), D: Jose Mojica Marins
This Night I Will Possess Your Soul (1967), D: Jose Mojica Marins
Awakening of the Beast (1970), D: Jose Mojica Marins
El Castillo de la Pureza (1973), D: Arturo Ripstein
El Laberinto del Fauno (English title: *Pan's Labyrinth*) (2006), D: Guillermo del Toro
Cidade de Deus (English title: *City of God*) (2002), D: Fernando Meirelles
Orfeu Negro (English title: *Black Orpheus*) (1959), D: Marcel Camus
La Virgen de los Sicarios (English title: *Our Lady of the Assassins*) (2000), D: Barbet Schroeder
Dracula (1931), D: George Melford, Enrique Tovar Avalos
Amores Perros (2000), D: Alejandro Gonzalez Iñarritu
El Angel Exterminador (English title: *Exterminating Angel*) (1962), D: Luis Buñuel
Santo vs. La Hija de Frankenstein (English title: *Santo vs. Frankenstein's Daughter*) (1972), D: Miguel M. Delgado
Nueve Reinas (English title: *Nine Queens*) (2000), D: Fabian Bielinsky
La Historia Oficial (English title: *The Official Story*) (1985), D: Luis Puenzo

Index

Numbers in italics indicate figures or tables.

About the Contributors

Adrian Guillermo Aguilar is researcher and director at the Institute of Geography, and professor of postgraduate studies in urban geography, at the National Autonomous University of Mexico (UNAM). His research is in the areas of urban-regional analysis, urban labor markets, globalization and megacities, and urban sustainability. His recent publications are related to urban development in the periphery of Mexico City, the restructuring of economic and urban space, and urbanization and environmental degradation.

Fernando J. Bosco is an assistant professor of geography at San Diego State University. His research focuses on the geographic dimensions of collective action, including networks of social movements and place and the politics of memory. His articles on these topics have been published in *The Annals of the Association of American Geographers*, *Social and Cultural Geography*, *Antipode*, and *Global Networks*. His most recent articles examined the relations between social movements, emotions, and geography and focused on the transnational dimensions of human rights activism in Latin America.

J. Christopher Brown is an assistant professor of geography and environmental studies at the University of Kansas, Lawrence. Dr. Brown's research on environment and development in Latin America focuses on the Brazilian Amazon. Specific research interests include rural development, rainforest conservation, and the politics and ecology of sustainable development. His most current research involves determining the impacts of the development of mechanized commercial agriculture in the Amazon.

Jim Craine is an assistant professor of geography at California State University, Northridge. His interests include media geography and geovisualization. He is editor of *Aether: The Journal of Media Geography*. He has recently published articles in *ACME: The Journal of Critical Geography* and *GeoJournal*.

Altha J. Cravey is associate professor of geography at the University of North Carolina at Chapel Hill. Author of *Women and Work in Mexico's Maquiladoras* (1998), she is completing a second book, titled *Racialized Spaces: Mexican Transnational Lives in the US South*. Her research interests include international development, globalization, and workers and labor unions, as well as gender and feminist theory.

John Davenport is a doctoral student (ABD) at the University of Kentucky. His interests are in cultural ecology and cultural geography. He has previously published in the *Columbia Journal of American Studies* and *California Geographer*.

Ross Flynn was a geography major in the Geography Department at Miami University, Oxford, Ohio, at the time of writing. He did the research for his undergraduate honors thesis in geography on sustainability themes advertised or practiced by ecotourism lodges in Dominica. He has since worked as a nature guide and camp counselor in the Smoky Mountains.

Larry Ford is a professor of geography at San Diego State University, where he teaches courses in urban geography, world cities, historic preservation, and urban design, and various courses in the cultural realm. He has taught and/or done research in a variety of regions including North America, Italy, Ireland, the United Kingdom, Indonesia, Mexico, Argentina, Spain, and Japan. He has published over 65 articles and book chapters as well as five books, including *Cities and Buildings*, *The Spaces between Buildings*, *America's New Downtowns*, and *Metropolitan San Diego*. He has also worked over the years on models of Latin American city structure.

Edward L. Jackiewicz is associate professor of geography at California State University, Northridge. His research interests are in development/postdevelopment, migration/transnationalism, and tourism. He has recently published in *The Professional Geographer*, *Annals of Tourism Research*, and *Latin American Perspectives*.

Joel Jennings is a doctoral candidate in the Department of Geography and a Gates Scholar at the University of Cambridge. His doctoral research focuses on Latino/a immigration, citizenship, and geographic scale. Joel has recently contributed to publications in *AREA* and *Childhood*.

Thomas Klak is professor of geography at Miami University, Oxford, Ohio. His research focuses on the theory, discourse, and practice of development in global context. He is the editor of *Globalization and Neoliberalism: The Caribbean Context* (1998), and co-author of *Alternative Capitalisms: Geographies of Emerging Regions* (2003) and *The Contemporary Caribbean* (2004). He annually convenes a course on ecotourism and sustainable development in Dominica.

London-born **Mirek Lipinski** has had a near lifelong interest in foreign *fantastique* ever since his parents took him to see Mario Bava's *Black Sunday* when they shouldn't have. His particular expertise is Spanish and Mexican horror. He is the webmaster of two highly regarded websites: *Latarnia: Fantastique International* (www.latarnia.com) and *The Mark of Naschy* (www.naschy.com), and has interviewed various luminaries in the world of Spanish and Latin cinema. Forthcoming is *Vampiros and Monstruos: The Mexican Horror Film of the 20th Century*, edited and partially written by Lipinski.

Susan P. Mains is lecturer in human geography at the University of the West Indies, Mona, in Kingston, Jamaica. Her research focuses on the themes of gender, diaspora, transnationalism, and postcolonialism in relation to Jamaican migration and tourism; Caribbean cities; and media representations of place. She is currently working on a documentary film titled *Ackee, Burgers, and Chips: An ABC of Jamaican Migration*, as well as an accompanying book. Her articles have appeared in *Social and Cultural Geography*, *GeoJournal*, *Journal of Geography in Higher Education*, and other publications.

Kent Mathewson is associate professor of geography at Louisiana State University in Baton Rouge. His research focuses on cultural and historical geography. He is widely published in these areas, and co-edited the book *Dangerous Harvest: Drug Plants and the Transformation of Indigenous Landscapes* in 2004.

Sarah A. Moore is assistant professor of Latin American studies and geography at the University of Arizona in Tucson. Her research focuses on the politics of the environment, including issues of urban development, struggles over environmental justice, and contradictions between the uses and hazards of garbage. Her current work, involving long-term fieldwork and archival research in Oaxaca, Mexico, is funded by a grant from the National Science Foundation. She has also explored the historical geography of urban gardening, race, and development in the United States, and contributed to collaborative projects on the development of nongovernmental organization networks in southern Mexico.

Linda Quiquivix is a geography graduate student at the University of North Carolina at Chapel Hill. Her research interests include migration over borders, identity/indigeneity, agrarian change in Latin America, and the Middle East. Her dissertation topic focuses on the Guatemalan Mam's seasonal migrations into Mexico to pick coffee.

Antonio Vieyra is researcher in the Institute of Geography, and professor of postgraduate courses in urban geography, at the National Autonomous University of Mexico (UNAM). His research areas include urban-regional analysis, urban labor markets, and urban sustainability. His recent publications deal with urban processes in the periphery of megacities, urbanization and environmental degradation, and globalization and change in urban structure.